Philip Augar is a former banker with a PhD in History. His previous books include four highly acclaimed business histories, and he contributes to the *Financial Times*, *Sunday Times* and the BBC. The Augar Review into post-18 education was published by the May government in 2019. He was knighted in 2021.

Keely Winstone is a writer and documentary-maker. The subjects of her documentaries range from the Gurkhas' summit of Everest and the D-Day landings, to Maradona's early demise and the spying career of John Stonehouse. She has a background as a print journalist and dramatist. *Agent Twister* is her first book.

AGENT TWISTER

JOHN STONEHOUSE AND THE SCANDAL
THAT GRIPPED A NATION

PHILIP AUGAR and
KEELY WINSTONE

**SIMON &
SCHUSTER**

London · New York · Sydney · Toronto · New Delhi

First published in Great Britain by Simon & Schuster UK Ltd, 2022
This edition published in Great Britain by Simon & Schuster UK Ltd, 2023

1 3 5 7 9 10 8 6 4 2

Simon & Schuster UK Ltd
1st Floor
222 Gray's Inn Road
London WC1X 8HB

www.simonandschuster.co.uk
www.simonandschuster.com.au
www.simonandschuster.co.in

Simon & Schuster Australia, Sydney
Simon & Schuster India, New Delhi

A CIP catalogue record for this book
is available from the British Library

Paperback ISBN: 978-1-3985-0543-8
eBook ISBN: 978-1-3985-0542-1

Typeset in Perpetua by M Rules
Printed and Bound in the UK using 100% Renewable
Electricity at CPI Group (UK) Ltd

MIX
Paper | Supporting
responsible forestry
FSC
www.fsc.org   FSC® C171272

Keely: For Matt, master of unconditional love
Philip: For Jessie, Samson and Adeline

CONTENTS

Part Three:
CROSSING THE LINE

Part Four:
THE GREAT ESCAPE

Part Five:
TO CATCH A THIEF

Part Six:

THE RECKONING

PART ONE

The Disappearance

I

MIAMI BEACH

The Right Honourable Member for Walsall North is packing. It's the morning of Tuesday 19 November 1974 at 21 Sancroft Street, an early 1960s townhouse in Kennington, south London. John Stonehouse puts three separate business suits and some shirts into his case. He adds some holiday items – casual shirt, slacks, sandals and swimming trunks – and then a raincoat. He's been to Miami Beach before and knows it has even more rain in the month of November than London. Last but not least, two black-and-white photographs of wife Barbara and the three children go into the case before he snaps it shut.[1]

Stonehouse turns his attention to packing his two briefcases. Passports? Check. Traveller's Cheques? Check. Credit cards? Naturally. Onward National Airlines ticket to Los Angeles, booked for 22 November? Check. Maps of the local area, always useful. And, of course, a paperback book. Stonehouse is currently reading John Le Carré's *Tinker, Tailor, Soldier, Spy*, but he's finding it hard going. In truth, he prefers the pacier work of Frederick Forsyth.

Barbara has agreed to drive her husband to Heathrow Airport before dashing back to central London and her job as a public relations consultant. She is beautifully groomed as always: immaculate mid-length blonde hair and a carefully co-ordinated outfit and accessories. Her husband, noted for his smart hairstyle and sharp suits, puts great store by how they look, not least because they are so regularly recognised. Not a day goes by without him saying he loves her. Just last week they celebrated twenty-six years of marriage with a candlelit dinner at La Busola in Covent Garden.[2]

Her husband is nearly ready. He looks around before he closes the door on the rented house they have called home for four and a half years. Barbara was once an aspiring interior designer and certainly knows how to put a room together. From the beige corduroy sofas and the white sideboard to the carefully appointed ferns and palms, it is all 1970s modernist, minimal chic. It's the perfect look for the perfect couple.[3]

They settle comfortably into their Rover 3500, barely six months old. Driving a British Leyland car says 'I'm Backing Britain' more than any slogan, especially for a West Midlands MP. They drive down Sancroft Street, past the Duchy Arms pub, and zigzag through the neo-Georgian estate, onto Black Prince Road, and then towards Lambeth Bridge. As they go across the Thames, Stonehouse can see the Palace of Westminster and Big Ben to his right. But he's not going there today. Heathrow Airport is fifteen miles away, and in no time at all he'll be through another familiar haunt, Victoria, and onto the Cromwell Road.

Before long, the Stonehouses are cruising down the Great West Road, home to London's finest stretch of 1920s architecture. It's a road that Stonehouse has travelled many times and he knows every landmark. Past the whitewashed Pyrene factory, stretched out like a lateral wedding cake, the more regal Firestone tyre factory, set back from the road with its lavish steps, columns and decorative lamps, and then the functional red-brick Gillette factory. Fifty years on though, it's all faded glory and heavy traffic into Hounslow West, where he and Barbara lived in the early days of their marriage.

They pull up in the drop-off zone outside Terminal 3. 'I'll see you in four days' time,' Stonehouse says, kissing his wife. He seems in a happy and buoyant mood, thinks Barbara as she watches him disappear into the futuristic building. Plans for the modernisation of the former 'Oceanic' terminal had been drawn up while Stonehouse was minister for aviation and it's a symbol of 1960s optimism. The automatic doors open onto shiny marble floors, wood-clad walls and lowered ceilings that soften the harsh fluorescent light. State-of-the-art escalators criss-cross the upper floors and the constant flick and rattle of the letters on the departures board stirs even the most seasoned of travellers.

Stonehouse checks in his baggage at a British Airways desk, retaining one of his two briefcases as hand luggage. The check-in attendant does a double-take, which Stonehouse takes as confirmation that he's on a VIP list. As he moves through light security – only Belfast flights get careful scrutiny – he feels the smiles of recognition there too, something he dislikes.

Today he isn't travelling alone. He turns towards the departure lounge, where he has arranged to meet James Overton Charlton, the chairman of London Capital Group, one of the companies Stonehouse founded after his ministerial career ended in 1970. They have known each other since 1967 and Stonehouse thinks Jim, a trained barrister with the manner of an English gentleman, will charm the American bankers they are going to meet.

Britain's first moving walkways take Stonehouse to the gate to meet Charlton. The two men greet each other and Charlton, who is not necessarily convinced by either the need or the prospects for this trip, is pleased to see that Stonehouse is in an ebullient mood. At the gate, drinks trolleys are loaded and the passengers soon follow. Flight BA 661 to Miami leaves on time at 13:00. As a minister, Stonehouse travelled first class, but he's now a Labour backbencher who combines business with politics. Every penny counts, so it's economy all the way these days. Neither the in-flight natural history film nor the Le Carré novel hold Stonehouse's attention; he's a people person and real life is much more interesting. Nine hours later, as the plane approaches Miami, they cross the Bermuda Triangle and land safely. They emerge to a beautiful day – no sign of rain – and temperatures in the mid-20s.

As they go through US customs and immigration, the officer asks Stonehouse how long he intends to be in the United States. A few days, he answers, and neither man is pulled over. A porter takes their cases to the car rental desk, where they pick up the keys to their car. It's a Plymouth Fury high-end sedan in the squared-off American tradition, complete with an elongated hood to house its powerful engine.

Stonehouse does the driving. It's a twenty-minute run to the Fontainebleau Hotel along the Interstate 195, across the causeway over Biscayne Bay and onto the island that makes up the centre of Miami Beach. It's another art deco backdrop but, just like the Great West Road, Miami Beach has seen better days. Once the home of glamour, the fading resort is now a place where package tourists and newly retired middle-managers rub along with drug smugglers and Cuban refugees.

Soon they're at the junction with Collins Avenue, where Stonehouse swings the Fury left alongside the Indian Creek until they get to the legendary Fontainebleau. The Mafia-backed hotel saw Sinatra welcome Elvis in 1960 when he finished military service in Germany, and they went on to film a TV special together inside. And it was home to the iconic opening shots of *Goldfinger* ten years ago. How Bond fans like

Stonehouse admired Sean Connery's elegant dive into the Olympic-sized pool.

Stonehouse and Charlton hand over the car to one of the attendants in the sweeping semi-circular drive of the hotel and give their luggage to a bellboy. They pass under the white layered slabs that make up the stylish portico roof, through the revolving gold-edged doors and into the main lobby where receptionists are waiting. The foyer bustles with a mix of corporate conference-goers and overseas holidaymakers trying to capture some of the hotel's former celebrity.

When Stonehouse stayed here earlier in the month, he was in the main building with an incredible view of the ocean, but this time he is put in the less glamorous multistorey tower, some 150 metres away, the other side of the tennis courts. A former owner deliberately built this standalone 'north tower' on the outer edge of the Fontainebleau land to cast a shadow over the neighbouring Eden Roc's swimming pool. The dastardly ploy eventually worked; on his previous visit, Stonehouse noticed that the Eden Roc was completely deserted, apparently closed indefinitely.

The Englishmen are shown to rooms on the same corridor and dine together in the main hotel. They drag out time until 10pm – 3am UK time – when they give in to their jetlag and make their way back to the tower. They agree to meet at 10am after Stonehouse has made his business calls.

Stonehouse is up well before then and dresses in a checked sports shirt and linen trousers. He doesn't approve of room 2425, which he thinks tastelessly ornate, but he won't be staying there long and has calls to make. One is to his secretary back in London, Sheila Buckley, another to his personal assistant, Philip Gay, and the rest don't take long. He suggests to Charlton that they go to the beach earlier than planned.

Stonehouse puts on his beach sandals and Charlton raps on the door to collect him. They make their way to the Cabana Club beach-side bathing area, past Sean Connery's diving board. Stonehouse isn't tempted: for him, the Atlantic Ocean is preferable to a chlorinated pool any day of the year. He is a keen open-water swimmer, a fact that has seen Barbara beg him not to swim out so far, for fear he'll never come back.

As guests of the hotel, Stonehouse and Charlton pass the manned cash desk and turnstile without charge. Stonehouse immediately slips off his sandals and trousers, revealing swimming trunks underneath. Charlton, on the other hand, is neither pre-equipped nor enthusiastic, and declines to go into the water. Stonehouse asks the Cabana Club attendant to look after his things and she recognises him from a previous visit.

He then heads straight past the lifeguard to the sea. The Atlantic hits the entire length of Miami Beach and Stonehouse plunges straight in. Charlton finds a spot in the sunshine on one of the breakwaters and watches his colleague swim out to sea some 200 metres. He is momentarily distracted by the local characters walking up and down the beach, and when he turns back to the ocean Stonehouse is nowhere in sight. Charlton anxiously scans the beach, the water, the horizon, looking for a recognisable silhouette. Then he spots Stonehouse emerging some way down the beach, and jogging back to join him.

Stonehouse takes a seat next to Charlton on the rubble breakwater and they chat away. Stonehouse begins to open up to Charlton about his plans for the future. He explains that he thinks his businesses need another four years to mature and then after that he'll be able to sell them and return to politics in a much more active capacity. Charlton isn't surprised: after all, this is a man who started his political journey in the 1950s thinking one day he would reach the top and become Labour leader and prime minister.[4]

The tête-à-tête over, Stonehouse gets his clothes back from the Cabana Club cash desk and they go to their rooms to get ready for their meeting. Stonehouse met the Southeast First National Bank of Miami last month and is hoping that the US regional bank will expand into Europe by acquiring shares in London Capital Group. They drive to the bank in the Plymouth Fury and arrive in good time for their midday appointment. They meet with Richard Stewart, a fellow Brit, and Charles Williams, respectively VP and assistant VP of the International Division of Southeast First National Bank of Miami. The two men take Charlton and Stonehouse to the McAllister Hotel for lunch, where they eat at the Bull and Bear, a British-themed restaurant. Stewart and Williams patiently listen to the pitch, but they're no more interested than their colleague John Odgers was two weeks earlier. You can't blame a chap for trying, thinks Stewart.[5]

From Charlton's point of view, the meeting is enjoyable enough but, as he suspected all along, the First National's international business doesn't extend to the type of deal Stonehouse is after. Stonehouse, however, appears to believe the meeting has been a success and seems happy. Charlton thinks that strange given they'd achieved nothing nor met any significant executives. He is glad he has other business to do in the States, so the trip won't be a complete waste of time.

After the meeting, they drive back to the hotel and hand over the Fury to the ever-attentive parking attendants. They cross the Fontainebleau lobby – its tiled floor depicting black bow ties – on the way to their tower. Stonehouse suggests they go their separate ways for a rest and meet again at 7pm for drinks in the hotel bar. He says he wants to do some shopping, and might even take another swim. At around 5pm, Stonehouse checks in his clothes with Cabana Club secretary Helen Fleming. She's the same woman as earlier, he notes. Older than him, hair set short in curls, this is not the kind of woman Stonehouse can easily flirt with, but he makes small talk anyway before heading for the beach.

A couple of hours later, Charlton finishes up a relaxing afternoon reading in his room and makes his way to the bar for seven o'clock sharp. He orders a drink and exchanges some idle chit-chat with the bartender, but after half an hour of people-watching, Charlton concludes that Stonehouse must either still be shopping or have fallen asleep. He's only a little annoyed. He phones Stonehouse's room but when there's no reply decides to go for a walk around the hotel grounds for half an hour. Back at the bar Charlton has a chat with a group of insurance brokers attending a convention but Stonehouse fails to materialise. An hour and a half after they were due to meet, Charlton becomes concerned: what if he's collapsed and is lying unconscious in his room?

He asks housekeeping to open up room 2425 and a maid comes along with a key. They enter the room, but there's no sign of Stonehouse – conscious or unconscious. In fact, the room just looks like that of someone who has gone to the beach for a swim. Belongings are strewn around randomly across the two double beds. One has a set of used clothes on it, and a zip document case with maps, a paperback novel, a photograph and some stationery. On the other bed, the sheets are pulled back as though it has been used. On the bedside table between the two beds lies Stonehouse's watch and another family photograph, and on top of the television is a confidential report, marked up for the Garrett Corporation of Los Angeles. And on the dresser is a brown combination-lock briefcase, loose change and keys, including those for a Plymouth Fury car. Charlton can't see the clothing Stonehouse wore to the beach that morning, which convinces him that his business associate went swimming.

Charlton double-checks for the car and their Plymouth Fury is still in the hotel garage. This alarms Charlton further and he reports the mystery to security staff and management. Then he remembers how Stonehouse left his clothes with the lady at the beach club cash desk that very morning. He calls the Miami Beach Police and tells them what has happened and then asks hotel security if they can go along with one of the guards to investigate the Cabana Club.

A security guard shines a torch through the window of the hut and there on the shelf is a bundle of clothes – mesh loafers, khaki trousers and an orange and black checked shirt – that Charlton recognises, without a doubt, as Stonehouse's. He and the security guard walk onto the beach, but there is no sign of Stonehouse. Charlton goes back to the hotel and then makes his way down to the Miami Beach Police office at 100 Meridian Avenue. But when he gets there, the police have disappointing news: there's really nothing they can do until daylight. Charlton is warned against contacting Stonehouse's wife, as experience shows that missing people often turn up within twenty-four hours. The police assure a distraught Charlton that they will issue a 'be on the lookout' message to any officers on patrol.

Charlton is utterly convinced that his long-time acquaintance and business associate went swimming that afternoon, never to return to collect his clothes. In fact, he is utterly convinced he has drowned. But this isn't the first time John Thomson Stonehouse has disappeared from the Fontainebleau Hotel, Miami Beach, Florida. It's just that no one had noticed before.

2

DEAD OR ALIVE?

At 9.30am on Thursday 21 November, Miami police officer Patricia Evans arrives at the Fontainebleau Hotel to search room 2425. She explains herself to reception in her nasal Florida twang and makes her way across to the multistorey annex where Stonehouse had been staying. There she meets James Charlton. They enter Stonehouse's hotel room and break into his brown combination-lock briefcase. Evans lists the contents: two British passports in the name of John Stonehouse, one expired, one current; a folder of personal business cards; an array of cheque books and credit cards; a Hertz rental contract for the Plymouth Fury; and a National Airlines ticket to LA for the following day.

Charlton phones Stonehouse's personal assistant Philip Gay to tell him that Stonehouse is officially missing. He thinks the time has come to tell Barbara and they agree that Gay should go to the family home on Sancroft Street. Barbara knows Gay and holds him in high esteem. The 30-year-old is an ex-army man in his first job on civvy street. He took it in the hope that John Stonehouse, MP and entrepreneur, could show him the ropes in the world of business. As Gay makes his way across London and heads south to Kennington, he tries to work out how to break it to Barbara, who thinks he is coming to deliver a package. He is no stranger to imparting sad news, but this is quite different to his army experiences. He has even brought his wife Caroline with him for support.[1]

Barbara is home alone when he arrives. She is surprised to see Caroline, and Gay has little choice but to tell her straight away. Barbara goes into complete shock and her anguish is plain to see. The Gays sit with her and try to comfort her, and then her two daughters arrive at the house. Gay has to repeat the news all over again. Jane, 24, and Julia, 23, are no less distraught. Now someone has to tell 14-year-old Mathew, who is away at boarding school.

John McGrath, an old business associate and non-executive director of Stonehouse's import-export business, is told too. He rings round colleagues, including Sheila Buckley, Stonehouse's long-serving secretary. 'Oh Sheila,' he says. 'Have you heard the news?' But she refuses to believe he is dead and then the phone in the hallway outside her Hampstead bedsit rings again. This time it's her sister Olwen, who has also heard that Stonehouse is dead. News of her boss's disappearance and suspected death is repeated, but Buckley remains unconvinced. She refuses her sister's offer to visit. It's hard to explain, she says, but her intuition tells her he is still alive.[2]

Buckley is not the only one who finds the news hard to believe. Prime minister Harold Wilson has just returned from the funeral of Irish president Erskine Childers in Dublin and is alone in his study with the head of his policy unit, Bernard Donoughue. In the general election six weeks earlier, Wilson became prime minister for the fourth time, equalling Gladstone's record. It was a satisfying triumph over Conservative leader Ted Heath, a man he dislikes, but his overall majority is now only three and the Labour party is far from united. Then there's the small detail of an unprecedented economic crisis driven by rocketing oil prices in the Middle East and striking coal miners at home. Northern Ireland is in turmoil and the IRA are bombing the mainland.

And there's one other difficult issue, the one that Wilson and Donoughue, a former academic who is now part of the inner circle, are discussing: the 'common market' of the European Economic Community. Britain joined nearly two years ago under Heath, and Labour, like the rest of the country, is bitterly divided on the subject. The PM knows it's tricky, but the veteran politician has seen everything before. Although not quite, it turns out.

The study door swings open and his private secretary for overseas affairs, Lord Tom Bridges – 2nd Baron, Eton and Oxford – glides in: 'It's John Stonehouse, the member for Walsall North. We've just heard via Washington that he's missing, presumed drowned off the coast of Miami.' Wilson takes a long puff on his pipe. It's a well-worn technique he uses to buy time. 'I wonder,' he asks, 'what is his majority?' Bridges has done his homework: with a majority of 15,885, Walsall North is one of Labour's safest seats. Wilson nods and Bridges leaves the room, pleased he saw the PM's question coming.[3]

The door closes and Wilson immediately turns to his policy chief. 'I very much doubt Stonehouse has drowned,' he says. Donoughue is never quite sure if his boss's pronouncements are based on shrewd insight, or a tip-off from one of his many highly connected friends. But before he can respond, Wilson carries on. 'It's probably some kind of trick. I never did trust him anyway.'[4]

That is not quite true. Wilson made Stonehouse an undersecretary in 1964 and gave him a succession of ministerial positions. It wasn't until 1970, and Labour's loss in that year's general election, that he dropped him. He will send condolences to Barbara, but any warm feelings for the man himself have long since gone. The loss of an MP is an irritation given the government's small majority but if Bridges is right, it will be only a temporary problem.

The meeting over, Wilson summons Joe Haines up to his study to tell him the news. Haines is a London docker's son with a fine turn of phrase and a nose for a story. He was a confidante of Wilson while political editor of *The Sun* before becoming his press secretary on 1 January 1969. They have an easy relationship. 'Our friend Stonehouse has disappeared. He went swimming, left his clothes folded up. They think it might be suicide. Do you believe it?' says Wilson. 'No,' says Haines. 'Neither do I,' replies the PM and they both laugh.

Wilson then makes his way along the corridor to the White Drawing Room, one of 10 Downing Street's state rooms, where he is giving a party for the journalists who followed his election campaign. Haines has a low regard for the lobby and keeps his distance, but the party morphs into a press conference, the guests are slow to leave and it is 10pm before the PM is ready to go home to Lord North Street where his wife Mary has insisted they live this time. Just as he opens the door of Number 10 to leave, he is called back. In Birmingham, IRA bombs have exploded in two pubs packed with socialising youngsters and there are reports of serious casualties. The soft Dublin rain and mournful crowds suddenly seem a long time ago.

Wilson wakes up on Friday 22 November to a Birmingham death toll of seventeen. All the papers lead on the bombing. 'Slaughter By IRA Bombs' is splashed across the front page of the *Daily Express*. But after the paper's initial pages of an hour-by-hour countdown to the horror of Birmingham, an entirely different story appears at the top of page seven: 'Riddle of Lost MP: Ex-minister feared drowned in sea off Miami Beach'. Stonehouse was considered one of the 'bright young men of the Labour Party,' says the article, with a 'meteoric rise under Harold Wilson'. It's a rise Wilson would rather the newspapers forgot.

Happily for the PM, the rest of the media don't mention their shared history. Bar the odd snippet taken from the news wires, it would seem Wilson's one-time bright young man no longer warrants media coverage. The American papers agree. Veteran detective Lieutenant Jack Webb of the Miami Beach Police says everything points to a drowning incident. It seems that police file no 383655 will soon be closed and consigned to a filing cabinet.[5]

But for Stonehouse's family and associates, the trauma is just beginning. Barbara is under sedation and is slowly coming to terms with the news. As she recovers from the initial shock, she remembers all the arguments she'd had with her husband about how far out he would swim whenever they were by the sea. How he'd go into the water and just swim straight towards the horizon and disappear. The whole family begged him not to, asking him to swim laterally instead, for fear he would get hit by a boat if he went too far out. In the end, they compromised on him checking back once an hour, but that is of no comfort to Barbara now that she is confronting the harsh reality of her husband's disappearance.

She is increasingly concerned that the usual air and sea search that's being undertaken by Miami police won't be enough. Perhaps her husband had swam so far out he'd been caught in an altogether different current or stream. She needs help on the ground and turns to Gay. She asks him to fly to Miami, as Charlton is coming back on Sunday, to take over as her eyes and ears. Barbara sees Gay as an extremely tough man, a man who has done three tours of Belfast, and she knows he'll leave no stone unturned. She also asks her sister Eileen, who lives in the US, to look into it. Stonehouse's cousin who lives in Miami might also be able to help.

In the Saturday papers, the press look to be giving up on the story, with hopes of Stonehouse being found alive fading even for the *Daily Express*. *The Times* tracks down Sheila Buckley, and she grants them an interview. She tells them that he is a very strong swimmer and tended to swim out a long way. 'It's the only recreation he had,' she says. 'He hated other sports.' But interest is waning and the story is relegated to 'overseas news'. The PM is relieved. In the left-leaning and well-briefed *Guardian*, talk is turning to slim majorities, by-elections and how out of favour Stonehouse was anyway. And he had once seemed destined for such high office, sighs the faux-lament of its political correspondent.[6]

On Sunday 24 November, James Charlton returns to London, and Gay flies in to Miami International. Barbara trusts both men: Charlton has her husband's best interests at heart and Gay will make sure everything is investigated thoroughly. She is sure she'll speak to Gay every few hours as she had been doing with Charlton; there's no need for her to fly out there herself. Gay moves into a room at the Fontainebleau. He thinks his boss drowned, but he wants to keep an open mind.

So do the FBI, who appear on the scene the following day. Miami Beach Police have changed their tune over the weekend. Lieutenant Jack Webb now says it's unprecedented for a drowned person not to be washed ashore within thirty-six hours and remarks that no one from the hotel saw him near or in the water that afternoon.

Stonehouse's disappearance goes from cop-shop enquiry to a national investigation. The Fontainebleau lifeguard Francisco Gordillo confirms he didn't see him in the water. 'There is no way he could have gone into the water without me seeing him,' says Gordillo. 'I would have seen him for sure. You can see anything for a long distance, a few miles out. I would have seen him swim out and I would keep my eye on him until he came back.' He says he clearly remembers blowing his whistle at the water's edge that evening to confirm he was going off duty, and there was no sign of anyone on the quarter-mile beach. Police are confident that no sharks were spotted on that day either. Police file no 383655 swells to seven pages and remains open.[7]

The secretary at the Cabana Beach Club, Helen Fleming, has also talked to the police. She is the last person to have seen Stonehouse alive. Fleming says that Stonehouse specifically asked her to look after his clothes twice on the same day, and made distinct small talk with her. She thinks it was all a deliberate ploy to make sure she remembered him. She had thought it strange on both occasions, given the number of lifeguards and attendants, that he wanted her to mind his belongings. 'I don't like this case,' says Webb. 'There are easy answers to some things, like the last time he was seen. But then – nothing.'

With the FBI on board, the hunt moves inland and dental records are sought. They are looking at the possibility that Stonehouse was kidnapped, or is still alive but suffering from amnesia. The FBI asks Scotland Yard to share any information they have on Stonehouse's business and personal interests, but Philip Gay assures both forces that his boss didn't have any unusual worries or a depressive illness. Stonehouse didn't seem to have any business problems, adds Kazi Ahmed, another close associate. Charlton backs this up. Accountants have recently checked his businesses' finances and everything is in order.[8]

Exactly a week after he left from Miami, Stonehouse's family break their silence. If, as the FBI suspect, he hasn't drowned, perhaps he will see the news and realise how well loved he is. Barbara has moved out of London to their rented country cottage in Hampshire – Faulkners Down House near Andover – but the press is still doorstepping her. She hopes a statement will give her some respite.

'I'm sitting here waiting and hoping,' she tells the *Daily Mirror*, and they run the story alongside a photograph of her with her husband looking glamorous and insouciant at a black-tie ball in 1968. She adds to Buckley's earlier statement: her husband was fond of open-water swimming any time of year, in any weather. Rosina Stonehouse, her mother-in-law, has reached a different conclusion: my son is dead, she tells the papers.[9]

Contrary to the view of Gay and Ahmed, Barbara does reveal that Stonehouse met with lawyers just before he went away. He wanted to sue *Private Eye* over an article on 15 November that was critical of his businesses. There was one key revelation: Keith White, a former general manager of London Capital Group, is suing Stonehouse for £10,000.[10]

Other rumours start to fly about his multiple intertwining companies and what was really going on. But Barbara isn't particularly surprised. Her husband had always been aggressive in everything he'd done and some people don't like that. This doesn't sound much different. She knows that her husband has work issues – she overhears him on the telephone sometimes – but who in business doesn't? His business worries were no greater than anyone else's, she concludes. They just get more press attention.

Barbara doesn't need these media distractions. She is focused on understanding how he could have drowned yet his body has not been discovered. Her sister Eileen approaches the School of Oceanography in Miami for details on the tides and currents. Barbara wants to know if it's possible that he got himself caught in the Gulf Stream. They didn't start looking for him until fourteen hours after he disappeared. If he was in the Gulf Stream, that travels between 5–10 knots an hour. His body could have gone a jolly long way, thinks Barbara.

But the whispers of those in the know are growing louder: about the British Bangladeshi Trust bank he co-founded and chaired (and since rebranded London Capital Group), and the adverse publicity around its share issue two years ago. There's also the question of the resignation of four directors from his various companies in recent months. They include White, who wants his £10,000, and it turns out that the publicly supportive Kazi Ahmed has also recently resigned from London Capital Group. Another of Stonehouse's twenty companies, Global Imex, saw directors resign too, while former managing director Peter Collaro claims Stonehouse owes him £5,000. Stonehouse had told Collaro he'll get his money once he's back from Miami.[11]

On 27 November, Joe Haines is called by the *Daily Mirror*. 'Have you seen the Stonehouse story?' he is asked. A member of the public has written to the prime minister making serious allegations. The *Daily Mirror* and the *Daily Mail* have been stirring the Stonehouse pot for a few days now, but this line is a new one. Haines's Downing Street team unearth the letter, which is from a Reverend Michael Scott, dated 24 November. Scott knows Stonehouse from their shared time in East Africa and he now claims that £1 million is missing from a relief fund for Bangladesh that Stonehouse chaired. Haines calls the *Mirror*'s political editor Terry Lancaster who says they have a copy of the letter and Scott is in their offices.

Elsewhere in Number 10, Bernard Donoughue also receives a Stonehouse call. This one is from a Winchester solicitor, Michael Hayes, a nephew of Stonehouse's. He has been approached by the *Daily Mail* who have heard that Stonehouse has not drowned but is still alive in the US. Stonehouse rumours are now running all over Fleet Street and Haines knows that the story needs to be gripped.

Then Haines notices something else in Scott's letter. He claims that a Czech defector by the name of Josef Frolík is about to break cover, and is going to name Stonehouse as a Soviet-bloc agent. This isn't necessarily surprising; after the Kim Philby and Cambridge Spies security scandal, any disappearance is looked at for espionage links. Haines takes the letter to the prime minister and they discuss it. The Czech story has political danger written all over it. Wilson recalls an investigation into the Czech allegation in 1969, but tells Haines it turned out to be baseless. You can deny that story completely, he says. Haines calls the *Daily Mirror* back to do so and when they carry a Stonehouse story on 28 November, Bangladesh is the issue they run with.

When it comes to Stonehouse's nephew and the *Daily Mail*'s story that he is still alive, Wilson chooses his words carefully. He tells Donoughue to tell Hayes that no information has reached the prime minister's office from a newspaper about the circumstances of Stonehouse's disappearance and that they know no more than they are reading in the papers. It's not a denial and it's not enough to kill the story. On the same day that the *Daily Mirror* run with the Bangladesh angle, the *Daily Mail* has an interview with Lieutenant Webb in Miami. He's officially no longer satisfied with drowning as an explanation.[12]

Number 10 needs to get to the bottom of this. The prime minister's office asks the Foreign Office whether the US authorities know anything about Stonehouse's fate – 'No,' they reply, but Interpol have been alerted – and the Department of Trade (DoT) are told to look into the Bangladesh allegations.[13]

Much to Number 10's dismay, the story ramps up again. An old business associate comes forward to say that, although Stonehouse always seemed very suave and in control, it was a big front. In reality, he was always bluffing, and just exploited his old political contacts and status as an ex-minister to win business. Family friends from back in Southampton, Stonehouse's hometown, emerge with their tuppence worth. The consensus is he lost sight of his youthful, idealistic vision and became seduced by the good things in life. One old friend who saw him just a couple of months ago says she was surprised he hadn't got a top job under Wilson this past February and thinks he has become sleek and pompous.[14]

When Stonehouse was missing, presumed drowned, his story was just a footnote. Now that there's darkness and intrigue, it takes on a momentum all of its own. The Miami Beach Police refuse to rule out that the disappearance was of 'a voluntary nature', and as a result the FBI is investigating an idea that both the prime minister and Barbara Stonehouse dread: that the MP for Walsall North hasn't drowned at all but has, in fact, faked his own death.[15]

3

THE PROBLEM THAT
WON'T GO AWAY

Stonehouse's personal assistant, Philip Gay, returns to the UK on 28 November. He updates Barbara, but the latest news from the so-called Sunshine State is anything but bright. The local police and FBI have now reverted to the theory that Stonehouse drowned, but there is still no evidence in the form of a body. It is a week since Stonehouse disappeared and without that body, public interest is growing.

The tabloids drag up rumours of other women in Stonehouse's life and Barbara issues a statement through family solicitor Michael Hayes. She says she and her husband are absolutely devoted to each other. 'There is no other woman,' Hayes says. And then, apropos of nothing: 'There is no other man.' The comment just hangs in the ether, at liberty to be interpreted whichever way. There's never been any public suggestion that Stonehouse was bisexual.[1]

The reporters at the nation's two broadcasters, the BBC and ITV, don't pick up on this when Barbara reluctantly agrees to be interviewed. The russet and mustard sitting room of the Stonehouse's country home is a colourful contrast to the muted tones of Sancroft Street and Barbara is as polished as ever. She presents Gay's latest findings and concludes, 'I'm afraid we think he must be dead. We've been waiting and hoping but we've been told it must have been a drowning accident.'

Her interviewer pushes her on this: 'Why are you so sure when others haven't been?' 'Because of the evidence,' explains Barbara, poised and calm. 'He was due to meet for drinks at seven o'clock, but he didn't turn up and didn't turn up for dinner either. At that stage, they broke into his room and found everything there – all his belongings, his passport, his money, quite a considerable sum of money – and then they went down to the beach to have a look in the beach hut and found the clothes he'd left were still there. Frankly, that is all the evidence that we have and any attempt to find any other evidence has come to a dead end.'

The reporter then puts another reading of events to this grieving woman. 'There is a suggestion,' he begins, 'that he may have disappeared . . .' – Barbara's gaze drops and she plays with her hands – '. . . Or committed suicide on account of business interests going wrong.' Barbara looks uncomfortable for the first time, but firmly responds: 'We discount all that. It's just, I'm afraid, rubbish. As a political family we get used to all kinds of non-stories making the headlines, but this is not on. It's not in his character. He liked life too much.'[2]

While Barbara is in the spotlight, the Labour Party annual conference, held in London for the first time since the Second World War, enters its second day. Every newspaper contains several column inches of Stonehouse backstory and his colleagues from the previous Labour government don't believe he's dead. Wilson, under pressure from the Labour left, could do without reminders of his once-close association with the man. His canny press secretary Haines briefs Gordon Greig, political correspondent for the *Daily Mail*, that Wilson long ago saw through him and that money had turned the young romantic into a hard-nosed businessman.[3]

Whatever she says publicly, Barbara thinks that it was odd,

the way her husband had taken to carrying two briefcases instead of one. She calls his loyal former parliamentary private secretary, William Molloy, now Labour MP for Ealing North, and tells him she hasn't heard anything from any of Stonehouse's close friends or the Foreign Office. In fact, she's only had one official call – from a mid-ranking police officer. She wonders if Molloy knows anything she does not? Molloy is non-committal. He suspects a lot but he doesn't want to share any of it with Barbara.

Instead, just before 4pm on Monday 2 December, Molloy makes his way to the Foreign Office on Whitehall, where he has arranged to meet junior minister Lord Owen Goronwy-Roberts. He tells the Welshman of his concerns that the ambitious Stonehouse was a man with enemies. His car had been blown up by a bomb in a Heathrow car park just six months before and Molloy wonders whether there was more to it than a suspected IRA act. He also doubts that his friend drowned, because he was such a strong swimmer. 'Perhaps he has been murdered?' he asks. Goronwy-Roberts says that, unfortunately, his hands are tied and no public statements can be put out until there is definitive information. However, he assures Molloy that the British ambassador in Washington is taking a personal interest and is about to pass on a personal message to Barbara. Molloy seems happy that Goronwy-Roberts is doing everything in his power and agrees to try to dampen the sensationalism of the press.[4]

It doesn't quite work out like that. The next day Molloy is quoted in all the newspapers, saying his friend had 'enemies everywhere' and that Stonehouse may well have been 'destroyed', possibly even at the hands of the Mafia. Barbara can't believe this. How could Molloy think that her husband could possibly have been in close contact with such people?

Banking and importing and exporting are so respectable. You're always going to make enemies in public life, thinks Barbara, but how could it be so serious they'd take his life? No. It's not possible, she tells herself.[5]

A couple of days later, Wilson sees the notes of Molloy's meeting with Goronwy-Roberts. In his own neat hand he writes, 'Do the police confirm it was JS's car which was bombed? Did they have any discussion with JS about it and did he mention possible enemies?' He asks the Home Office to look into it.

Home Secretary Roy Jenkins gets his principal private secretary Hayden Phillips on the case. Some ten days later, Phillips replies to Downing Street. He confirms that Stonehouse's car at the time, which he'd left at Heathrow, was indeed blown up during the explosion on 19 May, and that there is not much doubt that the Provisional IRA were responsible. Stonehouse didn't mention any enemies when he was interviewed by police after he returned to the country on 20 May, Phillips reports.[6]

With one conspiracy theory laid to rest, Number 10 should be able to breathe a sigh of relief, but Stonehouse's absence is affecting Wilson's ability to govern. Bob Mellish, Labour's chief whip and resident of 12 Downing Street, has the job of getting Labour's 319 MPs to stick together. Like Haines, he is Bermondsey born, supports Millwall and is the glue in Wilson's fourth administration. But to do his job, he needs to know where everyone is and there is one missing MP who never told Mellish he was going overseas in the first place. Stonehouse just left a note on the desk of fellow West Midlands MP and Labour whip, Betty Boothroyd, thanking her in advance for 'allowing me to pair today'.[7]

Mellish buttonholes Wilson on 4 December after the PM returns from a working dinner with the French president

Giscard d'Estaing. He reminds him that the absence of a sitting MP for the safe seat of Walsall North is problematical and that, were two more vacancies to occur, Labour would lose its overall majority. The standing committees, where the detail of parliamentary legislation is thrashed out, are already proving difficult and the situation needs to be sorted as soon as possible. He has discussed it with the national agent of the Labour Party who wants a February by-election, which means selecting a candidate in January. If death is established before the House resumes in January, there's no difficulty, but if this isn't the case, they need options. Mellish presents Wilson with two. They can encourage Barbara – 'in her own interests' – to apply for a presumption of death, something that hasn't been necessary in the House since the war. Or, leaving Barbara aside, they can invite the House to declare that the seat is vacant. Either way, the path would then be open for a by-election and Mellish encourages the PM to consider these alternatives.[8]

On 11 December, Stonehouse's 27-year-old secretary Sheila Buckley is back in the papers – but not because she's got more to say on her boss's extraordinary swimming ability. 'Why was Sheila at MP's Flat?' asks the *Daily Mirror*'s headline. The article describes her as an 'attractive' divorcee, and she has a striking facial resemblance to a young Barbara. The news they have is that Buckley lived at Stonehouse's one-bedroom flat at Vandon Court in Victoria. People from the block recognise photographs of her and claim she's lived there months, if not years. Only Buckley's father, Leslie Black, a butcher, says otherwise, claiming that she used to stay with her sister during the week and come back to the family home in Abbey Wood at the weekends. It is not lost on anyone that Stonehouse's family townhouse is only just over the river from his flat.[9]

Before that story can gather momentum, Barbara steps in.

'There's no mystery,' she tells reporters. 'It has been rented as an office-cum-pied-à-terre and for the past two years he has allowed Mrs Buckley to use it. She's been paying the rent, but has now found alternative accommodation.' The flat might not be news to Barbara, but it certainly is to Bob Mellish. Vandon Court, he notes, is definitely not registered with the Whip's Office.[10]

Friday 13 December, that unluckiest of days, brings the grimmest news yet for the Stonehouse family. Miami Beach Police find a concrete coffin in Fort Lauderdale, twenty miles along the coast from the scene of Stonehouse's disappearance. It has been smashed open, a body removed, and pieces of the concrete have been found on a beach within walking distance of the Fontainebleau. Albert Laine, a middle-aged plain clothes cop, is head of the Lauderdale Lakes Police. This so-called 'concrete overcoat' is typical of a Mafia killing, he drawls. Scotland Yard asks Laine to fly across samples of blood and hair taken from the coffin to determine if they belong to Stonehouse.[11]

But Stonehouse isn't the only man mysteriously missing in south-east Florida. A commodities broker called J. David Shaver has disappeared in similar circumstances, in the same time frame: belongings left behind, nobody notified, just gone. Laine considers Shaver, also believed to be six foot two inches, to be another possible inhabitant of the concrete coffin. Shaver was trying to finance a cement deal that involved both Stonehouse and a Nigerian businessman called Sylvester Okereke. It's one of many international deals of this kind that Stonehouse was trying to cut, and has now left in limbo. Even more intriguingly, Okereke was last seen on 18 November on a Thames houseboat in Teddington, south-west London and is now a third missing man.[12]

For the public, the complexities of the Stonehouse story is an escape from the grim reality of a strike-bound, IRA-bombed country, but for Barbara and her family it is an enormous strain. Jane, for one, already suffers from a terrifying recurring nightmare where her father is eaten by sharks. Journalists are camped outside Faulkners Down House and calling at all hours of the day and night. The family's idea of an honourable public servant has been replaced by an altogether different character, and Barbara is powerless to do anything about it.[13]

This has also been hard on Stonehouse's 80-year-old mother, Rosina. She's a former mayor of Southampton, but she's never been in the Westminster spotlight. Being called throughout the night and asked questions like 'Is your son the man they discovered in that slab of concrete having been killed by the Mafia?' or 'Did your son live apart from his wife between 1969 and 1972?' and 'Was he a womaniser who kept a flat just for this purpose?' is no fun for any mother, let alone an octogenarian. She and her daughter, Stonehouse's sister Elizabeth Hayes, are constantly doorstepped too, the press sometimes six deep. After a month of this, Rosina has a heart attack and is hospitalised.[14]

But a Stonehouse story of a different kind is troubling Harold Wilson. Although he thinks there's nothing in stories that Stonehouse was a Czech spy, these rumours won't go away. And Frolík the defector has memoirs he plans to publish, memoirs that will need publicity. Whispers of Stonehouse having flown from Cuba to Moscow and from Moscow to East Germany last month, under an assumed identity, seem wide of the mark, but Wilson's team can't yet rule them out. The prime minister's obsession with security and intelligence matters is well known – he thinks MI5 is trying to undermine his government – and Haines and his press team are on full alert.[15]

Sure enough, on Monday 16 December, the triple-deck headline 'Stonehouse Security Sensation' *is* the *Daily Mirror*'s front page. The paper reveals allegations of Stonehouse being a suspected spy when he was minister of posts and telecoms in 1969, and that he was investigated by MI5 at the time. They also report that the security services have been in Florida conducting their own enquiries on the missing MP. The *Daily Mirror* is not only the country's best-selling tabloid, it's also a stalwart Labour paper. Michael Hayes again acts as a mouthpiece for Barbara: 'The next thing we know people will be saying that he swam out from the Florida beach where he disappeared to a Russian submarine.' This intervention is of no help to the government.[16]

Wilson himself has been the victim of rumours ever since he negotiated with Russia as president of the Board of Trade. As a consequence, his instinct is to say nothing on any murmurings about colluding with the East. But he can remember the 1969 MI5 investigation into Stonehouse, he tells his team at Number 10, and it amounted to nothing. He once again tells Haines that he can deny the allegation completely.[17]

Labour's slender three-seat majority in the Commons prompts the opposition benches to seize every opportunity to make trouble. Tory MP Norman Tebbit writes to the prime minister to ask for sight of the MI5 'dossier' on Stonehouse. 'Normally one doesn't ask governments to deny rumours,' Tebbit tells BBC News, 'as they'd be at it all day and all night, but this particular one concerns a member of the House, his honour and national security. I think an exception should be made.' Using Barbara and the family as cover, he says: 'It is an undesirable situation when anything can be written about an MP and his family and they are unable to reply. The prime minister should waste no time in setting the record straight.' Barbara claims she wouldn't have known anything even if he was investigated; that's the kind of thing you just don't tell your wife if you're a minister. But this latest allegation is the worst yet. To accuse a man of being a traitor is the lowest of the low, she thinks.

On Tuesday 17 – and for the second day running – the *Daily Mirror* splashes the spy story, this time with a mugshot of Czech defector Frolík. The paper stops short of calling Stonehouse a 'spy', instead opting for 'contact for a spy ring'. But the rival *Daily Express* says MI5 is investigating claims that Stonehouse is still being blackmailed by the Czechs. The calls for a statement grow louder.[18]

After two days of pressure, Wilson decides to break with protocol and speak in the House of Commons on an intelligence rumour. Even though it was one of his own MPs who asked for this statement, Tory leader Edward Heath criticises Wilson: 'This might open up a situation where all sorts of stories might be given credence. I hope you will assure the House that this will not be taken as a precedent.' Wilson reminds Heath that this is from the leader who happily revealed Philby as 'the third man' in the Cambridge spy ring. Jeremy Thorpe, leader of the Liberal Party and the man holding the balance of power in the Commons, is quick to side with Wilson, saying the House is grateful he has made the decision to speak.[19]

The mandarins at Number 10 have drafted the speech, and Wilson, always careful with his choice of words, has adapted it personally. To a packed Commons, Wilson rises and asks the speaker's permission to make a statement 'on a security matter'. He claims one of the reasons he is making the statement is for the benefit of the family. He reveals Stonehouse's mother's heart attack and says his wife and children are being hounded, to which Labour MPs shout 'Hear, hear!' and 'Scurrilous!' Wilson adds that he doesn't have any information on the whereabouts of Stonehouse. 'I only wish I had,' he tells the House.[20]

As for the allegations that Stonehouse was spying for the

Czechs while in ministerial office, they were 'made by a Czechoslovak defector in 1969,' he says, and 'with my approval, the security services investigated these allegations fully at the time ... They interviewed the defector and questioned my right honourable friend about his contacts. The security services advised me there was no evidence to support the allegations.' He demands that the press stop making them, and leave the Stonehouse family alone. He adds that if there had been a 'scintilla' of evidence, Stonehouse would have been removed from office. He also says that he is again advised today that there is 'no evidence' to support the allegations. He does not, the sceptics note, go as far as to say they are untrue. That evening, a silhouetted Frolík appears on the BBC's *9 O'Clock News*, describing who it was that the Czechs targeted. 'Members of Parliament,' he says. 'People who had access to secrets.'[21]

PART TWO

Hooked

4

TWENTY-SEVEN YEARS EARLIER

It's 1947 and early evening at London's legendary Hammersmith Palais. Big band jazz fills the cavernous room and couples jitterbug and jive like their lives depend on it. This is a favourite haunt of the RAF – servicemen traded in boots for dance pumps at the door during the war – and a trainee pilot stands at the edge of the dancefloor in his uniform. John Thomson Stonehouse, 22 years old and from Southampton, is due to meet a girl he knows from the Armed Territorial Services.[1]

In the past, Stonehouse sought out companions based on shared interests, irrespective of gender. But as time has moved on, for close relationships, he's veered towards women. They're softer and more understanding, he thinks. Men can be so abrasive. He looks around the room in anticipation, then he finally faces the truth: his date isn't going to show up.[2]

Across the dancefloor is a 15-year-old brunette from east London in a white blouse and a pink skirt. Barbara Joan Smith is just two weeks out of secondary school and already working as a secretary. Music and dance trends come and go, but the Palais's real purpose is timeless: boy meets girl. When Barbara sees the stood-up twentysomething, it's love at first sight. She thinks this ex-serviceman devastatingly good-looking and he feels the same about her.[3]

It's also a meeting of minds as, after dancing, they discuss politics. Barbara can't believe that good looks and a sharp brain exist in one man. He is the son of Labour and Co-operative Party activists – he grew up in a family dedicated to supporting the politically persecuted from afar – and she's the daughter of a family steeped in local left-wing, socialist politics. Yet despite their humble backgrounds, both speak with carefully crafted received pronunciation accents, helped in Barbara's case by evacuation during the war. It's not discussed; everyone just knows that's how you get on in 1940s England.[4]

As the courtship develops, Stonehouse insists his girlfriend is too young for marriage, and his mother and Barbara's family emphatically agree. All underestimate this determined cockney woman, though. In November 1948, little more than a year after meeting, the couple get married at Hackney Town Hall. As a child of divorce who can count the stable years of her young life on one hand, Barbara is hellbent on making her own marriage go the distance. The memory of her father taking everything and disappearing, leaving them to move in with her grandmother, will always haunt her.[5]

Barbara is the breadwinner as they start married life together in an attic room in Hackney, to which they have to carry up water from the ground floor. Her husband is using his ex-serviceman's grant to study political science and economics at the London School of Economics under the Fabian academic Professor Harold Laski. Stonehouse becomes chair of the LSE's Labour Society and Laski encourages both him and his great friend Donald Chesworth to run for parliament. Stonehouse, a 23-year-old student with a now-pregnant wife, gets selected as the Labour candidate for Twickenham, a Tory safe seat.

Thursday 23 February 1950 sees a general election held at the conclusion of Labour prime minister Clement Attlee's near-five-year parliamentary term. As the contents of metal voting boxes get tipped onto tables up and down the country, Richard

Dimbleby gears up to host the country's first general election television coverage. Out of Lime Grove Studios in London Shepherd's Bush, Dimbleby shares the limelight with Oxford election boffin David Butler and at 10.45pm they go on air to address the country's two million TV owners.

Another landslide, such as that in 1945, is not on the table. The swing to the right is massive and Attlee's previous majority of 146 gets slashed to just five. Stonehouse and Chesworth can only dream of a seat in parliament, yet some left-wingers buck the trend: a Labour contemporary of Laski's, Fenner Brockway, gets a seat in Eton and Slough with an increased majority. It was always a long shot for Stonehouse and he returns to his studies. He becomes interested in the development of African co-operative farming and the movement towards independence from colonial rule – a particularly progressive cause, even among the left. He also takes a part-time job as travel secretary for the International Union of Socialist Youth, a voluntary organisation with seventy-three branches in more than fifty different countries.

The early defeat in Twickenham hasn't put Stonehouse off, and an easier seat might be a good idea. On 20 April, just two months after the election, the chairman of the Labour Society at the LSE and the international secretary of the National Association of Labour Student Organisations bounces back with an address to the Luton branch of the Fabian Society, of which both Barbara and he are still members.[6]

Stonehouse uses this platform to expound 'The Ultimate Aims of British Socialism'.[7] He maintains that it's not that socialism has failed in the UK; it's that it still hasn't been tried. 'The ultimate test of a socialist society is "Does it bring happiness to the community?"' Stonehouse says. 'It's no good achieving socialism if it is state-directed socialism; it must be firmly based on the mass of the people.'

It's the doctrine he's heard at home and at Co-op and Labour meetings from his domineering but much-admired mother Rosina, president of the Labour-aligned Co-operative Women's Guild, and his father William, a Post Office engineer and secretary of his trade union branch. When their son John joined the probation service after leaving school at 16, they were delighted and even more so when he followed their example in dedicating his life to improving the lot of the less fortunate.[8]

John and Barbara Stonehouse move west across London to a suburban street of inter-war semi-detached houses in Hounslow, just in time for the birth of their daughter Jane. In between his academic work and his part-time job, the budding politician takes on the household chores. It's unusual when the convention is for the working man and domestic housewife, and Barbara can't believe her luck. But before long, with Jane yet to reach her first birthday, Barbara realises she is pregnant again.[9]

This news does nothing to temper Stonehouse's parliamentary aspirations, even though he knows MPs who don't come from a moneyed background can't survive on that salary alone. Attlee is having a hard time getting anything done with his reduced majority and everyone can see another election coming. Stonehouse swaps Twickenham for Burton-on-Trent in Staffordshire and becomes the official Labour and Co-operative Party candidate. He's still only 25.[10]

On Saturday 7 April 1951, the Stonehouses make their inaugural trip to Burton-on-Trent as adopted candidate and wife. Once a Tory safe seat, the Conservatives won the constituency by only a whisker last year and it's all to play for. John and Barbara look like the perfect political couple as they arrive for a social at the working men's club. Stonehouse sports a thin neck tie and wavy brylcreemed hair, while his wife is the epitome of two-piece chic. More than 200 guests greet the couple who are moved by the warm welcome.

Once a boy with a crippling stammer, Stonehouse is now a fluent orator and the following evening wows a packed town hall audience of 300 people. He talks of winning back the progressive cause in Westminster and attacks the press for their 'false tales of woe'. He applauds the performance of the coal miners under state ownership, and says Labour's nationalisation has improved electricity and gas production. 'I do not believe that human beings are just selfish animals who have got to have their lives ruled for them by others – some of the things achieved by the Labour Government are the dreams and ideals of a generation ago.'

A week later, he's back in Burton. And the following week. And the one after. At the Annual Labour Party meeting, Stonehouse takes his vision global. The war in Korea may be necessary in the battle against communism, but re-armament mustn't take priority over the economic recovery. 'The only way to defeat communism is to build up economies,' he says. A month later, Stonehouse again looks beyond Britain's borders. He finds time for a trip to Paris for a conference on British and French colonies in Africa, even though Barbara is due to give birth any day. While he's away, their second daughter Julia is born.[11]

Stonehouse's rhetoric soon gets picked up by the national press. On Sunday 14 October, *The People*, the country's oldest Sunday tabloid, include him in a line-up of aspiring MPs. Under the headline 'Ten First-Class Young Men Whose Brain the Country Needs!', the paper implores its readers to take a good look at this now 26-year-old candidate, who they champion as 'the real voice of youth' and an antidote to 'jukebox' politicians of such limited repertoire. The following Tuesday, he and Barbara travel to Uttoxeter with his agent to hand over his nomination papers.[12]

On 23 October, just two days before the election, Stonehouse speaks at three separate events in between frantic canvassing. He claims that Thursday will decide the fate of the nation not just for the next five years, but the next twenty-five. Do the people of Burton believe in a fair share for all, or a 'mad scramble up a ladder', as advocated by Churchill?[13]

Election night, Thursday 25 October, is only twenty months after the last. It's been called this side of Christmas as the King has to tour the Commonwealth next year and wants to be in the country when the people go to the polls. For the second time, a general election is covered on television. David Butler keeps viewers on tenterhooks as results are chalked up across the country. The programme lasts until 4am, when it becomes clear that Churchill, the self-declared 'voice of Britain', is back in power.

In Burton-on-Trent, Stonehouse reduces the Tory MP's majority, but it's not enough. He has lost, as has his friend Donald Chesworth and so too a certain young woman by the name of Margaret Hilda Roberts on her first attempt to become a Conservative MP. On Friday 16 November, three weeks after his defeat, the Stonehouses return to Burton for a post-election social at the Co-operative Hall on Byrkley Street. He tells them that his associations with the Burton Constituency Labour Party, its members and supporters, have been very happy and something he and his wife will never forget. The crowd respond with a rousing 'For He's a Jolly Good Fellow' and top off the evening with a rendition of the Labour anthem, 'The Red Flag'. 'Though cowards flinch and traitors sneer,' they bellow, 'we'll keep the red flag flying here.' They also want to keep Stonehouse as their candidate, with the conviction that, come the next election, he'll get in.[14]

Stonehouse goes back to the LSE, where he picks up some lecturing work alongside his studies. He has also moved from travel secretary for the International Union of Socialist Youth to be the managing director of the travel business. Eager to try his hand at commerce, Stonehouse starts an affiliated travel agency and bases himself on a narrow Georgian street in Westminster. He takes bookings from his fellow academics for tours all over Europe. It's an admirable endeavour, but one for which Stonehouse is ill-suited. Complaints start to come in about cancelled trips and unfulfilled payments. Eventually, Alf Morris, Labour Co-op man and chairman of the International Union of Socialist Youth, is given the job of investigating. Stonehouse has a casual attitude to money and record keeping; Morris concludes that, while not dishonest, Stonehouse is guilty of gross incompetence.[15]

It's an undoubted setback for 'the real voice of youth', but soon he is approached by the recently re-elected Fenner Brockway. Brockway, who is already under security services surveillance for his far-left views on the British colonies, and American academic Dr George Shepherd, also an ardent campaigner for African independence, have a proposition for Stonehouse. Shepherd, an LSE alumnus, is going to Uganda to become the executive director of the Federation of Uganda African Farmers. He and Brockway want to set up a farmers' co-op there and they want Stonehouse to run it.[16]

Stonehouse rushes home to tell Barbara about the offer. She is not surprised: this man has an instinct for siding with the underdog. Their home in Hounslow has by now entertained many of the African men studying in London in preparation for independence. Stonehouse's eldest daughter Jane always lays out her toy tea set for them and, at Barbara's insistence, the startled men do the washing-up. Stonehouse tells his wife that the new Ugandan governor, Andrew Cohen, previously at the Colonial Office, is surprisingly progressive and supportive of the African fight for independence. The Stonehouses have two daughters under three and no money, but their idealism overwhelms them. They should go.[17]

In early March 1952, Stonehouse writes to the Burton Constituency Labour Party Executive Committee: 'It is with great reluctance that I have to decline the invitation to be re-adopted as the Labour candidate for the Burton constituency.' Parliament will have to wait; first, Africa.[18]

5

THE NEW RECRUIT

The Stonehouses return from Uganda in mid-1954 with £15 to their name and the 29-year-old father of two under a cloud. According to Fenner Brockway, there were complaints of 'a financial nature' against the man he persuaded to go to Uganda in March 1952 and he gently suggested that Stonehouse should wrap up his co-operative mission and come home. Stonehouse's story is that they were only ever supposed to be in Kampala for two years and he inherited a corrupt system because Dr George Shepherd hadn't been on top of affairs. But it's another money-related problem and, whichever way you cut it, the Stonehouse family are back in England and penniless.[1]

Barbara goes out to get work while her husband stays home and looks after their two daughters, now aged four and three. Barbara made the most of Uganda, speaking out on women's rights in between supporting the family with a job as a secretary at a local multinational company. Her husband, on a much lesser wage, found it harder to adjust to life there. He could feel the eyes of the colonial establishment on him, even when he became friends with the governor, Sir Andrew Cohen, and Barbara with Lady Helen Cohen. And he was right. Pressure for Ugandan independence is growing, do-gooders like Stonehouse are viewed as troublemakers, and the security branch of the local police were all over him.[2]

Back in London, Stonehouse takes on unpaid work for

Brockway's Movement for Colonial Freedom, but more than anything he wants a seat in parliament. First, though, he needs hard cash. The lack of income has put a real strain on their marriage and eventually Stonehouse finds a part-time job as an insurance salesman. This is just as well as the political climate does not help his parliamentary chances. After Churchill retires his successor, Anthony Eden, calls a snap general election on Thursday 26 May 1955 and wins a sixty-seat majority. There is not likely to be another general election for five years, but Stonehouse keeps his eye on by-election opportunities and works his old Labour network, including his friend Donald Chesworth, by now established in local politics as a London County Council councillor and radical campaigner.[3]

Stonehouse takes up an invitation to drinks at Chesworth's flat and, over cocktails, is introduced to a Czech diplomat – Lt Captain Václav Táborský. What Stonehouse doesn't know is that this man outranks the ambassador and is the London chief of the Czechoslovak Intelligence Service, the StB. Nor does he know that Chesworth has already been recruited to the StB's network of spies and they've named him 'Agent Knight'. They're working on the basis that Chesworth will move from local politics to win a seat in parliament, becoming, as they put it, 'influential and valuable'.[4]

A satellite state since the communist takeover in 1948, Czechoslovakia is Russia's way into the West. Its overseas residency staff are seen as less threatening than those of the Russian embassy, while Prague has influence in areas of the world that Moscow doesn't, especially post-colonial Africa. Like Europe and Asia before it, Africa is the latest continent to get caught in the ideological struggle between East and West. Táborský is on the lookout for talent and Stonehouse makes no secret of his parliamentary ambitions, nor of his interest in Africa. Táborský sees him as one step behind Chesworth and adds him to a growing list of 'acquaintances'. This man could prove handy.

In January 1956, a potential Commons seat opens up in Blaydon, deep in the mining communities of north-east England. It's as safe a seat as it's going to get, but Stonehouse loses out when a local coal miner is selected as the Labour candidate. Then he hears of an unpaid directorship on the London Co-operative Society board and his ears prick up. The co-operative ethos runs through his blood and, as the movement's political wing was crucial to Labour's 1945 success, this wouldn't do his political ambitions any harm at all.

Without delay, Stonehouse applies and gets the position – along with the ultimate perk of a chauffeured Daimler. But it is difficult to influence things from a part-time seat on the board. Co-op activists are suspicious of graduates like Stonehouse and, after only a year, the endless committees and conferences are getting to him.[5]

He still keeps his eye out for by-elections, and soon another looks likely. Labour won't support Eden's military action against Egypt, whose president, Gamal Abdel Nasser, has nationalised the Suez Canal, but Wednesbury's Labour MP Stanley Evans defies the party whip and supports the war. Passions run high on this divisive subject and constituents force him to resign. In between 'Stop the War' rallies in Trafalgar Square, and anger at the Soviet's violent crushing of the Hungarian uprising, Stonehouse sees another chance to become a member of parliament and heads to the West Midlands.

In the Black Country constituency of Wednesbury, Labour enjoys a majority of nearly 10,000. Stonehouse assures the local Labour Party that he'd never buck the party line like Evans. 'We must be loyal to decisions reached democratically within the party,' Stonehouse tells the management committee. Not that the British are staying in Egypt. The Anglo-French forces make a humiliating retreat, Eden resigns and, on 10 January 1957, Harold Macmillan becomes prime minister. A month later, on Saturday 9 February at the town hall, Stonehouse is adopted as Labour candidate for Wednesbury.[6]

Surely this is the one. Whatever happens, it can't be any worse than Burton in 1951, jokes Barbara. Then an independent candidate – Michael Wade, a local solicitor – enters the race at the eleventh hour. He proclaims he won't canvass at people's doors 'like a film star', a clear dig at Stonehouse's good looks, but will fight entirely on a cost-of-living ticket. Stonehouse is unruffled. He knows what these people want. They definitely don't want military action overseas, but more importantly they want job security, support for industry and not to be hit by Macmillan's pro-landlord Rent Bill.[7]

On Thursday 28 February, Stonehouse not only wins the by-election, but he increases Labour's majority by more than 3,000 votes. The following Tuesday, John Thomson Stonehouse, son of working-class co-operative campaigners, walks into the House of Commons as an official socialist, co-operative, Labour-aligned MP for the first time. He goes through the central lobby, past the larger-than-life marble statue of Gladstone, continues down the corridor to the members' lobby and finally makes his way into the chamber. Preferring affirmation to the biblical oath, he swears: 'I, John Thomson Stonehouse, do solemnly, sincerely, and truly declare and affirm, that I will be faithful and bear true allegiance to Her Majesty Queen Elizabeth the Second.'[8]

Barbara watches proudly from the public gallery, but it's not just she who is watching. So too are the Cold War intelligence officers masquerading as diplomats, stalking the public areas of the House and the diplomatic section of the gallery in search of the secrets of the British establishment and NATO. And they are especially alive to socialist new blood with a rebellious streak.

If they are disappointed by Stonehouse's maiden speech on 14 March, which is conventionally uncontroversial, a month later, he lets rip. On 16 April, Labour MP Barbara Castle wants to know why nearly 9,000 people have been arrested and imprisoned in Kenya, and Stonehouse, backed by Brockway, presses colonial secretary Alan Lennox-Boyd for their release. In May, he talks up the co-operatives in colonial territories: 'When I was in Uganda . . .' In June, he speaks up for his friend Achieng Oneko, detained without charge in Kenya since 1952 ('I beg for his release'). It becomes the Stonehouse and Brockway show as the two socialists regularly keep Lennox-Boyd and junior minister John Profumo on the run with accusations of racial discrimination and injustice in the British protectorates.[9]

The Czechs like what they're seeing. They know all about Stonehouse and his time in Uganda. They know he has become vice-chair of the Movement for Colonial Freedom to Brockway's chair. They know he is wildly ambitious. And they know he has a growing family, a Victorian villa in Islington to pay for and a burgeoning appetite for the finer things in life – not all of which can be supported by a parliamentary wage. The next step is to get him to Czechoslovakia and, in September, Stonehouse and another director of the London Co-operative Society, communist Harry Clayden, are invited to Prague. The Czechs roll out the red carpet with receptions, sightseeing and factory visits. These include a trip to Kladno, an industrial town twenty-five miles beyond Prague; Stonehouse decides that twinning it with his constituency would bring trade and cultural benefits to both sides.[10]

Back home, invitations to Czechoslovakia's stucco-fronted

embassy in Kensington Palace Gardens and to Villa Magnolia, the ambassador's sprawling Hampstead mansion, roll in. The Czechs, with their offer of free university education for thousands of African students in Prague, are Russia's secret weapon in colonial Africa, and the London embassy becomes a hub for visiting African independence leaders. Stonehouse thinks the parties are a great opportunity to make friends and influence people, but in fact he is the one who is being played.

Lt Captain Táborský knows exactly what he is doing and carefully introduces Stonehouse to one of his men, Vlado Koudelka. Over a series of lunch dates, a friendship develops. Stonehouse gets help with the Wednesbury–Kladno twinning project and, in exchange, Stonehouse tells Koudelka what is going on in the Labour Party. It's all innocent gossip, he tells himself.[11]

In October, Stonehouse agrees to do a favour for Koudelka. He'll ask a question at the Parliamentary Labour Party meeting on 6 November about foreign troops in Czechoslovakia. It's not quite the House of Commons, thinks Koudelka, but it will do for now. They have another lunch on 19 November at a Hungarian restaurant on Regent Street. 'It's a promising contact,' reports Koudelka and, in the run-up to Christmas, he sends Stonehouse two bottles of wine, along with a box of chocolates for Barbara.[12]

Three weeks later, on 14 January 1958, Barbara and her husband get ready to go out for the evening. It's only a couple of miles from Canonbury to 32 Chatsworth Road, Brondesbury, an early Edwardian semi-detached house opposite the local bowls club. They knock on the door and are greeted by Vlado Koudelka. He welcomes them into his home for drinks.[13]

Soon after, Stonehouse makes a flying visit to Uganda, at the invitation of African farmers who want his advice on coffee marketing. When he arrives, his money-management issues come back to haunt him. He is briefly arrested for a long-standing unpaid debt, then released after the locals have a whip-round. But it's his return that counts, when he makes a forceful speech in the Commons, tearing into the government's attitude to under-developed countries. 'It appears that the West, because of the various alliances that have been created, is inflexible. It may even be true that the Communist bloc is more flexible than the West . . . The assistance which Russia gives to under-developed countries is every bit as valuable as that which we and the United States can give.' Koudelka is more than pleased.[14]

The relationship grows throughout 1958 with more drinks and lunches. The Wednesbury–Kladno twinning progresses, but Stonehouse is frustrated by bureaucracy on the Czech side and asks Koudelka to help again. On 30 October, Koudelka says he'll intervene to speed up exchange visits between the two towns.

Early in 1959, Stonehouse is invited back to East Africa by leaders pushing for independence. He is keen to go, but these trips are expensive and he is unable to find a commercial or political sponsor. Then he has a brainwave. On 8 January 1959, in the 'personals' section of *The Times* – in among 'lady, chauffeur or companion' and 'exceptional young man requires opportunity' – another advertisement appears: 'Kenya, Tanganyika, Rhodesia. Director of Independent Economic and Commercial organisation making extensive tour February invites discussion of future assignments.' As if by magic, the money appears and on Friday 13 February, Stonehouse is on a BOAC plane to Nairobi.[15]

It's a whirlwind tour of, yes, Kenya, Tanganyika and Rhodesia. In Southern Rhodesia, he meets three African leaders of the Southern Rhodesian African National Congress and protests when they are refused alcohol at his hotel in Salisbury and denied entry to other buildings. Having stirred up trouble for the white settlers of Southern Rhodesia, he does it again in Northern Rhodesia encouraging Africans to 'hold your heads high, and behave as if the country belongs to you'.[16]

He has been under security-service surveillance throughout and the Rhodesians cable Labour leader Hugh Gaitskell in London: 'Urge immediate recall of Stonehouse. He is inflaming critical situation.' There is no response from Gaitskell but, on 28 February, the chief immigration officer of the federal government tells Stonehouse to leave Rhodesia within twenty-four hours and declares him a 'prohibited immigrant', along with other expelled anti-colonialists including radical campaigner Reverend Michael Scott. Barbara meets him off the plane in London. She is pleased to have him home after a sinister late-night call threatening to reveal 'urgent information about your husband'.[17]

Stonehouse tells Koudelka all about his adventures in Rhodesia, not to mention the costs involved, and Koudelka reports back to Přemysl Holan, an intelligence officer at StB HQ in Prague. Holan spots an opportunity and writes to his seniors in the Ministry of the Interior in July 1959: 'Stonehouse is complaining that he has spent a lot of his money on trips to Africa and he is now in debt. I think he would accept rewards in return for active intervention. Let me know whether we can take advantage of this situation.'

He is a good prospect and they identify his thirst for money as something they can exploit. It's not unusual. Ideological commitment disappeared as the motive for most agents years ago and the vast majority now have to be bought. They decide to bring Stonehouse onto the payroll. In November, they give him a codename, Agent Kolon, after his involvement with African colonies. Koudelka writes up his new recruit. 'He is energetic, self-confident and believes his abilities will deliver a great career for him. He makes many interventions in parliament to draw attention to himself; he wants to be recognised and noticed.' It's an astute observation. 'They are not well thought-through but he is improving. He is pleasant and friendly and easy to discuss things with. He is not driven by any one political concept he would fight for; he is more interested in becoming someone in public life.'[18]

Koudelka also notes Stonehouse has a 'pretty, pleasant wife', one who 'suspects him of infidelity'. Unfortunately for Barbara, he's right. Her husband's numerous affairs are something she tolerates as long as they remain hidden from their children and the rest of the world. But that doesn't mean she likes the situation. Stonehouse admits his extra-marital liaisons to the Czechs, but claims he is careful that they are of no disturbance to either his wife and family, or his parliamentary career.[19]

Stonehouse eventually agrees to receive a Christmas present in return for asking questions. His first active intervention was asking the transition government in Nigeria to establish a Czech consulate in Lagos and allow a trade delegation to visit. It didn't bring results. There are only nine Czechs in Nigeria and, following British influence, the Nigerians reject the consulate and the proposed delegation, saying individual businessmen can come, as they already do.

The next request is for the MP to ask an easy question. Stonehouse wastes no time and he asks Tory minister Ernest Marples if any decision has been made about nuclear propulsion for ships. In a timely fashion, Marples replies in the affirmative: nuclear reactors with propelling machinery will be used. Invitations for tender will be issued shortly. It is useful information for the Czechs and Stonehouse tells himself he is doing a friend favours in return for petty cash. His new controller in Prague, Robert Husak (cover name Hanc), tells Koudelka to give Stonehouse £50. The Czechs are clear: he has been hired to work for the StB, and he knows it.[20]

6

SUCKED IN

On 18 February 1960, Stonehouse makes his way to 10 Downing Street. Not as prime minister – that's still in his dreams – but as head of a five-man Movement for Colonial Freedom deputation. They have with them a petition calling for the release of independence leaders Dr Hastings Banda and Jomo Kenyatta from prison and it is an opportune moment as Harold Macmillan has just made a daring, anti-apartheid speech in Cape Town. 'The wind of change is blowing through this continent' he says, 'whether we like it or not.'[1]

Macmillan returns from South Africa with some news for Stonehouse and his fellow Labour MP and campaigner Barbara Castle. When he was in Northern Rhodesia, he was invited to lunch with the mayor of Lusaka, a white colonial who insisted on discussing both Castle and Stonehouse. 'They come here to create trouble,' he complained to Macmillan. 'They come to write sensational articles and slam the white man in Africa without regard for the truth.' It's reported in the *Daily Mail* and, after Stonehouse consults with Castle, they both decide to sue for defamation.[2]

If only the mayor knew how Stonehouse spends his lunch-breaks. In the week beginning 22 February 1960, he meets Captain Koudelka at Le Matelot (The Sailor) on Elizabeth Street, SW1, and it's an unexpectedly eccentric start to the week. The restaurant's owner, Dr Hillary James, is a psychiatrist at the

Middlesex Hospital in Fitzrovia, and moonlights as the chef here in Belgravia. Television chef Fanny Cradock declared that Le Matelot will either 'enchant or embarrass', as behind its anodyne candy-striped awning and floral curtains, exotically dressed staff fight for space with mounds of draped fishing net. On each table sits an ashtray depicting well-endowed, muscle-bound sailors.[3]

Compared to their usual staid haunts of the Café Royal on Regent Street or Boulestin in St James's, it's certainly quirky. But these two men have shared enough lunches and secrets over the past two years not to be embarrassed by a display of camp extravagance. And, anyway, Stonehouse needs to avoid the obvious see-and-be-seen lunch circuit. The Czechs always do due diligence – neither was followed here – but it doesn't hurt to keep out of Mayfair. The British MP and Czech diplomat scan the menu: ratatouille, avocado vinaigrette and coquilles Saint-Jacques.

Over lunch, Koudelka establishes – in order to report back to Prague HQ – that Stonehouse considers himself sexually 'normal', by which he means both straight in having only female partners and in what he does with them. Stonehouse says he's not interested in any wild parties that might damage his reputation. He has a 'moral profile' among his parliamentary colleagues as a happily married family man, and he intends to keep it that way, despite his affairs.[4]

That item ticked off, Koudelka gets down to business. If he is going to get the authority to pay Agent Kolon regularly, he needs to get some solid intelligence in return. Unbeknown to Stonehouse, he has other paid agents on his books, including Agent Lee – aka Labour MP Will Owen – and wants to make sure that, between 'Lee' and 'Kolon', various select committees are covered. Owen, also known by his handlers as Dedek

(Grandad) because of his advancing years, has got defence sub-committees A, B and D sewn up. But Stonehouse isn't a member of any select committees and has no interest in joining any of them. They're boring, he tells Koudelka.[5]

Frustrated, Koudelka moves the conversation on to Stonehouse's personal views. The man likes to talk about himself, this much his handler knows. What does Stonehouse think about the current infighting within the Labour camp between leader Hugh Gaitskell's right wing of the party and the remnants of predecessor Aneurin Bevan's left wing? The pure Bevanites are no longer in the fight as Bevan is ill, but shadow chancellor Harold Wilson is emerging as the centre-left leader. Koudelka wants to know who Stonehouse will support if the Labour split continues? Stonehouse tells Koudelka he is a fan of Wilson, but the squabbling will do the party no good.[6]

Now it's Stonehouse's turn. He asks Koudelka if people at the embassy ever discuss their 'co-operation'. He's worried that the British will have their own agents in the London residencies: after all, the Cold War is intensifying and there are rumours of double agents in every embassy. Koudelka is amused; of course not! Stonehouse is never discussed, except with one top person at HQ in Prague. And, anyway, this is about friendship and shared goals. Even if I were to go back to Prague, says Koudelka, you will be looked after on the same terms.

By way of a top-secret document, news reaches the minister of the interior in Prague of their latest London catch. Koudelka tells Prague that Stonehouse is shaping up and could develop into an interesting agent. 'We should focus on making him an expert on colonial issues in Africa,' he says. The trust is growing and he will fund Stonehouse's membership of the Reform Club where Stonehouse's friend and fellow Czech informant Donald Chesworth is already a member. He says that the information shared is of good quality and predicts Stonehouse will be part of the leadership of the Labour Party within ten years. Koudelka also notes how Stonehouse enjoys the sense of conspiracy. By this, the Czech means all aspects of hidden intelligence activity and says he will give him a further £25 at their next meeting.

But Stonehouse is far from in the bag. He's enjoying the intrigue, but the nagging fear of being found out haunts him and he demands hard cash to compensate. He's paranoid that the regular embassy staff know about him. He refuses to sign anything, even though Koudelka says he must in order for the money to continue to flow. They never have this problem with Chesworth; he just uses a pseudonym. Stonehouse has also turned up to several 'lunches' empty-handed. Where are the long, typed reports his friend supplies?

There is no report on senior shadow cabinet member George Brown – they are keen for Stonehouse to get close to him – and no minutes of the Labour Party's foreign policy committee. In fact, there is no written material at all. He didn't tell me anything, Koudelka concludes after a lunch on 3 October, that I couldn't have read about in the *Guardian*. What's more, he didn't reveal anything to Koudelka that could be used to black-mail him. Fortunately for the Czechs, Stonehouse's thirst for cash is all they need to exploit this reluctant agent.[7]

Barbara is pregnant with their third child, their rambling, book-strewn house in Canonbury doesn't come cheap and he's only on an MP's package of £1,750. At their next lunch, at the restaurant of the riverside Pier Hotel on Cheyne Walk in Chelsea, far from either of their social or business circles and jammed full of boating memorabilia, Stonehouse asks for money. He wants a £25-per-month retainer, regardless of results, guaran-teed security and no written reports. Koudelka responds that he will of course make sure Stonehouse is safe – that's in both their interests. As for the money, he will up that £300 to £500 a year 'basic', guaranteed, with no ceiling, but he needs something, even if it's just a list of annotated contacts. Stonehouse agrees.[8]

In the House of Commons, Stonehouse continues to speak on Africa. On 22 March, the only MP with the distinction of being forcibly removed from one of the territories of the Crown tables a motion urging the government to protest against the South African police shooting dead sixty-nine apartheid protesters at Sharpeville. His name comes up in the ballot for motions and, on 8 April, he gets his say. If the Europeans in South Africa go on with this insane military dictatorship in an attempt to suppress eleven million people, they are inviting disaster and more widespread violence, he tells the Commons, referencing Macmillan's 'wind of change' speech.[9]

When he is not busy on Africa, Stonehouse keeps his eye on issues in his Wednesbury constituency. On 11 April, he takes the minister of health to task. Walsall General Hospital does not have enough beds for this part of the Black Country and he has heard that fee-paying patients are being given priority over those reliant on the National Health Service. Stonehouse doesn't want the hospital staff to think he's sniping at them and makes it clear that they are doing a good job.[10]

The next weekend, with his and Barbara's third baby due any day, Stonehouse takes his daughters on the final stage of a Campaign for Nuclear Disarmament march to Trafalgar Square, a cause he champions along with Fenner Brockway, now 72, and his former African colleague, the Reverend Michael Scott. Barbara gives birth to a son. They call him Mathew, and following in the Ghanaian tradition of naming children after the day of the week on which they are born – in this case, Monday – he is given the middle-name of Kojo.[11]

At the end of May, Stonehouse sees Koudelka again, this time at the trendy Chelsea Grill on the King's Road. Stonehouse wants to go back to East Africa and visit friends who are becoming politically important there. Will Koudelka be able to help? Koudelka isn't inclined, as Stonehouse has failed to bring the list of contacts he promised. Stonehouse says he burned it; he was worried about all the notes he'd written and, as they hadn't met for so long, he didn't want to keep it on him. But the tables in the restaurant are too close together for any meaningful conversation about this or any other sensitive subject. They won't meet there again.[12]

The African independence movement is gathering pace and so too is the battle for influence on the continent between East and West. Being in on Stonehouse's next Africa trip would be a short-term win for the Czechs and the conspirators arrange to meet. Stonehouse brings a draft itinerary for the trip with him. He's talked to shadow colonial secretary James Callaghan and it's set for September. Koudelka and Prague get stuck in, writing up their own itinerary of people for him to see there but, once again, Stonehouse has no idea how he will fund it.

Koudelka agrees to a 'loan' and then a 'reward' if Stonehouse delivers the intelligence required as a result of the trip. Not oral information, he says, but a proper written report. And the trip must be planned together. They want him to see President Kwame Nkrumah in Ghana, for example. Koudelka tries to find out if Stonehouse is planning to see a woman he had an affair with in Rhodesia, but Stonehouse won't discuss it. He tells Koudelka that he won't 'entertain' anyone while he is away; the press will be all over him.[13]

Stonehouse is taking more than enough risks already, especially since every week brings fresh news of rising tension between East and West. The Russians have just shot down an American U2 spy plane and taken the pilot prisoner, and Stonehouse worries about being uncovered as part of a counter-espionage power game.

Sensing that making arrangements to meet up will become more complex given his man's anxieties, Koudelka offers a solution. They'll stick to the Pier Hotel on Cheyne Walk. It's on a busy corner at the junction with Oakley Street and, as they've established, no one that either of them knows goes there. They'll meet on the second Monday of the month, at 1pm in the saloon bar. After then, Koudelka decides, he will introduce Stonehouse to the newspaper cuttings method of making a date: send a page, and one week from the newspaper's date, they will meet at the Pier.

In his parallel public life, Stonehouse's recourse to the courts pays off. On 9 May, the High Court sits to hear the case of Stonehouse and Barbara Castle against the *Daily Mail*. The judge finds no proof of untruthful articles written by either claimant and the *Daily Mail* rescinds, apologises and pays compensation and costs.[14]

The Czechs want Stonehouse to ask a question in parliament about whether the Spanish minister of foreign affairs, who is visiting the UK, will discuss joining NATO. On Wednesday 29 June, he duly asks the foreign secretary, Selwyn Lloyd, to confirm that there is no question of Spain being admitted to NATO. Lloyd is trying to improve relations with the country and evades the question: '350,000 Britons went to Spain for their holidays last year,' he says. 'Señor Castiella will be coming as a guest of Britain.'[15]

While Koudelka builds his relationship with Agent Kolon, his big boss – Czech minister for the interior and de facto head of the StB, Rudolf Barák – is getting closer to Moscow. He initiated the first conference for all the security heads across the communist world in Prague, and Russia is impressed. They also like the headway the Czech security services have been making at home and call a top-level meeting between the StB and the KGB in Moscow. There they launch a joint initiative to evaluate 300 CIA employees and decide to work together in London on the political groups supporting colonial freedom in Africa. The StB says it could do with some assistance in handling a British agent who goes by the name of 'Kolon'. There have been missed opportunities to use him in Africa, they say.[16]

Kolon himself is happy to take Koudelka's money, but still refuses to sign for it. At a tense meeting on the small strip of park on Cheyne Walk by the banks of the Thames on 21 July, Koudelka pushes the issue again. 'What will you do with this signed receipt?' demands Stonehouse. 'Put it into a safe at the embassy,' replies Koudelka. He means the secret room at 6–7 Kensington Palace Gardens that's hidden behind the double doors of an oversized green filing cupboard. Not even the ambassador knows about it. 'Someone may find out, five years down the line,' says Stonehouse, and again refuses. Koudelka relents once more and gives him £250 for the Africa trip without a signature. He'll find a solution to this later; with his Africa connections and the KGB's interest, Stonehouse is still too good a catch to upset, and they haven't ensnared him properly yet.

On 30 August, Stonehouse flies back to Africa and spends the first ten days in Nairobi where he is well received. On 10 September, he flies from Nairobi to Bechuanaland, and there his expulsion from Rhodesia the previous year catches up with him. He has picked up a transit visa from the Rhodesian Federal Commission in Nairobi, but that doesn't mean he can leave a Rhodesian airport. Stopped at Immigration, Stonehouse tells reporters he will demand to see the Commonwealth relationships secretary as he is being prevented from carrying out his duties as a British MP. But he doesn't get that far and has no option but to fly on. In Ndola, Northern Rhodesia, and Salisbury, Southern Rhodesia, Stonehouse is not even allowed into the airport building. Then, when he crosses into South Africa from Bechuanaland, the police are waiting for him. There is no way forward and, on 28 September, he returns from his 15,000-mile trip round Africa and prepares to update his paymasters.[17]

He hands over a fountain-penned report, but Koudelka is not happy. These are notes Stonehouse could have written for anyone, as he well knows. Yet he still asks for more money, complaining that his trip to Africa ended up costing him. Koudelka says no, 'not until you have written a proper report as instructed'.

Koudelka reports back to his bosses in Prague: 'I have confirmed Stonehouse's main worry is getting compromised. From our point of view, this is a positive finding as we could well use it in the future. He is also under financial pressure. It is only a matter of time before he will be fulfilling his tasks.' But Robert Husak, Stonehouse's invisible controller in Prague, wants some ground rules laid down. Any future financial reward must depend on providing the sources of information, more meaningful active interventions and the signing of receipts.

The Czechs really need Stonehouse to be closer to power and, that autumn, they watch as Wilson mounts a serious challenge to Gaitskell's leadership of the Labour Party. This time he is unsuccessful, but when the votes are counted on 3 November, nearly a third of the Parliamentary Labour Party has registered its dissatisfaction with their leader. Stonehouse is among them. Wilson has drawn his line in the sand and Stonehouse is standing right by him.

This is potentially interesting to Prague, but right now they need their pound of flesh and Stonehouse is still reluctant. On 23 November 1960, he says he knows the signing of receipts is a way of making him do things that he wouldn't do ordinarily; he knows they'll use them to blackmail him. 'I'm upset that you're trying to take advantage of my financial pressures in this way,' Stonehouse says. It's the first time in the three years that Koudelka has seen him lose his cool.[18]

Koudelka gently reminds him that he never said he'd give him money in return for nothing. 'Do you think the work you have done has been worth over £300?' Koudelka asks. 'More or less, yes,' says Stonehouse. Koudelka disagrees; he could pay a journalist £50 for it. A report on a discussion with Callaghan contained less than what was apparent at the press conference! How can Koudelka tell his bosses he paid £300 for what Stonehouse has delivered? Stonehouse is shocked. He backtracks and says he didn't realise they wanted such detailed information.

'I'm away from London for the rest of this year now,' Koudelka says, 'so focus on extending your relationships with regards to the Colonial Office and their activities.' He will top up the money to reach £500 by Christmas, as per their agreement, but won't be able to give Stonehouse a bonus until he fulfils his tasks properly. They create pseudonyms so that they can communicate discreetly. Stonehouse will become 'Paul Barnes' and will sign receipts in that name. Koudelka becomes 'Harold Poulter' which he says stands for 'hot pen' as he chastises Stonehouse for writing his reports too hastily and with little attention to detail. The meeting ends jovially enough, but Koudelka needs much more, while Stonehouse wants to get away with the bare minimum.[19]

And with good reason it turns out. On 7 January, Stonehouse hears of the dramatic arrest of two men and a woman at their meeting place near Waterloo Bridge. They are Harry Houghton and Ethel Gee, two civil servants working at the Portland naval base, and Gordon Lonsdale, thought to be a Canadian businessman working for the KGB. Gee's handbag contains details of HMS *Dreadnought*, Britain's first nuclear submarine, and they become known as the Portland Spy Ring. The security services have been tracking them for some time and it is a huge story in Cold War-obsessed Britain. It's not just Stonehouse who is spooked by the arrests. So too are the Soviets; Lonsdale is actually their man from Moscow, Konon Molody, sent to Canada in 1953 on the passport of a dead man called Lonsdale. What a ruse.[20]

Molody has been working in Britain as Lonsdale since 1955. MI5 case officer, interrogator and Colditz prisoner of war Charles Elwell gets stuck into him. Molody puts up little resistance to the spy allegation, but Elwell does not discover his true identity. Lonsdale is jailed for twenty-five years in March and the civil servants get fifteen years each.[21]

Koudelka relaxes on Stonehouse during the Portland brouhaha. They're both worried and Koudelka knows he for one is being watched by British security services. Then, in mid-1961, he gets word that his rotation in London is drawing to a close. Přemysl Holan will take his place, but not to worry – he knows all about Agent Kolon, having previously managed the Prague end of the relationship.

The Czechs reconsider the Kolon relationship. Stonehouse has great contacts in the East–West battleground of Africa, is ambitious in his political career and believes in co-operation between the worlds either side of the Iron Curtain. He's also money-motivated and a rising star in British politics. Koudelka definitely needs to introduce him to Holan. Prague decide that the Kladno–Wednesbury twinning is gaining momentum and can be used as cover for a handover. On 9 March, the *Birmingham Daily Post* announces that an invitation has been sent to the mayor of Kladno to join Wednesbury in celebrating its 75th anniversary as a borough.[22]

Before then, Koudelka needs to keep Stonehouse warm. Money is how he can do it. With all the paranoia around Soviet spies, in-person handovers are seen as too risky. Getting the 'rewards' to Stonehouse is increasingly fraught – and he keeps asking for more. Táborský's successor in London, a Major Kroupa, agrees Koudelka can give Stonehouse £250, part of the annual £500 previously agreed, as a sweetener before the switch to Holan.

There are a few options, a dead drop being the most obvious. However, the Czechs doubt whether Stonehouse will remember the exact location without a sketch. They consider hiring a lock-up or a beach hut to which both parties could have access. Or perhaps fixing a container to the underside of his car and leaving the money there at a set place and time. When Koudelka sees Stonehouse again, these ideas are all dismissed. A live drop is fine, he says.

But Koudelka refuses to do this for his agent's own safety and eventually Stonehouse accepts that a device must be fitted to his car. Koudelka promises the money will be there by 3 July, a few days before the Czechs come to Wednesbury. Stonehouse remarks that transfers to a Swiss bank account may be easier.[23]

On 20 June 1961, the Wednesbury Housing Committee meet and decide to name a new road Stonehouse Crescent in his honour. The people of Wednesbury have no idea that they've named a road after a man in the pay of the Czechs and one who is using the town's twinning as cover.[24]

Both Koudelka and Stonehouse now use the newspaper cutting method to set up meetings. If this fails, Koudelka is allowed to phone Stonehouse at home, or he visits parliament using the standard visitor's 'green' pass available to the public. If Koudelka sends someone else, the coded greeting is 'Mr Kolon, Harold Poulter says hello to you'.[25]

Koudelka's time in London is up and he travels back to Prague by car. He leaves a parting shot on Stonehouse: 'Kolon is ambitious, energetic and brave. But he won't be subjected to signing anything in case of conflict.' Holan, his new handler, arrives just in time for the Wednesbury 75th anniversary party and the carnival parade through the town centre, along with officials from the twin town of Kladno.[26]

Stonehouse meets with his new handler Holan after the Wednesbury event, but not as often as the Czechs would like. Still keen to stay off the beaten track, they meet at Beal's, a restaurant in a row of grungy shops on the Holloway Road. It's near Stonehouse's family home, but it's a definite downgrade from the bright lights of Chelsea. The next meeting is in the saloon bar of the Black Horse and Harrow pub in Catford, south-east London. Stonehouse explains that his parliamentary duties are preventing him from meeting more often; for the next meeting scheduled at Casa Prada on the Euston Road, Stonehouse fails to turn up.

This doesn't stop Holan and friends from approaching Barák's successor as head of the Ministry for the Interior, Lubomír Štrougal, with a request to send Stonehouse to Tanganyika as it approaches independence. Štrougal needs convincing that Stonehouse can deliver the inside story on shifting allegiances in East Africa, as well as make some key introductions, but the London residency has already promised to help fund the trip. Stonehouse then announces he can no longer go because of parliamentary duties, but still asks for another 'reward'. Holan tells him no, not without some real intelligence.

As Christmas approaches, and with Stonehouse now having three children, as usual he needs money. He meets Holan for lunch on 6 December at Lucullus on Mincing Lane in the financial district of the City of London and comes armed with a short report on Tanganyika. Although Holan is appreciative, his bosses in Prague say Stonehouse's evaluation is exaggerated and the value of the report is inadequate. And his idea that Britain is lobbying for a nuclear-free zone in Central Europe is dismissed as he is the only source. He can perhaps be given something in January, they say, but not now. There have only been six meetings in the entire year and, for an agent who started off with so much promise, the Czechs are sorely disappointed.

But Holan, like Koudelka before him, wants to keep his man in play, and the only way to do that is with hard cash. On Friday 8 December, Stonehouse parks his car at the dead-end of Eden Street, off the Euston Road. He leaves it there for ninety minutes between 8 and 9.30pm, during which time the Czechs creep in and put £100 under the passenger seat – just in time for Christmas. Next year, they tell themselves, they're not going to be so easy.[27]

7

ON AND OFF THE HOOK

Stonehouse starts the year of 1962 with another march to Trafalgar Square for the Movement for Colonial Freedom, but he has a new ambition: to become president of the London Co-operative Society. The movement played an important role in winning London voters over to Labour in the 1945 election and is still aligned with the party. The presidency would help his political profile, as well as increasing his pay and expense allowance.[1]

Before then, he also needs to keep the unofficial sources open and drip-feeds 'reports' to the Czechs to ensure regular money drops to his parked car, left on deserted back streets. The communist states are eager to use post-colonial liberation to gain a foothold in Africa. Holan is impressed by his insights on matters such as Kenyan independence, the Portuguese in Angola, the break-up of Rhodesia and the evacuation of the British Army HQ, but Prague is less so. The controllers there want his reports to be more substantive with exact sources to justify the outlay and there is a chance to do so at the beginning of March.

Stonehouse and other British socialists are invited to East Germany's Spring Trade Fair in Leipzig, one of the first visits east since the Berlin Wall went up in August 1961. Stonehouse wants to be on the trip and he can fly via Prague – with a one-night stop-over – on the excuse that there are no convenient direct flights to Leipzig.[2]

He tells Holan about the trip but, on arrival at Prague International Airport, there is no sign of recognition in Immigration or Arrivals. He calls at the Czech Foreign Office in Prague and leaves a message for Koudelka, who is furious with London when he picks it up. What is Holan up to? Trying to retrieve the situation, Koudelka turns up at Stonehouse's hotel, insisting that they have lunch the next day before the Englishman goes on to Leipzig. Now they've found each other, he's going to give Stonehouse the red carpet treatment that London should have set up.[3]

They go to a restaurant in the hills overlooking the Vltava River. A waiter tells Stonehouse that the Czech government is making a mess of things and Koudelka notes that he'll have to report this as the restaurant frequently entertains foreign delegations. Stonehouse declines an all-expenses-paid trip to Czechoslovakia for Barbara and the children, but misses his connection to Leipzig and goes bar hopping and sightseeing with Koudelka instead.

Koudelka takes him to the dancing tea parlours where Stonehouse is amazed that you can pick up strange women for a dance, no questions asked. He is also impressed with the quality of people's clothes, the service and the sensible prices. He thinks the standard of living has improved vastly since he was last here four years ago and could well be on a par with the UK. Koudelka thinks this is pushing it. 'His ideas about us are much better than the reality,' he reports back to his seniors.[4]

Once Stonehouse's day with Koudelka is over, he finally gets on a plane to Leipzig. At the trade fair, he introduces the East German communist leader Herr Walter Ulbricht and Russian first deputy premier Anastas Mikoyan to the Midlands companies that are present. 'My constituents are very interested in increasing trade with the East,' says Stonehouse and they move their discussion beyond the stand into the British pavil-ion. There, over whisky, Mikoyan jokes with Ulbricht that he's already had a Czech beer and that whisky is stronger than the vodka he's used to, and they drink to closer trade links. Later that evening, Stonehouse and his fellow British socialists go to a reception with Ulbricht at the town hall. Labour MP Ian Mikardo, who too has many dubious contacts behind the Iron Curtain, is in full flight. He tells Ulbricht and Mikoyan that the British can't export any weapons as they haven't made any since 1919, and the entire room of Eastern Europeans bursts into laughter. Ulbricht then opens champagne and toasts the Brits.[5]

Soon after Stonehouse's return, Holan, eager to restore his reputation with Koudelka, debriefs Stonehouse over Greek meze at the Acropolis restaurant in Hammersmith. Stonehouse contrasts Czechoslovakia with East Germany: reserving certain hotels for VIPs and excluding ordinary East Germans is not exactly socialist equality in action. He also understands that it's necessary to control the border, but the wall?[6]

The conversation then moves on to money. Stonehouse asks for more, saying his political work is costing him and he tells Holan of his plans to run for the presidency of the London Co-operative Society. He'll need money for a promotional campaign. Holan says the information he's providing needs to be more precise and valuable before that happens. But Prague senses victory. Stonehouse's fear of revelation, combined with his demands for more money, mean he is almost at the point when they can really start to push him.

The next time they meet, on 2 April, Holan chastises Stonehouse for rescheduling an earlier meeting. He is told in no uncertain terms that if he can't make a meeting, he needs to await instruction or come the following week. They have noticed that the intelligence is getting better the more pressure they put on him and now they give him a shopping list of required information, including details of Harold Wilson's forthcoming visit to the United States. Stonehouse says that this will take a long time to gather and he needs money now. They compromise on £100 now, £100 later, and the car is left on Tonbridge Street, another backwater just off the Euston Road. Holan decides to surprise his agent and when Stonehouse returns to his car, he finds the full £200.[7]

The Co-op campaign, funded out of his own pocket, is Stonehouse's main focus and for weeks he travels the shops and households of the capital making his case. On 5 May, London Co-op members get their chance to vote for their new president, and as voting goes on across the capital, Stonehouse is tense. Will his visits to the Women's Guilds in the suburbs pay off, or will Harry Clayden, his communist opponent and one-time travel companion to Prague, be victorious? Stonehouse scrapes home by 118 votes out of a turnout of around 12,000 and, at 37, becomes head of the largest retail co-op in the world. But although Stonehouse has won the presidency, Clayden's supporters dominate the management committee and they won't step aside without a fight.[8]

Stonehouse dives straight into his new job. He slashes prices in the Co-op's 170 self-service shops in London in order to show the emerging supermarket giants a thing or two. 'If our competitors try to retaliate,' he says, managers will 'slash prices even further to maintain [our position] as the lowest priced shop.' He hires an American ad agency, BBDO, to run a campaign to back this aggressive grab for market share and pays them £50,000. He boasts that he's going to take over a national chain of shoe shops and 'get into the footwear business in a big way'. Clayden's supporters are appalled.[9]

Stonehouse's wife and children are also disappointed. The

Co-op campaign has left him so broke that he needs to sell their much-loved north London villa to release some capital. The Stonehouse clan move wholesale to a smaller house, north of London. Home is now Potters Bar, deep in the home counties commuter belt.

The Czechs have no complaints though. Their man is in a new position of power and he is most grateful for their financial contributions that covered part of his costs. His new role also suits minister of the interior/StB overlord Štrougal and KGB chief Vladimír Semichastny, who want to deepen their connections to organisations like the Co-op. Anxious to avoid a competing power block in Western Europe, the Czechs also want Stonehouse to push their anti-Common Market agenda and he obliges, becoming secretary of the new Socialist Committee on Britain and the Common Market. On Friday 20 July, he takes another £100 from Holan after lunch on Putney High Street.[10]

A general election must be held in two years' time and Macmillan's Conservative government is struggling to control wage claims. After a series of by-election losses, the prime minister sacks his chancellor Selwyn Lloyd – 'invited to resign', as it is politely described – and replaces seven of the twenty-one members of his cabinet. The 'Supermac' who presided over the 1950s boom becomes 'Mac the Knife' as the economy frays at the edges and Labour look like a sure bet to take office.

Stonehouse promises his handler that, once he's a junior minister, he'll deliver better service. Then he once again seeks reassurance that no one at the embassy knows about him. Holan says that only two officers – he and Koudelka – and the big boss in Prague know his true identity. But Holan is lying to his informant: at least ten individuals know that Agent Kolon is in fact John Stonehouse MP.[11]

The Co-op position helps Stonehouse's profile but, as he gets busier, he is even harder for the Czechs to pin down. On a rare day off, Sunday 9 September, he joins an anti-Common Market march to Trafalgar Square. He takes to the plinth: 'The Conservative government has no mandate from the British people to take us into the Common Market. The Labour Party will come out against it at conference. It will come off the fence.' But such optimism is misleading as the party is bitterly divided. Influential MPs such as Roy Jenkins are on the other side of the argument and Stonehouse thinks nothing of dismissing Jenkins's pro-European assertions as 'foolish, misleading and dishonest'.[12]

A few days after Trafalgar Square, Stonehouse's Czech alter ego haunts him when MI5's Charles Elwell strikes again. John Vassall, a civil servant working in naval intelligence, has been named as a Soviet agent by a KGB defector. Security services find a Praktina document-copying camera in Vassall's flat and he confesses to everything. The case immediately goes to the Old Bailey and causes a press sensation. Vassall receives an eighteen-year sentence and, so soon after Portland, public interest in communist infiltration reaches an all-time high.[13]

It's a salutary reminder to Stonehouse of the risks he is taking, but the Czechs want more. He's taking their money but only handing over 'intelligence' when he accidentally comes across it. They consider him lazy and decide to stop the retainer and pay him only for bespoke work. They note that he's moving away from East Africa but, on the flipside, he's becoming more vocal against the integration of Western Europe, which they like. Could they make getting closer to both Wilson and Gaitskell his next project? Stonehouse is known to be a Wilson man, but once the visibly ageing Gaitskell goes, and there's a new leader, who knows? Either way they're in it for the long haul, and Stonehouse knows it.[14]

In October, the Cold War steps up another notch. US spy planes confirm that Russia has deployed nuclear weapons in Cuba and President Kennedy says that any launch from Cuba to a Western nation would be interpreted as an attack by the Soviets on the United States. The world trembles on the brink of nuclear war, but then Russia withdraws the weapons.

While Russia and the US stare each other out, Stonehouse again backs Wilson in Labour's deputy leadership contest against Gaitskell's man George Brown. Brown sees him off and it looks as though Stonehouse has backed the wrong horse. But by Christmas, Gaitskell is hospitalised and, in January 1963, he dies. Over lunch at the Angus Steakhouse on Blandford Street in Marylebone, Stonehouse boasts to Holan that he was the person charged with calling Wilson in the US to tell him the news.[15]

True or not, his man Wilson becomes the party's new leader in February and the Czechs reappraise Stonehouse's value. At the end of the month, they tot up how much 'Kolon pravýn jménem (real name) John Stonehouse' has cost them so far. Just a £50 Christmas present in 1959, £580 in 1960, £350 in 1961, and a top-up over the agreed basic of £500 to £750 in 1962. That's just the cash 'rewards'; the Africa trips, club memberships, political and campaigning expenses are all extra. He has been a disappointment so far, but now that he is closer to Wilson, they offer him further encouragement. A general election has to be held by October 1964 and Stonehouse is positive Labour are going to win. The Blandford Street meeting is soon followed by another at the Peppercorn restaurant near the Tower of London's Traitors' Gate and a money drop in his car in Bloomsbury Square.[16]

Then Stonehouse goes cold. In March, war minister John Profumo resigns over his dalliances with other women and their KGB connections. It's a steamy affair that whips up public interest in espionage. In April, a 50,000-word report on John Vassall criticises the civil servant's security clearance and aspects of government security. While these scandals reverberate and his money worries ease thanks to the move out of town, Stonehouse wants out.[17]

The Czechs are disappointed but, while Agent Lee is using his position on House of Commons sub-committees on military expenditure to fill the files of the Czech's security services with secret documents, Stonehouse still hasn't handed over any top-secret documents. And although they have seen that he will allow himself to be corrupted for money, they still haven't found his Achilles heel.[18]

A crackdown at the Czech embassy in light of Vassall and Profumo settles things. Holan is observed trying to persuade a member of the navy to give up secret information and is expelled from Britain. He slopes back to Prague with his tail firmly between his legs, ready for a rebuke, or worse. Until this blows over and the Czechs can re-establish the London residency, they decide the Kolon relationship should be suspended. Stonehouse is off the hook.[19]

This means he can concentrate on the Co-op, which is just as well as there he is facing opposition everywhere he looks. His only ally is his close friend John McGrath, the London Co-operative Society's chief accountant who has been in post since 1948. Yet McGrath has secretly set up a company, Economic Planning Services, without the knowledge of the board, and is also in trouble for obtaining amphetamines from the Co-op chemist without a prescription. His days are numbered and Stonehouse isn't looking much better.[20]

There are rumours that he took a back-hander as part of the contract to ad agency BBDO and that he's sleeping with one of the men on their team. Stonehouse puts this absurd gossip down to Communist Party members and forms the Anti-Communist Reform Group to counter them. He briefs the nationals that the London Co-op has been taken over by a communist insurgency, but the society at large fights back, calling this defamatory.[21]

The schism in the London Co-op makes national television in May ahead of elections to the board of directors. Richard Dimbleby interviews both Stonehouse and fellow Labour MP and Co-op member Ronald Ledger, the latter saying that there's nothing to substantiate Stonehouse's allegations of communist disruption. Rather, Ledger claims, it is the speed of Stonehouse's changes that is at the bottom of any disagreement. The television programme does Stonehouse no favours and, when the board election results are in, the so-called communists of the 1960 Committee trounce Stonehouse's Reform Group. The president calls it a tragic blow, but is clearly in retreat.[22]

As a Co-op sponsored Labour MP, Stonehouse appeals to his party leader about his situation. But while Wilson is sympathetic, he says he really can't intervene in Co-op business. At a meeting on 29 July, the London Co-op Society calls for Stonehouse's resignation in a 784–331 vote. Stonehouse refuses to resign, citing the independent arbitration that won't reveal its findings until September. Yet Labour contemporaries, such as Anthony Wedgwood Benn and Richard Crossman, are muttering about how Stonehouse uses rough tactics. He doesn't come out of the whole affair very well at all.[23]

Before then, there's an unexpected offer from Harold Wilson: the use of his holiday bungalow, Lowenva, in the Isles of Scilly for a family holiday. It was Mary Wilson's idea, but it's a sure sign of the party leader's approval.

Back from holiday, Stonehouse steps into the fray over what is now the 'Profumo Affair' after Tory MPs suggest Lord Denning's report on the scandal shouldn't be published. 'Labour MPs who are still very suspicious about his handling of the affair will not allow other scandals to be swept under the carpet,' Stonehouse says in a September speech in his constituency. 'There's been enough gossip in the last few months to bring down half-a-dozen governments. This can only do harm to political life in Britain. The public will develop a cynical disrespect for all politicians unless the facts are brought out.'[24]

At the Labour Party conference in Scarborough, Wilson makes a triumphant speech that not only captures the imagination of the whole party, but also the public at large. 'We are redefining and restating our socialism in terms of the scientific revolution,' comes the stirring rhetoric as he brings his speech to its conclusion. 'The Britain that is going to be forged in the white heat of this revolution will be no place for restrictive practices or for outdated methods ... For the commanding heights of British industry to be controlled by men whose only claim is their aristocratic connections or the power of inherited wealth or speculative finance is irrelevant to the 20th century.' We can't be a nation of 'gentlemen' in a world of 'players', concludes Wilson.

A general election is due by the end of 1964 and Harold Macmillan's government has run its course. Thought to have mishandled both Profumo and Vassall, and satirised as out of touch in *Private Eye* and the BBC's cutting Saturday-night programme TW3 (*That Was the Week That Was*), the contrast with Wilson's vision of a new Britain is stark. Macmillan resigns and, on 18 October, foreign secretary Sir Alec Douglas-Home takes over from him. 'He had an expensive education,' Wilson had once said of the outgoing Tory leader. 'Eton and Suez.'

On 20 November, Stonehouse feels it's time to remind a few people of his background in the RAF – and that Britain can only fail if it cowers to American dominance. His erstwhile handler Koudelka was right: this man loves attention. It's Stonehouse's oxygen – what he needs to feel alive, to survive. The government has failed to sell the TSR2 bomber to Australia, Stonehouse says to a packed House, and instead they are buying American TFX bombers. Why? The Tories suggest his comments won't help with the deal-making but, to cheers from his own benches, Stonehouse says this claim is contemptible. The Common Market negotiations and the impact on the Commonwealth countries is a more likely story, he insists, to more roars of approval.[25]

It's interpellations like this that make Stonehouse realise that it's time to get serious. No more Czechs, no more Co-op infighting. He's gone over and above in helping Wilson to the leadership and got to stay in his holiday home as a reward. Now he must do everything in his power to ensure that Wilson's Labour Party wins a general election again after thirteen years in opposition. If ever there was a time to go big on his political ambitions, this is it.

8

AGENT TWISTER

On 10 January 1964, Stonehouse finally throws in the towel and formally announces his resignation from the London Co-op Society, effective 1 May. He cites parliamentary and political commitments ahead of this year's general election but, for the management committee, it is a clear victory. The post was supposed to be for three years and Stonehouse will serve only two. The world's biggest co-operative society will get a new president in Stonehouse's now-bitter rival, the communist Harry Clayden.[1]

It's a relief in a way, but despite downsizing to Potters Bar, money is tight. Stonehouse is one of a new breed of MPs without independent means and will soon have no other income to top up his MP's salary. But 1964 might be a good year for him, he thinks. With Labour the favourites for the election due this autumn, his loyalty to Wilson could just pay off – perhaps with an appointment to the Colonial Office.

Prime Minister Douglas-Home hangs on until the last moment before he calls the election for Thursday 15 October. The campaign is only a month long and the country is on a knife edge. Merseybeat bands are rocking Britain, mini-skirted Cilla Black is the year's big number one and the grouse-shooting Etonian prime minister looks out of touch. Wilson is a television natural but the wartime generation aren't yet convinced by Labour's promises. The 1950s boom is still going strong and the middle class have never had it so good. Why rock the boat?

It is a close-run, highly charged campaign. Tory grandee Quintin Hogg lashes out at a poster of Wilson with his walking cane while Labour hecklers shout down Douglas-Home on the hustings. The Tories are ahead in the opinion polls for most of the campaign, but in the final days, Labour edges ahead.

Stonehouse needs to make sure that he keeps his own seat *and* maintains a national profile. On Wednesday 7 October, one week before the election, he chooses to stand on a makeshift box in Wednesbury marketplace as he prefers it to 'a disembodied voice over a loudspeaker'. 'I tried to get a soap box,' he jokes, as he makes his final case to keep his seat. 'The Tories like to claim they are patriotic. But is it patriotic to sneer at the success of nationalised industry?' he shouts. 'They've tried to make nationalisation a dirty word, but the Electricity Council has made £70m profit. I ask you, Tories, aren't you proud of that?'[2]

His Tory opponent criticises the time Stonehouse spends campaigning in other constituencies, but this is all key to his push for a position under Wilson. And in these surrounding constituencies, there is one Tory who Stonehouse keeps running into: Enoch Powell, the Conservative candidate for Wolverhampton South West. Powell says immigration or, as the papers would have it, 'the colour problem', is already 'so formidable' that any further immigration must be halted while Commonwealth newcomers assimilate. Stonehouse says that, under Labour, immigration would have been organised at source and these kind of problems would never have arisen.[3]

'Labour is poised for a great victory,' Wilson says on 10 October at his last regular London press conference. But, he cautions, 'the Conservative leadership is rattled and at panic stations. I must warn the electorate of the possibility of last-minute stunts, scares or diversions.' Asked about the type of cabinet he might form, he says young members especially should be given a chance – and that is just what 39-year-old John Stonehouse wants to hear.[4]

On the BBC, fourteen years after the first election coverage on TV, Richard Dimbleby leads the nation through the night, while election expert David Butler takes centre stage once more – this time with an innovation: the swingometer. 'We hope to give you a firm prediction before many results are reported,' says Butler, reminding viewers that Labour needs a 4 per cent swing to achieve a working majority. Robin Day joins the studio presenters, as he talks to candidates up and down the country. Alan Whicker is under an umbrella and a giant TV screen in Trafalgar Square, while TW3's dinner-jacketed David Frost is the 'man about town' dropping in on celebrations throughout the night.

Then the teleprinters start clattering, the first results come in and as Dimbleby keeps viewers updated, he explains that the snack he is eating is Italian and is called pizza. The swingometer oscillates as Roy Jenkins keeps Birmingham Stechford and is predicted to get a role in a Wilson cabinet. Then to Huyton, Wilson's seat. It's a startling 19,000 majority to huge cheers from the crowd and the BBC predicts a Labour majority of twenty-nine seats. 'Do you feel like a prime minister?' he is asked. 'Quite honestly, I feel like a drink,' he quips.

The nation is gripped. Wilson watches as Richard Crossman, Denis Healey, George Wigg and other favourites for his government win decent majorities. He is quick to condemn the racist, anti-immigration campaign in Smethwick, which has seen the only major Tory swing of the election. Fenner Brockway also loses his seat in Slough in another anti-immigration vote.

At 12.55am on Friday 16 October, Wednesbury is called.

'Mr Stonehouse, a well-known member of Parliament,' says Dimbleby – all his parliamentary grandstanding and briefings with journalists have paid off – 'is holding the seat for Labour Co-op.' But it's a disappointing swing to the Conservatives as Stonehouse's margin is halved to 3,222. 'In that Black Country area,' says Butler, 'it isn't just Smethwick on the racial issue.' By dawn, Labour's predicted majority of twenty-nine is downgraded to nineteen, and ultimately ends up at just four. It's a mandate, but it's not going to keep Wilson in business for the full five years.[5]

The PM-in-waiting makes his way to London and, before he's met the civil servants in Number 10, details of his front bench are leaking out. Callaghan has already been made chancellor. Ted Short moves into 12 Downing Street as chief whip. Barbara Castle becomes overseas development minister, Healey gets defence. Jenkins, a heavyweight Gaitskellite foe, is given aviation. Wilson makes his most loyal lieutenant George Wigg paymaster general – in effect, minister without portfolio – and gives him a special brief of liaising with the security services. Post-Profumo, he sees this as an essential protection against future scandal.[6]

At her new and significantly less glamorous house in Potters Bar, Barbara waits and wonders if her husband will make the cut. He's been staring at the telephone, hoping for a call from Wilson. And with each passing hour, he's convinced it will never come. By late afternoon on Saturday 17 October, it's time to take his mind off things. The new Bond film is out. He and Barbara will go to the pictures, leaving their daughters behind to look after their 4-year-old brother.

Goldfinger, beams the illuminated listing. Sean Connery is back as Bond and Honor Blackman joins him as Pussy Galore. The police had their hands full at the black-tie world premiere in Trafalgar Square as excited fans waited for a glimpse of the stars; the buzz around this one is huge. After Shirley Bassey's rousing theme, Stonehouse and Barbara settle down to the post-title shots of Miami Beach and the Fontainebleau Hotel. 'I doubt that the Miami Beach Police would take kindly to what you're doing,' smirks Connery to one of a long line of villains, while sipping a cocktail and having suntan lotion masterfully applied by yet another beautiful woman. In London, the new secretary of state for aviation, Roy Jenkins, is watching the same film with his family.[7]

The Stonehouses return home to be greeted by their teenage daughters: 'He's called!' Before long, the phone rings again: 'Harold here, John. Will you come and see me tomorrow?' Stonehouse knows there are plenty of ministerial positions left and there's a spring in his step as he knocks on the door of Number 10. He's taken down a long corridor and shown to a round table in an alcove ante-room. Soon a door opens and there is Wilson, sat behind the table in the Cabinet Room, huge ashtray and pipe in front of him, alongside a biography of Abraham Lincoln. 'I want you to join Roy Jenkins at the Ministry of Aviation,' Wilson says with little ado. 'You were a pilot in the RAF, weren't you? You should do well there, and I think you can get on with Roy.' With a love of James Bond in common, what could possibly go wrong?[8]

Stonehouse's MP's pay is bolstered by a salary of £3,750 and he says he is delighted that Jenkins is his new boss, describing him as urbane and cultured and dismissing his reputation for conceit. But pundits predict fireworks, given that Stonehouse is on the record as calling Jenkins foolish over his pro-Common Market views. Suffice to say, Jenkins does not share his new junior minister's warm feelings. When Wilson sprung Stonehouse upon him, Jenkins protested but unusually the prime minister wouldn't listen. Within a month, 'personal differences' are reported, and Jenkins says he is fed up with Stonehouse patronising him.[9]

Regardless, Stonehouse goes about carving out a role for himself as the jet-setting champion of British aviation exports. The country needs to pay its way in the world, thinks Stonehouse, and he makes aviation his business. But it has its downside: the Czechs are back on his case.

With military and civil aircraft in his brief, they're pleased about Stonehouse's promotion and make moves to re-establish contact. The expulsion of Holan from the London residency has died down and Stonehouse's previous silent controller at HQ, Robert Husak (aka Hanc), is the new man in town. Husak, a so-called 'Romeo agent', is a party animal in the mould of Profumo's Captain Ivanov. For a man who likes to play, 1960s London is perfect. The fleshpots of Soho are heaving, the women look incredible and there's a socialist government. He's also a determined and persuasive intelligence officer.[10]

Stonehouse becomes one of his top targets and he sees to it that the new junior minister of aviation is invited to a cocktail party at 6–7 Kensington Palace Gardens. Inside the vast embassy on this gated 'Millionaire's Row', Husak spots Stonehouse across the room and makes a beeline for him. Stonehouse is surprised when Husak moves in as though he knows him. He is sure he'd remember the tall, handsome diplomat, yet has no recollection of having seen him before. Husak, however, knows all about Stonehouse: the 'friendship' with Koudelka, Kladno, his Co-operative background. Stonehouse tries to shake him off, but Husak is persistent and suggests they have lunch. Husak mainly uses his charm to get the wives of diplomats into bed, but it works on Stonehouse too and he agrees to meet. After all, no one will be watching now that Wilson has forbidden MI5 from carrying out surveillance of his MPs.[11]

Over lunch in December, Husak invites him to Czechoslovakia, but Stonehouse explains that there are more pressing overseas trips for him to take. He's due to fly to South America just after Christmas to promote Britain's VC10 passenger jet and has to justify such trips with Jenkins and the Foreign Office. Undeterred, Husak insists on looking at other options, but Stonehouse remains non-committal. He is determined not to get further compromised, so he carefully reports this lunch and Husak's interest in him to the department's intelligence officer David Purnell, who in turn tells Wilson's security supremo, George Wigg.[12]

During the Christmas break, Husak develops his plan and, in February 1965, Stonehouse receives an official invitation to visit Kladno. Unfortunately for the Czechs, it's turned down as 'unnecessary' by civil servants at the Ministry of Aviation and Foreign Office. Stonehouse does get approval to go to Beirut though, where he believes Middle East Airlines are ripe to buy seven VC10s, and also to Saudi Arabia to sell an air defence system. And then, on the recommendation of the Saudis, Kuwait also puts in an order.[13]

He is proving to be a brilliant salesman. Taller than most men of his generation, charming and authoritative with just a hint of steel, he has found his metier and, on 1 April 1965, he is rewarded with a personal minute from the prime minister. 'I would just like to offer you my congratulations on the assiduous and successful work you have been putting in on sales of British aircraft,' writes Wilson. 'I know that this is calling for a great deal of travel all over the world, with all the inconvenience and disruption to your private life that that involves; but I do not need to tell you how valuable the work is to the Government and to the country.'[14]

Shortly after, at the end of June, Stonehouse's visit to

Czechoslovakia comes back onto the agenda. Hawker Siddeley are trying to sell their medium-haul Trident aircraft there and the company thinks Stonehouse might help. This time he is up for it, but again there is a hurdle: the Foreign Office doesn't want to overdo visits to the Eastern bloc and word comes back from Cecil Parrott, the British ambassador in Prague, that it's too early for a visit.[15]

However, Stonehouse's Labour colleague Ian Mikardo is going to Czechoslovakia on private business – he's a specialist in international reciprocal trade agreements – so Stonehouse asks him to 'lend a hand' with the Hawker Siddeley deal. Mikardo – another MP rumoured to be an Eastern bloc agent – agrees to this, even though secretly he thinks Stonehouse a man whose talents fall well short of his growing reputation. Meanwhile Stonehouse makes sure his staff at the ministry don't let up on Parrott: 'The new role Mr Stonehouse is playing in the promotion of aircraft exports might not be apparent to the ambassador. With this in mind you may feel that it is not too early to intervene.'[16]

Make no mistake, Stonehouse wants to go to Prague, yet in Cecil Parrott he encounters a formidable barrier. The ambassador replies: 'We appreciate the new role Mr Stonehouse is playing in the promotion of our aircraft exports and his willingness to visit Czechoslovakia. The Czechs dislike being rushed and are reluctant to openly defy the Russians, which discussions with a British minister on sales of Western aircraft would imply. A representative of Hawker Siddeley could probably make useful progress.' Stonehouse gives in – with the caveat that it might be appropriate for him to go later in the year.[17]

He leaves it until August before he tries again. Hawker Siddeley are giving a presentation there in October and

Stonehouse offers to go in September to smooth the way, to which foreign secretary Michael Stewart gives his approval. Parrott sounds out the Czech Ministry of Foreign Affairs and is surprised to find that Stonehouse's visit would be 'much welcomed' by the Czechs. So much so, in fact, that Parrott now thinks it should take place even though the Czech minister of transport is away in Moscow at the time. He invites Stonehouse to stay at his residence, but warns that a visit to the communist stronghold of Kladno will mean enduring speeches on the communists' take on the Vietnam War and West Germany.

The Foreign Office also briefs him. Those persecuted in the Stalinist era have been rehabilitated; listening to foreign broadcasts or receiving Western visitors won't land you in jail; and some debate and criticism is now tolerated, he is told. The Vietnam War has made little practical difference to Anglo-Czech relations, continues the briefing, nor to the current exchange of visiting personalities that has been in play since late 1963. However, there is no question of a sudden political volte-face by the Czechs; the present regime is consistent in its support of the Soviet Union on all major issues.[18]

What neither the Foreign Office nor Stonehouse know is that the StB, led by the latest interior minister Josef Kudrna, have tightened their co-operation with the KGB and its chairman Vladimir Semichastny. Developing the intelligence services of the satellite states is one of Semichastny's priorities and none are better placed than the Czechs. There are to be joint operations and closer co-ordination between residencies in Western capitals – including London – and well-placed agents become even more important.[19]

Husak tries to get hold of Stonehouse at regular intervals on his home phone to arrange more meetings, but Stonehouse is elusive. When Stonehouse finally arrives in Prague, he is never out of the British embassy's sight, listening devices are everywhere and the StB do not even attempt to make contact.

For the Czechs, it is a missed opportunity and, from the British business perspective, it also proves to be a wasted trip. The Czechs aren't interested in the Trident after all. Their medium-haul requirements are being met by Russian aircraft and they plan to buy Boeing planes for long-haul routes. Stonehouse persuades them at least to consider British Overseas Aircraft Corporation's long-haul VC10. Ever the optimist, he tells the *Birmingham Daily Post* that Britain has very good prospects of selling aircraft to Czechoslovakia.[20]

He also has a new fan. In his despatch to foreign secretary Michael Stewart, Parrott applauds Stonehouse's vigour, unstinting energy and good humour, and reports back that the visit was extremely valuable. News that a team from BOAC are in fact coming to Prague to promote the VC10 confirms his enthusiasm for the minister of aviation.[21]

At the end of the month, Stonehouse avoids Husak at September's Labour Party conference in Blackpool where Wilson hints of an early general election to bolster his standing. Husak is frustrated but eventually meets him again at another party at the ambassador Zdeněk Trhlík's Villa Magnolia in Hampstead, which Stonehouse attends in his official capacity. He tells Husak to call on him in parliament and just before Christmas, on 21 December, Husak arrives in the Central Lobby. They have lunch in the Grill at the nearby St Ermin's Hotel. It's an appropriate enough venue: during the Second World War, the Special Operations Executive and MI6 were based there and it was a favourite meeting place for Guy Burgess and his Russian handler in the 1950s.

Husak is armed with Christmas presents for Stonehouse and

his wife Barbara, but Stonehouse is frosty. He explains that although he had good relationships with Koudelka and Holan, he is in government now, has long-term ambitions and can't afford any scandal in his career. Husak reassures him that he realises his status is changing and the cover story needs to be watertight. 'What do you want and what are the limits on the financial rewards on offer?' asks Stonehouse. Husak tells him that the compensation will be the same as before – a basic with no upward ceiling – but they need good-quality information. It doesn't have to be military, but it does have to be of quality.

They agree to meet again at the beginning of February but Stonehouse, who has been on another sales tour, this time to Australia and New Zealand, doesn't turn up. And then he misses the next two dates as well. But Husak, much like his quarry, is a man who won't take no for an answer.[22]

On 28 February 1966, Wilson calls a snap election and, ten days later, parliament is dissolved. Polling is set for three weeks' time and Stonehouse, who has spent a lot of time away, needs to focus on Wednesbury, seen as marginal after the Tories took a chunk out of his majority seventeen months ago. But, as usual, he's positive and tells the press he'll retrieve those lost votes. 'The government is very popular in the area,' he says. When asked if some top politicians will be drafted in to support his campaign, he replies: 'We have got enough talent in the constituency already.' It's talent who's chosen to greet the Queen at London Airport on her return from a tour of the Caribbean the very next week, and Stonehouse makes sure the West Midlands press give it the attention he believes it deserves.[23]

Ted Heath has replaced Alec Douglas-Home, but he's only eight months into the job and his first election campaign as party leader is not a success. Thursday 31 March is polling day and results in a Labour landslide with an overall majority of 97 and a majority over the Conservatives of 110. Stonehouse holds Wednesbury where he increases his margin by 4,000 votes; Wilson is particularly pleased by the recapture of Smethwick.[24]

The new mandate gives Wilson a chance to refresh his team and over the weekend he brings in some new faces. He still regards Stonehouse as a bright prospect and calls him into Downing Street. He is given a new brief: a return to his political roots as undersecretary of state in the Colonial Office. It's a sideways move – he's still the number two and his income will remain the same – but dismantling the remains of the British Empire is a passion and he's soon on a jet-setting tour of East Africa and Mauritius accompanied by Barbara.

During the spring and early summer, while Stonehouse is getting stuck into his new role, Husak is at his wits' end. Stonehouse has missed countless meetings and has remained elusive. If this carries on, he will have to go and stake out the family home in Potters Bar.[25]

Then on 14 June, Czech deputy prime minister Oldřich Černík comes to London and, a week later, Stonehouse attends a dinner in his honour. There he runs into Husak. It's a tense exchange. Stonehouse tells Husak he's been promised a ministerial post come the autumn, when the Colonial Office will be reorganised, but that will make it even harder to co-operate. We need to talk about it properly, insists Husak, and Stonehouse gives in, just as he did last time. They set a lunch date for 19 July.

Both need to be careful and the Czechs are vigilant on both of their behalfs. After inspections and surveillance hours ahead of time, the two men meet at Vivian's, an anonymous and unglamorous restaurant on the edges of north-west London. Husak wants to know why Stonehouse hasn't been attending their scheduled meetings. Stonehouse explains that he has just been very busy, but concedes that he is still willing to 'co-operate'. He reiterates that in the autumn, when the Colonial and Commonwealth offices are merged, he hopes to be promoted. They will then have to be even more careful, but it also means he'll be more valuable. They inevitably discuss money. His previous basic was £500 a year, but he wants to be compensated for the lack of money since Holan was expelled. Stonehouse promises to share government views on Germany, the USA and Africa and pushes for £1,500.

While Husak and Stonehouse negotiate, the country cavorts. On a glorious late July afternoon, England win the World Cup and Wilson milks it, appearing with team manager Alf Ramsey on the balcony of the Royal Garden Hotel in Kensington during the evening celebrations. The prime minister would have been less happy if he knew that, less than a mile away in Kensington Palace Gardens, the Czech's London residency chief, Captain Josef Minx (cover name Malena), was compiling a report on one of his ministers.

Husak has told Minx what Stonehouse wants and, at this level, Czech minister of the interior Josef Kudrna has to sign it off. Minx and Husak say that Stonehouse's gap in service should be reflected in the cash reward, and reassure Kudrna of their agent's career prospects. Minx adds that when they hand over the money, a sound recording will be made to compromise Stonehouse further. They already have photographs of him heading for a lunch date with Husak.[26]

While they put his case, Stonehouse goes to the House of Commons for a debate on Gibraltar. Things have changed significantly since he and his great friend Fenner Brockway sparred with John Profumo over the British colonies nearly ten years ago. Now he is the one charged with finding solutions and there is a change in tone: 'This is not the time for extravagant solutions that cannot work in practice. This is the time for patience and statesmanship.' He is sounding more and more like the statesman he proclaims to be and Terry Lancaster declares in *The People* that Stonehouse will be a winner in the upcoming reshuffle, while other papers say he's going to become minister of state in the new ministry to come out of Colonial and Commonwealth. The Czechs are delighted.[27]

But Wilson knows who talks to the press and who doesn't, and he's the one who likes to make the announcements. Fortunately for Stonehouse, he is usually loyal to those who have backed him and very rarely cuts them off completely, even when they disappoint him. It is a trait that baffles his closest colleagues. In the July 1966 reshuffle, the Colonial Office disappears, but there is still a Commonwealth relations secretary. That job goes to the leader of the House, Herbert 'Bert' Bowden, and Stonehouse stays in post. No promotion, no demotion.

Stonehouse next meets Husak for lunch on 29 November at another obscure out-of-town restaurant. It's what Husak would describe as a 'working lunch' and he finds Stonehouse relatively relaxed and co-operative. But the same old problems soon emerge: the information Stonehouse is selling is not worth the price they're paying. And Stonehouse is worried that, like Koudelka and Holan before, Husak will leave London and even more people will know about him. Husak is frustrated yet again and vows to talk about how exactly he can apply the thumbscrews when he goes back to Prague HQ.

Stonehouse knows he has to do more to stay in the money and when they meet again before Christmas, he thinks he has intel that will please Husak and his bosses. He reports that the UK is not going to reduce the number of its troops in West Germany; Wilson considers the situation with Southern Rhodesia hopeless; and there's the possibility of an 'Atlantic alliance' forming between the UK and the US, if the former can't achieve membership of the European Economic Community (EEC). But apart from the news on troops in West Germany, the Czechs either already know what Stonehouse has revealed or it's contradicted by another source. They hand over some money regardless.[28]

Wilson spends his Christmas break in the Isles of Scilly, working on a major reshuffle and a government reorganisation. Early in 1967, Aviation is folded into the Ministry of Technology and, on Friday 7 January, Wilson makes Stonehouse a minister of state in the enlarged department, a promotion from under-secretary and a pay rise to £5,625, plus allowance. It's not quite the big promotion he's been talking about, but the extra money is useful for Stonehouse and selling planes is something he knows he can do under new boss Anthony Wedgwood Benn, who has been promoted out of his position of postmaster general and into the cabinet.

Stonehouse joins defence minister Denis Healey in Paris for his first outing in the new role. They discuss the Anglo-French 'swing-wing' combat aircraft that the two countries have been working on together. The following week he is off to Bonn to meet with the West German minister of economics about building a European airbus. After years of fighting the Common Market, Stonehouse now sees sense in a 'European project'. He has become an important figure on the political stage and, when a by-election is called in Nuneaton, Stonehouse is now one of the Labour 'big guns' called in to campaign. But he's back in the pay of the Czechs and this time their claws are digging deeper. They rename him Agent Twister and prepare to draw blood.[29]

9

FALLING STAR

At the beginning of 1967, enthused by the cash he's now receiving, Stonehouse raises his game and gives the Czechs some serious intel. He reveals that, contrary to reports, a base for the American fighter jets (F111s) *is* being built on Diego Garcia, a British-owned atoll in the Indian Ocean; he comments on rumours that Polaris submarines are being deployed in the Indian Ocean; and he details the reality of West Germany's nuclear plans – the chief stumbling block to East–West negotiations.

As well as these globally significant insights, Stonehouse says he might also be able to provide the technical specification on a revolutionary new plastic that is being used in British military aircraft – if he can have payment before Easter. Husak's bosses at the First Directorate of Foreign Intelligence back in Prague ask their chief Josef Kudrna if he can clear a payment of £750 for the next meeting and, on 13 March, the money is handed over.[1]

Two weeks later, Stonehouse and the Czechs switch to official business. A Czech delegation descends on London for two-day talks about a possible £10 million deal to buy three Super VC10s and their interpreter is a certain Robert Husak. Speaking as the UK government's minister of aviation, Stonehouse offers landing rights in London if Czechoslovakia buys the VC10 – but they must decide soon or the rights will go to Austria. To the Czechs, it's like everything with Stonehouse: promises, promises.

Back undercover, at their next one to one, Stonehouse asks Husak, just as he had Koudelka before, if he records their meetings; after all, it seems the logical thing to do. Husak laughs and dismisses this. The truth is they do keep trying, but the restaurants are too noisy to get a clear recording. What they have got, however, are those shots of Stonehouse and Husak together in Belgravia's Lowndes Street.

Husak is under pressure to get more out of Stonehouse. The defence intel is good, but he will only give oral briefings and takes back any documents he shares. This makes compromise and blackmail near impossible and, without that, moving him into top-level espionage is going to be hard work. Husak is told to find more private meeting places in the hope that Stonehouse will give them more. Until then, no more money is to be handed over.[2]

At home, Barbara notices that her husband is increasingly stressed. He is losing faith in Labour and often comes home to Potters Bar sick to the heart after debates in the Commons. She puts some of his bad temper down to the 'male menopause', but with every rising star Wilson promotes, he seems to get more paranoid and threatened, and she struggles to understand why. He says he's getting old and MPs are becoming hard-bitten and cynical.[3]

Stonehouse chooses July next to give the Czechs something of value. He tells them about the forthcoming visit of West German defence minister Gerhard Schröder, but he refuses to hand over any information about the top-secret military aspect. He always stops just short of fully compromising himself, laments Husak. Even so, they will have to give him some money for his efforts – which, with summer holidays fast approaching, is what it's all about for Agent Twister, and £200 is approved. Throughout the summer, Stonehouse puffs himself up to Husak. He has the full support of Wilson. He'll be a cabinet minister soon and then, eventually, foreign secretary.[4]

He's on the road in the autumn of 1967, buying and selling planes for Britain, visiting Moscow, Bonn, Canada and the US. Britain is committed to buying US swing-wing fighters, the F111, and when he gets to Fort Worth, Texas, donning an orange flying suit, he takes an eighty-minute flight in one, but refuses the offer to actually fly it. The Americans dub him 'Mr Aviation'. By the end of the month, Stonehouse is in Paris with Healey, signing another deal to co-produce helicopters. Come November, he predicts that Concorde will be flying early in 1968.[5]

But while Healey and Stonehouse are talking up British industry, foreign exchange speculators are talking it down. Under the 1944 Bretton Woods international agreement, currencies are pegged at fixed rates to the US dollar, but Britain's widening trade gap and deteriorating industrial relations lead dealers to form a bleak view of the country's economic prospects. They sell sterling, forcing the chancellor, James Callaghan, to raise interest rates and buy sterling to maintain the peg with the dollar. But the pressure is irresistible. At 9.30pm on Saturday 18 November, Callaghan announces that the pound will be devalued from \$2.80 to \$2.40, the official bank rate is increased to 8 per cent, and credit controls are tightened. Banks and stock exchanges are told to stay closed the following Monday and Wilson appears on television on Sunday evening in a sombre broadcast. He assures a shocked and uncomprehending public that 'although the pound abroad is worth 14 per cent or so less in terms of other currencies, that doesn't mean of course that the pound here in Britain, in your pocket or purse or in your bank, has been devalued'. It's a poor choice of words that his political opponents never forget.[6]

Nor, it would seem, does John Stonehouse. When he meets with Husak the following month, he eventually confides that he is depressed by the failures of Labour policy and that the devaluation will backfire. Husak also has a confidence to share. He will be leaving London in the near future, news that Stonehouse takes very calmly. They are lunching at the Carlton Tower Hotel on Cadogan Place – it's a return to the glamour days of this unlikely union – but it's hard to talk as the restaurant is packed with Christmas bookings. Stonehouse suggests they go on to the Royal Automobile Club on Pall Mall, where he is now a member.

They settle down to drinks amid the plush velvets, crystal chandeliers and gold leaf panelling, with only a handful of elderly gentlemen slumbering in their armchairs as company. Stonehouse shows a desire to drink more than usual and eventually Husak notices his informant is in fact, for the first time in their relationship, quite drunk.

Stonehouse says that he is becoming more ideologically inclined towards the regime in Czechoslovakia. It's been the year of great social reform and modernisation at the Home Office under Jenkins, with the legalisation of abortion, decriminalisation of homosexuality and a promised race relations act. But why is it, laments Stonehouse, that when it comes to economic progress, Russia is doing so well and British industry is so lacking? Could Husak perhaps put him in touch with a Communist Party economist so he can understand more about their way of doing things?

It's hard to confirm if it's a drunk mind speaking sober thoughts, but for the first time Husak feels ideological motives may play a bigger part than he thought. Stonehouse says that he will be visiting Czechoslovakia in the new year and agrees to meet Husak's replacement for a detailed 'operative' debriefing.

Contact will be made by the phrase 'best regards from Robert (Husak) and your friends in Kladno'. And this time, he doesn't even mention money.[7]

Husak is at pains not to overestimate the situation. It might just be a momentary crisis for Stonehouse, but on the basis of this day in late December, it's hard for the Czechs not to get excited again. They may finally get something decent out of their investment. And with Wilson's security supremo George Wigg moving upstairs to the House of Lords, there will be even less chance of Stonehouse being discovered.

In January 1968, Czechoslovakia gets a new leader in Alexander Dubček and he leads the Prague Spring of liberalisation under the banner 'Socialism with a Human Face'. Stonehouse tells the London residency chief Captain Josef Kalina that he wants to meet Dubček when he's in Prague on a forthcoming ministerial visit. Kalina, who is looking after Stonehouse until the handover to Husak's successor, lets him down gently.[8]

As Stonehouse continues to wear three hats – minister, spy and MP – it is no wonder he is stressed. He needs help and looks for an exceptional secretary to work in his House of Commons office. He gets an ad placed in *The Times*, and shortlists some candidates. One evening at 6.30pm, a young woman in a neat suit enters Central Lobby. Stonehouse approaches her: 'Miss Black?' They shake hands and Sheila Elizabeth Black notices how debonair he seems, this Labour minister. She follows him along to his parliamentary office and, within half an hour, he offers her the job.

Stonehouse thinks Black – 22 years old, efficient and attract ive – is not unlike Barbara in her secretarial days. For her part, she is thrilled to be working for an MP. She did wonder how a True Blue like herself will get on working for a socialist. Never mind, she thinks, he's born under the same star sign. Two Leos will be strong together.[9]

As well as being a Tory, Black is also engaged to be married, which is just as well as Stonehouse mustn't get distracted by new women when there's so much to do. The following month, on Saturday 10 February, his duties to his constituents include hospital visits to check out complaints about working conditions and overcrowding. Ten sisters have all resigned in protest from the West Bromwich Hospitals Group, which runs crucial A&E units. Stonehouse agrees that non-emergency surgeries need to be cut back until the situation is rectified. He launches a 'Can I help you?' campaign among his constituents, to an overwhelming response.[10]

Ignoring Kalina's hints, Stonehouse continues to push to see Dubček on his upcoming visit; he even tells *The Observer* of his request and they duly report it on their front page. The Czechs don't respond well to these kind of games; anyway, Dubček has somewhat bigger fish to fry. He's been summoned to an emergency meeting of Warsaw Pact leaders to explain his liberalisation programme, which includes a curb of the secret police and a transition to democratic elections.[11]

When Stonehouse gets to Prague, he is again staying at the residence of Ambassador Cecil Parrott. He has a room with a view of the enchanting rooftops of old Prague, but he's not in it long. Little does Parrott know that Stonehouse has been handing over ministry documents that detail a new way of reinforcing structural plastics with carbon fibres, complete with scientific formulas. The British hope this alternative to metal and fibreglass will revolutionise the construction of aircraft and, as the document states, the Royal Aircraft Establishment is hoping to patent it for the nation. On Thursday, back on ministerial duty at the first Anglo-Czech press conference for twenty years, Stonehouse announces a technological pact of joint enterprise between the two countries, simultaneously serving his official and unofficial paymasters.[12]

He does so again when he moves on to Kladno and to the Low Tatras for some skiing. It has all been agreed with Husak and, in a brief encounter on the slopes, Stonehouse is told that Husak and his replacement will come to his hotel room at 10pm that evening.

Armed with wine and glasses, Husak officially introduces Stonehouse to the new man, Karel Pravec, who is also being lined up to take over the handling of Agent Lee, Labour MP Will Owen. Stonehouse is told to concentrate on German issues, UK–German and UK–US relations. And, of course, continuing to get close to Wilson. They emphasise that they need valuable written information. As the Czechs leave, Husak is confident that Pravec and Stonehouse will get on well.[13]

But that relationship will have to wait as Mr Aviation is on the road again in May, visiting Australia and the US west coast to keep up his contacts there with Lockheed, Boeing and Garrett. When he's back on Friday 28 June, Wilson comes good on a promise to elevate him and Stonehouse is made a member of the Privy Council for 'services to exports'. In front of the other privy counsellors and the Queen at Buckingham Palace, Stonehouse takes the biblical oath, swearing to do everything 'a faithful and true Servant ought to do to Her Majesty'. 'Approved,' says the Queen, as the unseasonal rain lashes down outside. And later on, his boss Wedgwood Benn throws a huge Private Office party to celebrate.[14]

It is with this new title that the Rt Hon. John Stonehouse goes to the Czech ambassador's mansion in Hampstead on 16 July for a reception (and later dinner) with Dubček's deputy Ota Šik. The Czechs have been trying in vain to reach him since the Low Tatras handover and, across the room, he spots Pravec, his new handler. But despite Pravec's attempts, Stonehouse refuses to get cornered alone with him. As he leaves, he tells Pravec to call him at home from a phone box, but when Pravec tries, the Potters Bar number they have for him no longer works. It seems the personal crisis has passed and the flow of high-quality intel has dried up with it. Agent Twister is proving as slippery as ever.[15]

In the summer's reshuffle, Wilson moves Stonehouse to postmaster general. It's a promotion of sorts, as he gets a bump in pay to £9,750, which is twelve times a postman's wage, but it's not the big cabinet ministry he dreamed of. Worse still, it's a time-limited appointment – in fifteen months, the Post Office will move from being a government department to a public company – and it soon turns sour. He's blamed for an increase in the television licence fee from £5 to £6 and has to call short his family holiday in Ireland when a postal price increase and the introduction of a second-class system creates a public furore. The *Daily Mirror* says he's fast qualifying for the title of Britain's Most Unpopular Minister, but Stonehouse comforts himself with the notion that sorting out the Post Office can't be any harder than pushing through reforms at the London Co-operative Society. He lets it be known that these problems are inherited from Wedgwood Benn and not his fault at all.[16]

But it's not just the Post Office that's going wrong. Russia does not approve of the Prague Spring and, despite talks between Leonid Brezhnev and Dubček, in the early morning of 21 August, Soviet paratroopers seize Prague International Airport and 250,000 troops and 2,000 tanks from Warsaw Pact countries invade Czechoslovakia. As many as 300,000 Czechs, including a number of StB defectors, flee the country, taking their secrets with them.[17]

At the Labour Party conference in Blackpool, Pravec is in town, and when he approaches, Stonehouse initially runs away in horror. But later he sees Pravec talking to other high-ranking Labourites, and concludes it is safe to have a conversation. Don't phone me at home, says Stonehouse, my phones are routinely tapped. He agrees they'll see each other again at a Polish cocktail party back in London and boasts that he'll be getting a very attractive new post next year.[18]

On Friday 4 October, John Stonehouse is a guest on David Frost's TV talkshow. At a time when he faces unprecedented public criticism, it takes a lot of nerve, but somehow he hits the right note. Bedecked with a flower-power tie, he laughs at jokes about the new two-class postage system and makes a series of droll comments that has reviewers wondering if the real comedians are hiding out in parliament. It's only a brief respite from the faux pas though: on a visit to Manchester, he tells reporters that there is a telephone exchange 150 feet below the city, in case of national emergency, and this is also true of London, Birmingham and Glasgow. 'It's extremely important for defence reasons,' says Stonehouse, not quite getting that that's why there is a D-notice in place against mentioning it.[19]

He also doesn't quite understand that you don't just walk away from a relationship with a Soviet bloc intelligence officer. Stonehouse never made the cocktail party at the Polish embassy and has been avoiding Pravec ever since. The Czech tries to get his attention across the House, but Stonehouse won't hold eye contact. Pravec knows if he chases him too often in parliament, his presence will be challenged. Instead he reverts to calling Stonehouse's home, this time on the correct number. Barbara claims he's never there – and she may have a point as his private office often wonder where the postmaster general is sleeping.

Pravec doesn't buy it. 'I'll have to find another solution for meeting him,' he tells her ominously.[20]

At this point, Stonehouse regularly works eighteen-hour days. He opens an exhibition at the Post Office Art Club, revealing a display of two of his own swirly abstract oils where dark and gloomy colours predominate. 'Some may argue they can't see what Mr Stonehouse is getting at in his work,' quip the critics. 'He has heard the same about the way he runs the Post Office.' Then there's another crisis: threatened strikes by postal workers, just in time for Christmas. More than 100,000 postmen, 20,000 sorters and 50,000 telephonists could be involved. Meanwhile, over in cabinet, the discussion is on whether or not to send Christmas cards to Russians.[21]

The strike threat is temporarily averted in time for Stonehouse to throw a showy Christmas party in the elegant surroundings of Queen Anne's Gate, Westminster, but come the new year, it still looms. The Union of Post Office Workers refuses Stonehouse's appeal to take the dispute to arbitration, and overseas telegraphists dealing with cables are the first to strike. Union leader Tom Jackson says services will be in utter chaos soon and Wilson calls Stonehouse to Downing Street for a top-level meeting. Those round the cabinet table include old foe Roy Jenkins who urges him not to give in to Jackson's demands. Soon he has ten cabinet ministers telling him, 'You can't do this! The government can't afford to relax on this!' Stonehouse, furious at being told what to do, proceeds to leak details of the meeting to the press. 'Stonehouse "mad" at Cabinet' is the big headline on the front page of the *Daily Mail*. He wanted to work with the union, it's reported across other newspapers, but he was 'straitjacketed' by members of cabinet – specifically Jenkins and Barbara Castle.[22]

Stonehouse's skilful manipulation of the media outrages his

senior colleagues, while at the same time making them feel distinctly uneasy. It's highly unusual for a minister to take on the PM, the chancellor (Jenkins) and the first secretary (Castle) in the pages of the newspapers. And he has this canny ability to present his wishes as a fait accompli. Had Stonehouse been weak and relented, he might have been sacked, but this show of power through the papers confirms that he is the kind of character who is definitely less dangerous inside the tent.[23]

Still, Wilson is furious and tells press secretary Joe Haines to find out who leaked it – even though they all already know. Haines's first move is to phone the *Daily Mail*'s industrial correspondent Monty Meth. 'How are you? I saw your article. I'm ringing to commiserate, Stonehouse must have been talking for hours.' Haines called it right. 'Bloody man, three quarters of an hour, I couldn't get rid of him,' says Meth. 'Cheerio,' says Haines and reports back to Wilson.[24]

Wilson summons Stonehouse to Number 10 and delivers the nearest thing to a rebuke that a prime minister who avoids personal confrontation ever gives. 'It's intolerable that these leaks are happening!' he says. Later that evening, amid rumours that he is going to resign, Stonehouse is forced to make a statement in the Commons: 'I deeply deplore attempts to drive a wedge between ministers on this question,' says the leaker. 'The government is united and any suggestion I do not entirely support that policy is totally untrue.' It's enough to hang onto his job. 'Stonehouse will have to go, of course,' Jenkins tells Castle, 'but he can't go yet.' If nothing else, it would be too much of a gift to the Tories.[25]

Beset by delays and failed deliveries, the reputation of the postal service is in tatters. A Tory MP presents him with melted and squashed chocolates that he was supposed to get as a Christmas present but has only just received due to delays, and when a meeting with Post Office union leader Tom Jackson finally takes place, Stonehouse is not allowed to take the chair. The strike is eventually settled, but Terry Lancaster in *The People* likens Stonehouse to John Wilder in television's *The Power Game*, permanently engaged in a battle of stroppy one-upmanship.[26]

Stonehouse pushes his luck again on Wednesday 26 March, the eve of three crucial by-elections and just before the Budget. Without consulting the Treasury or Number 10, he says in an uncleared speech that Wilson's devaluation of the pound had not been 'as successful as hoped' and Britain is now in a 'critical position' where living standards may in fact fall. He claims his intention was to encourage industry and raise investment in technology, but the cabinet can barely believe their ears, not least Roy Jenkins, the chancellor of the exchequer. Stonehouse has gone from gaffe prone to a faux pas merchant to an out-and-out liability. The Tories are ecstatic. The Labour postmaster general has 'let the cat out of the bag' and, by Friday, the results are in. Labour has lost all three by-elections to the Conservatives, with a 16 per cent swing.[27]

No wonder Stonehouse doesn't have time to engage with Pravec, as he ricochets from disaster to crisis and back again. He fails to turn up to countless meetings and the Czechs are angry. This man has been on their books for nearly ten years, bar a few breaks in service, and has been paid £2,450 between 1966 and last year. It's time to threaten him. Prague instructs Pravec at the end of May to tell Twister that the current situation is unfair. We stuck to the agreement and fulfilled our financial commitments. Three to four meetings a year with quality oral information – that's all we're asking for. If necessary, doorstep him in Potters Bar until he talks, he is told.[28]

Despite the ever-present threat from the Czechs and his

less-than-optimal ministerial performance, when Stonehouse is unexpectedly summoned to Number 10, he doesn't even consider the possibility of the sack. His intrinsic confidence in his own ability, combined with an overriding optimism, is in full force yet again. Stonehouse thinks that a reshuffle is in the offing, and that he might be about to receive some good news. He and Barbara Castle have publicly denounced a rumoured plot to replace Wilson, the prime minister thinks he's a great salesman, and even those colleagues whose trust he's lost concede he has an extraordinary way of dealing with the public. He fantasises that he's about to get offered a job at the Board of Trade and is feeling positive when at 11.30am, he knocks on the big black door.[29]

He makes for the Cabinet Room, but is redirected upstairs to one of the state rooms. He enters to find Wilson standing, alongside his principal private secretary Michael Halls. 'You know Michael, don't you?' says Wilson. Stonehouse indicates that he does and his eyes move beyond Halls to another man. 'This is Elwell, of counter-intelligence,' says Wilson. Stonehouse's blood runs cold. 'A Czech intelligence officer has defected to America and named you as an informer to the Czech Secret Service.'

Elwell, an unremarkable middle-aged man who combs his hair over to disguise a bald spot, starts reading from a report. He explains that the Czech officer has been debriefed by the Americans and claims a senior British minister is working with the Czechs. Halls is scribbling furiously to keep up. That officer named you, Stonehouse is told. 'We must get to the bottom of this,' says Wilson. 'It's important that you co-operate.'[30]

It's Stonehouse's worse fear come true: his handlers and the top brass in Prague aren't the only people who know his identity. His paranoia that it was all over the London residency was well founded. What's more, although the Czechs know their man Josef Frolík has defected to the US, they think the likes of Stonehouse and Will Owen are still safe. Or at least that's what they're telling themselves.

Elwell calls Stonehouse to arrange a series of interviews, which take place on Stonehouse's home territory, the Royal Automobile Club on Pall Mall. Using Frolík's debriefing, he questions Stonehouse about the defector's allegations, but the minister is an accomplished liar – he's been lying to his wife for years – and has explanations and alibis for absolutely everything. Then Wilson intervenes. In one of his routine meetings with MI5 director general Martin Furnival Jones, he says he wants the Stonehouse investigation stopped. The security services have got a reputation for going too far since the recent suicide of another MP, Bernard Floud, after a heavy-handed MI5 inquisition. Wilson doesn't trust them not to do it again. There is to be no full-scale interrogation of John Stonehouse. Based on what they have gleaned, however, Elwell and the security service assure the prime minister that there is no evidence that Stonehouse gave the Czechs any information he shouldn't have given them, much less consciously acted as an agent for the StB.[31]

Elwell moves on to other cases, but Wilson concludes that suddenly sacking Stonehouse would look suspicious. Even though he has performed poorly as postmaster general, he does not drop Stonehouse when that role disappears and instead makes him the minister of the new department of Posts and Telecommunications. It baffles Labour colleagues after Stonehouse's recent performance, but Wilson is notorious in his refusal to sack anyone. The human frailties of his MPs amuse him, rather than infuriate him. It's both his strength in keeping all sides of the party happy, and his weakness in sticking with those who are dangerously past their sell-by date. But keeping him inside the tent is just a short-term public solution to the Stonehouse problem. In private, Wilson has changed his mind for good about his once rising star.[32]

PART THREE

Crossing the Line

THE IDEALIST RIDES AGAIN

After the prime minister's rebuff, Charles Elwell and his friends in MI5 counter-intelligence move on from Stonehouse and follow up on another of Frolík's tip-offs. In the early hours of 14 January 1970, they swoop on an ordinary semi in the London suburb of Carshalton and interview another Labour MP, Will Owen, the Czechs' Agent Lee, under caution.

They search Owen's house and find two packets stuffed with cash. One contains £300 in notes, the other £250. The 69-year-old former coal miner, an MP since 1954, claims it's his holiday money, but when taken to Scotland Yard, he admits it comes from Czech embassy 'officials'. He is arrested the following day and charged with eight counts of communicating information useful to an enemy. The white-haired, bespectacled backbencher is front-page news.[1]

It is not good news for the prime minister. He is obsessed by security issues – he suspects MI5 of trying to undermine him – and he knows that the public is equally interested. Profumo, Philby, Blake and Burgess: newspaper barons know what sells papers and it all gets lapped up. Wilson plans a general election this year and this political embarrassment is unwelcome. It's just as well voters don't know that he had dismissed security-service suspicions of Owen just a few months ago.[2]

For Wilson's serving minister of posts and telecommunications, Owen's arrest is even more worrying. 'To jail in the rain' is not the kind of headline John Stonehouse wants to see among his morning papers. He might not be taking their money anymore, but he has had too many Czech handlers to feel secure. Stonehouse might not yet know they're the same men as the ones who controlled Owen, but his old boss, Anthony Wedgwood Benn, does.[3]

Still in charge at the Ministry of Technology, the rebranded Tony Benn asks David Purnell – the ministry's security officer Stonehouse had told about his lunch with Robert Husak – if he'll come and see him. He's concerned that Stonehouse's name will come out at the Owen trial. Husak is going to be named, and Benn knows he's linked to Stonehouse. But Purnell is unperturbed; he has records of the Stonehouse meeting, as Benn knows, and there's nothing more to say.[4]

That does not stop the looks and murmurs Stonehouse notices as he walks through the House. He is also familiar with Wilson's legendary paranoia about MI5 interference in his government – rooted in the fact that Wilson himself was wrongly under suspicion after his trips to Moscow when he was at the Board of Trade. He may not have been sacked on the spot, but whatever happens come election day, Stonehouse knows he is unlikely to feature on any front bench whether in government or in opposition. Post-Elwell, it is time to reassess his career. The 43-year-old is fed up with politics, and politics is fed up with him.

Out of ministerial office, his income would be reduced from £9,750 to £3,250 and that would be a problem. That sharp Stonehouse look is expensive to put together and, following a move back to London, Barbara has got her eye on a house in the country, in addition to their rented Kennington town-house. Their 10-year-old son is soon to start boarding school. Stonehouse has developed a taste for fine wines and cigars. And extra-marital affairs don't come cheap.

His secretary Sheila Black, who has proved to be most dedicated in her role, got married to trainee accountant Roger Buckley just a year ago. He and Barbara took the young couple to the Proms to celebrate. But when the marriage quickly falls apart, Stonehouse steps in to comfort his secretary, and a relationship develops. Buckley can't believe this man is interested in someone with such an ordinary brain as hers.[5]

Stonehouse has seen other ex-ministers struggling to come to terms with the loss of power and money, and he's determined not to go there. Fawning businessmen have told Mr Aviation that he is a rather good salesman – and he has a 'services to exports' position on the Privy Council and a personal note from the prime minister to prove it. All those global contacts in aviation and technology are just waiting to be revived. And, of course, if it hadn't been for those interfering communists, his entrepreneurial flair would have made the London Co-operative Society a raging success too.

Stonehouse seeks advice from an old friend who has shadowed him ever since their time together at the LCS. When John McGrath was forced to resign as the Co-op's chief accountant for having an undisclosed company on the side, Stonehouse got him a position as financial controller of British Airports Authority (BAA); he later became a director of Stonehouse's Post Office. Encouraged by his friend, Stonehouse decides that business is indeed the way forward. It is a disastrous decision for a man who has never been able to manage his own money or that of any organisation he has been involved with. He establishes Export Promotion and Consultancy Services (Epacs) on 5 March 1970 and McGrath soon becomes a board member.[6]

For this new business venture, everything must be done in style. He leases a beautiful Georgian townhouse at 26 Dover Street – in Mayfair, no less. Along the road at Number 19 is

Berolina, an East German travel agency run by Will Owen, and a daily reminder that Stonehouse needs to move on from the Czechs.

The interior of his new premises must be equally stylish. His secretary (and now mistress) Buckley is good at a lot of things, but for this he needs his wife. Barbara has been dabbling in interior design and, under her company Interior Décor and Design, she decorates and furnishes the offices for a total of £5,500. Now 26 Dover Street is a faux-colonial dream of deep green carpets, bamboo furniture and broad-blade ceiling fans.[7]

Stonehouse needs no advice from McGrath for another business he establishes later on in the month: Connoisseurs of Claret. Wine is his hobby and he's sure it's the next big thing. Stubby bottles of Mateus Rosé – ideal for a candle when the wine has gone – adorn middle-class dining tables and 'plonk' enters the lexicon. The Wine Society's red vans drop off cases to the cognoscenti and Stonehouse also thinks that mail order is the way to go. He does it big time, buying in large quantities and launching an expensive advertising campaign.[8]

For Stonehouse, it's a relief to be working on something different, but there's no escaping the past. On 1 April, Will Owen resigns his position as MP using the arcane method of applying for the Chiltern Hundreds. His trial starts shortly afterwards and Frolík gives evidence. Fearful of being assassinated while in London, he is named only as 'Mr A' and appears in court behind a screen. Husak's name is all over the papers – 'the smooth tongued spy who lured Mr Owen with flattery', as one has it – and Stonehouse can only pray that the publicity doesn't persuade Elwell to take another look.[9]

Owen admits that, over a nine-year period, he accepted £2,300 from the Czechs, but insists he never passed on classified information. In fact, he says, any intelligent person could have gleaned what he told them from reading official publications. It is a useful defence for anyone else facing similar accusations. Owen describes his actions as 'folly, folly to the point of madness' and he looks frail and stooped as his story plays out.

Owen is not a celebrity outside his Morpeth constituency and he's had limited access to top-secret information, so the national press go gently. But stories of furtive meetings with Czech intelligence officers, pressure from Husak ('I got into their hands, they squeezed and squeezed') and clandestine payments are all too familiar. And for Harold Wilson, the prospect of one of his former MPs being convicted as an Eastern bloc agent is another factor to consider as he weighs up a general election.

No one has too long to wait. On 6 May, after a thirteen-day trial, the jury are back. The prosecution's decision to exclude 'hearsay' evidence from defectors has weakened their case and the jury return not guilty verdicts on the eight counts. Owen tells the papers he has never been happier and gives a 'kiss of freedom' to his wife Anne. It is one less thing for Wilson to worry about. But Labour Party whips warn MPs to be careful in their relationships with foreign embassies and, on Friday 8 May, Wilson tells the Commons that despite the 'not guilty' verdict, the Security Commission will look into the affair.[10]

Less than a fortnight later, the front door of Number 10 closes gently behind the prime minister. He waves to the tourists and photographers, and takes the few steps across the pavement to his waiting car. It is 5pm on a spring afternoon and he's on his way to Buckingham Palace. That evening, puffing on his pipe in the sunlit garden of Number 10, Wilson tells the nation that a general election will be held on 18 June.

Three hours later, five thousand miles away in the Mexican city of Guadalajara, the captain of the England football team,

Bobby Moore, is arrested on suspicion of shoplifting a bracelet. The team are there defending the World Cup and British journalists decide not to report the story to avoid upsetting preparations for the next match. Wilson is informed the next morning, but he too says nothing. He is banking on a good run in the World Cup to keep the country happy and help him win the election.

For three weeks he gets his wish. The Bobby Moore arrest looks like a set-up. On 11 June, England finally gets one over on the Czechs. The national team beats their Czech counterparts 1-0 and progresses into the quarter-finals. The squad's song *Back Home* is number one in the charts and World Cup fever grips the land. Wilson tours the country with wife Mary in a relaxed, folksy progress, while Conservative leader Ted Heath, a bachelor, looks stiff and frumpy in comparison. Wilson dismisses the Tory plan to cut public spending and state benefits as 'a system of society for the ruthless and the pushing, the uncaring' and the public stay with him.

But it's the weather and the World Cup, not the election, that really captivate the public. It stays bright and hot, everyone is in shirt sleeves or summer dresses and a few enterprising pubs and cafés daringly put tables on the pavement. It is all very un-British and as the team prepares for its quarter-final against West Germany on 14 June, there's a holiday atmosphere across the land.

On Friday 12 June, the well-regarded National Opinion Poll shows Labour 12.4 per cent ahead; most people assume Wilson is home and dry. 'For heaven's sake, wake up,' Heath tells the electorate the following day, imploring them to 'recognise what the real issues are because Labour has pursued a policy of diversion with a bogus story of sham sunshine'.[11]

The quarter-final kicks off at 7pm that Sunday. Millions of families gather round their new television sets; it is the first

World Cup broadcast in colour. It's another glorious summer evening in Britain, but over in Mexico, the heat is stifling. Star goalkeeper Gordon Banks is taken ill with a mysterious stomach bug an hour before kick-off and reserve Peter Bonetti is called in. The roar of a nation is heard as England move into a two-goal lead, but then it all goes wrong and the Germans draw level. The match goes into extra time, but the momentum is with the Germans who score a decisive third. England are no longer world champions.

Back home on a sober Monday morning, attention finally turns to politics. The day starts with news that the number of days lost to strikes is increasing again, another blow to Labour's 'In Place of Strife' white paper, an attempt by employment minister Barbara Castle to regulate the unions. It has split the cabinet, antagonised the unions and given Heath's opposition party another stick with which to beat Labour. There hasn't been this much disruption since the General Strike of 1926 and Labour's credibility at managing industrial relations takes a further blow.[12]

There is worse to come at noon when new trade figures are released, showing a trade deficit of £31 million. It is the opening that the Tories have been craving. 'The economic lights are flashing amber,' says Heath. It's a bad start to election week for Wilson.[13]

The weather briefly breaks in London the following day. Wilson leaves Number 10 for the Liverpool train in the rain, and arrives to the same weather. He spends Wednesday campaigning in his Huyton constituency, but the bookmakers are so certain Labour will be back in power that they stop taking bets. The prime minister, however, for reasons he can't yet rationalise, feels uneasy.[14]

Polling day on the 18th is again hot; in the cities, it is

oppressive and clammy. Labour worries that, after a hard day down the mines and in the factories, its voters will go home rather than turn out to vote. They are right. It is the lowest voter turnout in decades.

When the polls close at 10pm, Wilson gives a party for the journalists who have followed him up to Liverpool, before retiring to his suite at the Adelphi Hotel with his entourage. He is sitting on a sofa with Mary when the first result comes in. It's from Guildford and shows a 5.3 per cent swing to the Tories. The next two results confirm that there is a nationwide swing to the Conservatives. Wilson goes to Huyton for the formality of the results in his own constituency – he increases his majority from 41,132 to 45,583 – and then drives to London a beaten man. On Friday 19 June, Heath's Tories are declared the winners with a thirty-seat majority. Stonehouse holds his seat, though. His Black Country constituency has been Labour since 1931 and remains so, even if his majority has been more than halved.

Wilson is in deep shock after the defeat. If he's going to come back from this, he needs people he can trust to work alongside him and that no longer includes Stonehouse. Wilson doesn't necessarily believe the Czech accusations, but mud sticks and Stonehouse has long been a liability. His inept performance and repeated faux pas as postmaster general, along with the press leaks, means it is finally time to put him out to pasture. Wilson secretly thinks him 'corruptible' and a 'crook' and tells Stonehouse that there will be no place for him in future Labour governments. Meanwhile, as the security service briefs the new prime minister Heath, they repeat their assertion about Stonehouse: there is no evidence that he gave the Czechs any information he shouldn't have given them.[15]

Instead of meekly retreating into his role as an opposition

MP, Stonehouse seeks his revenge at being dumped, as his colleagues had always feared he would. He writes to his constituents after the election and leaks it to the *Evening Standard*. They duly oblige with 'Stonehouse on why Labour lost'. It was because of 'smug complacency', he says. 'Our supporters need something more than the status quo to vote for. They have to be stirred by a vision and we failed to give them that.'[16]

It's difficult to say if this is Stonehouse bowing out, or the start of a long-term counter-attack, but what is undeniable is that he cannot let anything drop. He is ever-present in the House as he weighs in on Post Office matters to defend the fallout from his time in office, and he's still a fixture at the Commons chess tables during the long nights when he routinely votes against Tory legislation. But he knows that he can't go back to his full-time idealistic hobby-horsing of the 1950s: money has to be the focus.[17]

Supplementary Czech cash is no longer on the table. After the Agent Lee trial – and despite the acquittal – they are in retreat. Husak has been kicked out of the Ministry of the Interior back in Prague, and Pravec is about to leave London. Without ministerial position, even as part of the shadow team, Prague HQ doesn't see how Stonehouse's most fruitful period under Husak in 1967 can ever be repeated. Plus, they think he's now more likely to reveal himself to his political colleagues than to co-operate. They decide to leave it for two or three years to see what happens. In the meantime, they ask other Soviet bloc countries if they have an intelligence use for Twister.[18]

Discarded by his party and put on ice by the Czechs, Stonehouse turns his attention to business. Drawing on years of globetrotting and domestic networking, he hits on all his old contacts for Epacs work. The Clark brothers at Ilford-based electronics company Plessey and military communications entrepreneur Ernie Harrison at Racal give the former minister some of his first consultancy work. Epacs turns over £33,000 in its first year, quadrupling his former government income. It's a promising beginning to his new career; this business lark is easy.

Or not. Stonehouse is not the first wine lover to find that making money from it is harder than drinking it. He has no experience of buying and makes rookie errors. He orders far too much stock which sits unsold in a bonded warehouse. It's a marketing problem, Stonehouse decides, not for the first time, and embarks on an expensive advertising campaign. But the bills mount up and Connoisseurs loses a thousand pounds a month. John McGrath and Stonehouse's trainee solicitor nephew Michael Hayes counsel caution on all fronts, but Stonehouse isn't one to listen. When he finds a new passion, 5,000 miles away in Bengal, they can only hold their breath.[19]

On 25 March 1971, the West Pakistan army cracks down on Bengali separatists in Dacca, causing millions of East Pakistan Bengalis to pour over the border into India. In London, there are emergency meetings at the major relief charities including War on Want, which is chaired by Stonehouse's old friend and fellow Czech employee Donald Chesworth. He remembers Stonehouse's passion for post-colonial emancipation and asks him to go to India on a fact-finding mission. Stonehouse, champion of the underdog, is back in business.[20]

The man of action who loves to travel quickly gets jabs for typhoid and cholera, and by Saturday 17 April is on a flight to Calcutta. There he meets leaders of the newly self-declared independent state of Bangladesh. He sees thousands of destitute families crowded together with no hygiene, no possessions and no roof over their heads. Shocked, he returns to London and files a report recommending an immediate aid programme.

A delegation from the charities meets the foreign secretary, the former prime minister Alec Douglas-Home, and the government authorises RAF planes to commence relief flights. Bangladeshis in Britain march on Downing Street and hold rallies in Hyde Park demanding British recognition. Stonehouse and Chesworth become trustees of Bangladesh Fund, a new British charity raising relief money.[21]

On 7 June 1971, Stonehouse writes to *The Times* calling for the recognition of Bangladesh and UN Security Council action, but the definitive article comes a few days later in the *Sunday Times*. It is written by Anthony Mascarenhas, a Karachi-based Christian Goan journalist who evacuated his family by air while he escaped overland. Under the headline 'Genocide', it says 'I have witnessed the brutality of "kill and burn missions" as the army units, after clearing out the rebels, pursued the pogrom in the towns and villages.'[22]

Pakistan denies the story, but international opinion mobilises and Stonehouse and other British politicians step up their campaign. In July, more than 200 MPs sign a House of Commons motion calling for recognition of Bangladesh. Stonehouse organises the design and printing of millions of stamps for a new state, which he launches in a ceremony at the Commons, but most of the stamps remain unused in a garage in Willesden, leaving him to foot the bill.[23]

On Sunday 1 August, Stonehouse addresses a crowd of 10,000 Bangladesh supporters in Trafalgar Square. He has barely finished speaking when, across the Atlantic, a crowd gathers in Midtown Manhattan. Limousines crawl along Eighth Avenue, the crowds getting thicker near Madison Square Garden as they press against the tinted windows to see who is inside. The limos stop at West 33rd and Eighth as they reach the stage door and, one by one, some of the world's biggest rock stars wave to the fans and dash into the building. It's the biggest assembly of rock music talent the world has ever seen. Two Beatles – George Harrison and Ringo Starr – have put the band's squabbles behind them. The guitar god Eric Clapton is there, and even Bob Dylan puts in an appearance. Harrison spent the previous month calling in favours to stage this, the world's first rock benefit concert.[24]

It isn't jazz-loving John Stonehouse's kind of music, but it is his kind of cause. He's momentarily distracted on 9 August with a fine of £15 from Andover magistrates for reversing into another car and driving off without leaving his name and address. Always inclined to overlook the damage his actions cause other people, he's on a much more important mission than dealing with minor road traffic accidents. He becomes the go-to man for William Hardcastle's *World at One* on BBC Radio 4 and vies with Mascarenhas as the unofficial voice of Bangladesh in Britain.

Radical left MP and secret Soviet sympathiser Ian Mikardo chairs the Labour Party conference in Brighton in October – just a month after the Foreign Office, acting on information from a KGB defector, expelled an unprecedented ninety Soviet diplomats for being spies. The priority for Wilson is to agree an economic policy for the next election, but Mikardo and the far left are more interested in a commitment to extreme nationalisation. Stonehouse's fiery speech of famine, rape and murder in Bangladesh is one of the few moments that raises the still wounded and ideologically divided party out of introspection, but it does little to dampen his nagging fears that rise up whenever he's in Labour circles: that they know he was named by a defector and investigated by MI5, that they know he's been accused of being a spy.[25]

And Stonehouse is right: his party colleagues have all

heard the rumours by now. They also engulf Michael Foot (wrongly), Wilson's old private secretary Ernest Fernyhough (rightly) and Tom Driberg (probably more KGB than StB). Even Ted Short, erstwhile chief whip, has a codename as a result of meeting the Czechs, but he's never taken their money and there are no rumours about him. Meanwhile, it doesn't escape Stonehouse's notice that Nicholas Prager, an ex-RAF man who sold secrets to the Czechs a decade ago, has just gone to jail for twelve years. Josef Frolík was behind this arrest, as well as Owen's.[26]

As autumn turns to winter, Stonehouse tries to put this to one side. His latest dalliance certainly helps take his mind off things. The situation with his secretary Sheila Buckley is hotting up to the point that it's starting to feel less like an affair and more like a permanent relationship. Buckley, looking for a place to live pending her divorce, has moved into his one-bedroom pied-à-terre in Vandon Court in Victoria. Barbara has no idea that her husband keeps a flat in town and even less of an idea that his secretary is now living there.

Whenever Buckley feels guilty about their relationship, Stonehouse assures her that she couldn't break up his marriage; it is broken already. He portrays Barbara as a nag who is constantly demanding things from him and who he has been unhappy with for years. But when Buckley asks him why he won't divorce her, he says he can't as it would harm his career. Barbara's impression is that he is still having the odd affair. She sees that he loves the conquest, but he always returns to her and she'll continue to tolerate the affairs, as long as he comes home at night and the family unit remains tight. There is much, it seems, that a woman will forgive a good father – and at home he's an entertaining presence the children adore.[27]

With his new cause of Bangladesh to champion, and a permanent mistress, Stonehouse is outwardly happier than he has been for a long time. Then, on 16 December 1971, as he sits in his Dover Street office working through his consultancy projects, his ears prick up at an item on the *World at One*. The number of Bangladeshi Hindu refugees pouring into India has prompted Indian prime minister Indira Gandhi to take military action and Stonehouse has been following the thirteen-day war closely. When he hears that the Pakistan army has been defeated, he rings the Indian high commissioner and asks if he can get to Bangladesh as soon as possible. It is difficult because most civil aircraft have stopped flying in the region, they say, but if Stonehouse can get to Bombay, the Indians will take him north. He is on a plane that night and then on a crowded internal flight to Calcutta. He gets a lift in an Indian army helicopter and lands amid burned-out aircraft at Dacca Airport less than two days after the ceasefire. There's not much he can do except to gather evidence for a relief effort and he's back home for Christmas. But there's no time to waste. Over the holiday season, he works the phones and his contacts hard to whip up publicity and support.[28]

Then, on 3 January 1972, he is off to Dacca again on a ten-day visit with Chesworth. They hold a party at the Intercontinental Hotel for the newly arrived diplomatic corps and present a cheque for several hundred thousand pounds from the Bangladesh Fund. Back in London, on 18 January he speaks in the House of Commons to congratulate foreign secretary Alec Douglas-Home on his diplomatic efforts to get formal recognition of Bangladesh. He writes in *The Times* about 'getting a devastated new nation off its knees' and praises Chesworth's relief efforts.[29]

When exiled Bangladesh leader Sheikh Mujibur is released

from prison and becomes the new prime minister, he makes Stonehouse a citizen of Bangladesh. The new citizen doesn't yet know what rights it brings, but you never know when a new passport might come in handy.

I I

DIRTY WORK

On 25 January 1972, a handsome and smartly suited Asian man presents himself at the Central Lobby in the Houses of Parliament. He is handed a green slip and fills in the name of the MP he wishes to see. 'John Stonehouse' he writes. Name? 'KB Ahmed.' Purpose of visit? 'Bangladesh.' A formally dressed attendant clad in a white wing-collared shirt, bow tie and a black tailcoat takes the card and disappears along the corridor.

Ahmed waits beneath the high Gothic dome of the lobby. MPs, messengers and visitors scurry about their business past the statues of distinguished parliamentarians. The clickety-clack of high-heeled shoes echoes on the stone floor as a bored policeman looks on. After a few minutes, Stonehouse appears and escorts his visitor to one of the small interview rooms underneath the Commons debating chamber.

Kazi Ahmed, a 27-year-old Bengali businessman living with his family in a 1930s semi in High Barnet, tells Stonehouse that the 83,000 Bengali migrants in the UK have as much as £15 million waiting to be sent home. They don't trust the Pakistani banks and Ahmed proposes that a Bengali bank be set up in the UK to help them. Bank, you say? It's the worst kind of business possible for a man with a money touch like his, but Stonehouse is all ears.[1]

The meeting lasts for two hours and ends with Stonehouse inviting Ahmed over to the Epacs offices the following day.

Stonehouse wants him to meet his right-hand man McGrath. Ahmed moves negotiations on by proposing that Stonehouse becomes chairman of the new bank. McGrath shows no objections and Stonehouse agrees in principle. Then he grandly adds that, of course, if he were to do so, he would naturally forego payment.

Stonehouse says that the support of British institutions would be needed and offers to sound out the Bank of England. Not being a man to mess about, he contacts the governor, Sir Leslie O'Brien, whom he knows from the Privy Council. In no time, he is marching along Threadneedle Street with Ahmed and McGrath in tow.

A meeting with the governor of the Bank of England is a ceremonial event. Here the frock coats are pink not black but, as in the House of Commons, history is everywhere as the bank's messengers lead the visitors along the gloomy corridors to the governor's parlour. Antique tables and leather sofas reek of old wax polish and the Establishment, and French doors lead on to an impeccable lawn. It's hard to believe they are in the middle of the City of London.

The governor, a quiet and reserved grammar school boy, is courteous to his fellow privy counsellor, but he has a lot on his plate. Ted Heath's government has lost control of the economy: unemployment recently passed the one million mark for the first time since the 1930s and a five-week coal strike has led to power cuts, a state of emergency and a three-day working week. Chancellor Anthony Barber's solution is to turbo-charge the economy with tax cuts and easier credit, risking inflation. A footling bank is the last thing the governor wants to think about. He politely asks his visitors a few questions and then deputes Jim Keogh, one of the Bank of England's top officials, to look after them.

Keogh is friendly, but he too pushes the idea down the line as he insists there has to be a process. The would-be bankers are told in no uncertain terms that the word 'bank' cannot be used in its name until a certificate is issued by the Department of Trade. Also, at least one year's normal trading is required to get the certificate and the authorities need to be certain it is 'soundly based' and 'operating fairly'. Experience in banking among the management team is also essential. This is stern stuff and it doesn't sound like an empty threat. But although the founders can't yet call it a bank, that is in essence what it will be. They look for an alternative name, one they hope will be only temporary, and settle on the British Bangladesh Trust (BBT).[2]

BBT is not the only entity that Stonehouse establishes in spring of 1972. On the advice of an old RAF friend, the Canadian Gerald Hastings who is now a successful businessman, he decides he needs a Swiss company and bank account for when he gets paid for his Epacs work in dollars.[3] He works with a lawyer in Liechtenstein, Oswald Bühler, to set up Victa International, and sends Bühler a cheque for $5,000 to put into its new bank account. His newly divorced lover and parliamentary secretary Sheila Buckley, now based at Dover Street, is the only person in the building who knows about it.

Like everyone else, Buckley finds her boss overly domineering in the workplace, yet she too accedes to his demands and begins to value their friendship as much as their love life. It's like being with a walking encyclopedia, she muses – he's such an intellectual! But she's noticed that, in private, he's a man who needs an awful lot of reassurance. He's forever telling her that he loves her, but then immediately asking if she loves him back. The contrast with his bullish public persona couldn't be greater.[4]

Stonehouse's reputation as the parliamentary voice of Bangladesh now becomes crucial if Bengali savings are to be attracted. In April, he introduces a motion in the Commons to muster international support for the new country. It is well received by British Bangladeshis, but it's already obvious that their savings won't provide enough capital to support Ahmed's member-run mutual society. Outside investors will be needed if the business is to be viable and that means becoming a public company.[5]

They need professional advisers for this and, as usual, Stonehouse goes straight to the top, which is none other than City grandee Sir Charles Hardie. This is the age of the gifted amateur and, in Britain in 1972, few businessmen are as gifted or as amateur as Sir Charles. He is chairman of five companies, deputy chairman of another two and a director of eight more. Once asked how long it took to work out his audacious plan to merge the merchant bank Hill Samuel with the Metropolitan Estates Property Company, he replied, 'Oh, about a quarter of an hour.'[6]

The pair had met when Stonehouse was minister of aviation and Hardie was chairman of BOAC, British Airways' predecessor; he is now senior partner of the accountants Dixon Wilson. Hardie agrees that his venerable firm will be BBT's auditors and puts Marius Gray, one of his younger partners, on the job. Hardie also introduces BBT to solicitors, beginning the letter: 'The governor of the Bank of England has given permission for the formation of the above company on the basis that it will be categorised as a bank.' Reassured by this misinterpretation of the company's true position, well-respected City solicitors Stanleys are only too pleased to act and, in May, they draft the prospectus that the directors will sign.[7]

The Bank of England advises Stonehouse to seek the formal sponsorship of a merchant bank to show investors that the City club is on board. He uses his numerous contacts from his ministerial time and within days Stonehouse and Ahmed are treated to silver-service boardroom lunches all over the City. But although keen at first, all the merchant banks he approaches, including Hambros and Kleinwort Benson, eventually decline. The club has spoken. High-street bank Barclays agrees to do the administration, but there will be no blue-blooded sponsor standing behind the share issue.

Undeterred, Stonehouse hits the fundraising trail. He wines and dines leading businessmen in the House of Commons and pitches his idea in boardrooms up and down the country. Welsh financier Julian Hodge proffers £50,000. Stonehouse also lunches the chairman of Crown Agents, the government's international trade arm, thinking he's clocking up support wherever he goes.[8]

Money from the Bengali community is still vital to the enterprise. Ahmed's £15 million has been reduced to a more realistic target of half a million pounds, but it's still ambitious. To help with this, the British Bengalese newspaper *Janomot* is asked to translate a handbill setting out BBT's aims into Bengali.[9] The handbill includes the audacious claim that the Bank of England, in somewhere between twelve and eighteen months' time, will give permission for BBT's name to change to British Bangladesh Bank. This is backed up by a photograph of the Bank of England's Jim Keogh and British Bangladeshis are offered a 5 per cent commission on any investment they bring in. Two nationalised Bangladesh banks are wrongly named as supporters.[10]

The Bank of England and BBT's professional advisers are given copies of the handbill, but whether or not they take the time to read a translation remains a moot point. Either way, they don't pick up Stonehouse's use of the word 'bank' when they explicitly told him he could *not* use it and the handbill moves into circulation.

Stonehouse and Ahmed tour British towns and cities where there's a Bengali population, including Bradford, Sheffield, Birmingham, Manchester, Rochdale, Portsmouth, Newcastle, Swansea, Cardiff and Bristol. At first Stonehouse is a big draw, but British Bengalis are politically factionalised and attendance at the meetings soon dwindles as one of the factions turns against him. At one meeting in Rochdale, only Stonehouse, Ahmed and two reporters turn up.

The economic background does not help. Bretton Woods, the wartime agreement by which exchange rates were pegged to the US dollar, is being dismantled. The Tory government is grappling with accelerating inflation, industrial relations problems and rising unemployment. Chancellor Anthony Barber's spring Budget promises tax cuts and investment incentives in a dash for growth, but currency dealers are not impressed. The Bank of England's foreign currency reserves are being run down in a desperate attempt to prop up sterling, but it's a losing battle. On 23 June, the government gives up.

Barber announces that the pound will be allowed to float freely as a temporary measure until Britain joins the Common Market on 1 January 1973 and the markets take fright. It's a terrible backdrop to a new issue, but BBT is small and it has an incredibly well-connected chairman whose determination knows no bounds.

As the prospectus nears publication, Stonehouse interviews bankers to staff the business. He knows a good man when he sees one, regardless of his own lack of experience in banking. Keith White, for example, is a former National Westminster branch manager and a fellow of the Institute of Bankers. He agrees to join BBT as general manager, the most senior banking position in the business, and will start six weeks before the bank opens for business. John Broad, fifteen years with Lloyds, agrees to join too, as assistant general manager. He fails to mention that, since 1971, he is an undischarged bankrupt.[11]

The prospectus is published on 22 October with BBT's premises given as 27 Dover Street. Not revealed in the prospectus is the fact that BBT will be a rent-paying tenant of Epacs and that John Thomson Stonehouse is chairman of both companies. Alongside Stonehouse (unpaid chair), the other directors are Ahmed (non-exec, unpaid), McGrath (non-exec, £5,000 per annum) and White (executive, £10,000 per annum).

With a privy counsellor as chairman, a qualified banker as general manager, a chartered accountant as one non-executive and a Bengali as the other, on paper it's a strong board and to start with it behaves like one. When, for example, on 20 October the lawyers point out that applications from the board and their connected parties exceed the 10 per cent allowed in the prospectus, quite properly, the directors scale down their applications.

One million pounds is the target for the issue, but half a million will be enough and with a month to go before the subscription lists open on 27 November, Stonehouse goes on the road again. At a meeting in Bradford, he is approached by Anthony Mascarenhas, by now an award-winning *Sunday Times* reporter.[12]

Stonehouse is not pleased to see him. He has been tipped off that the *Sunday Times* are snooping into his business activities. He decides that the best way is to co-operate and so explains BBT's objectives, mentioning some of his leading backers. He hopes he has done enough to kill the story, but hears that the *Sunday Times* have been cross-checking with the potential investors he had named. There follows another frosty meeting with Mascarenhas back at Dover Street.

Any negative publicity at this stage is unwelcome, particularly from the *Sunday Times,* the paper whose pace-setting editor Harold Evans is the most famous and admired newspaper man in Britain. Naturally Stonehouse knows him. They are both members of the Royal Automobile Club and have played squash together there – never on an Elwell interrogation day, Stonehouse made sure – and he calls him up. Evans invites him over to his office on Gray's Inn Road. There he tells Stonehouse that he will be given a right-of-reply before they go to press, but if Evans decides the article is fair and accurate, it will be published on Sunday 19 November in the Business section, a week before the list opens. 'Ring me up on the Saturday,' he says, 'and I will read the article over to you.'[13]

While Stonehouse waits it out until that Saturday, parliamentary business offers him the diversion he needs. He still attends in the evenings, and some debates are too good to miss. 'It is not necessary to imagine fanciful situations where my right hon. and learned friend might require a managing director to produce his grandmother's birth certificate,' says Peter Rees, Conservative MP for Dover, on a Power to Obtain Information amendment. 'But it is possible to envisage situations where he might require a company or a trade union to produce all its books of accounts, records, correspondence, and so on. That would be oppressive and vexatious in the extreme.' Increasingly, the aspiring entrepreneur finds the Tories are talking his language.[14]

And the following morning, Friday the 17th, he's Stonehouse the salesman again, as he confidently tells journalists 'that nearly £620,000' of subscriptions have 'already been found' for the BBT issue. On Saturday, he drives down the M1 from the

West Midlands to London, stopping off at every service station, calling Evans to see if it is ready. 'Not yet,' Evans tells him. 'It hasn't come down yet.'

Trust Houses Forte's Scratchwood Services is the last before London. It has only been open for two years but is already looking tired. Dodging the truck drivers and families, and opting out of the Grill & Griddle restaurant, Stonehouse finds a call box. Evans now has the article and reads it out over the phone. It is far worse than Stonehouse is expecting. He protests that there is not a single good word about BBT and that his motives have been misunderstood, but Evans only agrees to correct one factual error. He concedes that he will consider the rest, but really he just wants to get him off the phone. For Evans, who is trying to get justice for the thousands of disabled thalidomide children, Stonehouse is just another story.

Stonehouse is in a stew all evening and towards midnight he hurries across town to the Ludgate Circus newsstand at the bottom of Fleet Street where the early editions of the Sunday papers are sold. He flicks through the *Sunday Times* and stops at the headline 'Five Questions on the British Bangladesh Trust'. 'Stonehouse and his BBT colleagues have adopted somewhat unorthodox methods of soliciting investment funds for this banking trust,' writes Mascarenhas. The article criticises the unauthorised naming of the two Bangladesh national banks, calls the 5 per cent commission generous and says they've used Keogh's photograph without the Bank of England's permission. As for the suggestion that the name will change to 'bank' in the fullness of time, this is yet to be approved by the Bank of England, *Sunday Times* readers are told.[15]

Stonehouse takes it personally, identifying himself with BBT and raging at a challenge from what he regards as an unjustly powerful enemy. And the timing couldn't be worse. BBT has taken ad space in the Monday papers for the final push, but if this article sticks, thinks Stonehouse, that's the end of the share issue and my business career. If the issue fails, he thinks that his credibility in the City and beyond would be blown. He has worked his contacts book hard, boasted to the press and put all his energy into making it a success. It is the turning point in his career; he has been told by the leader of his party that he won't hold a ministerial job in any future Wilson government and he can't bear the thought of returning to a humble and lowly-paid career on the backbenches. He is staring into an abyss and he will do anything to get out of it, losing all sense of proportion and judgement.[16]

Stonehouse spends that night drafting a press release and it has some effect. Although the Monday edition of the *Guardian* bluntly says there is no justification for offering shares to the public, the *Daily Telegraph*'s City doyen Kenneth Fleet is supportive. But Stonehouse is still furious with the *Sunday Times* and orders his solicitors to fire off a strong letter.[17]

Still, Fleet's article and the punchy advertisements complete with cut-out coupon are enough to give Stonehouse hope. They say that Bank of England approval will be sought in two years' time and that there are firm applications for over £200,000 shares. With the Rt Hon. John Stonehouse, BSc (Econ), MP, heading the board as chairman and a pristine set of advisers named in the advertisement, they might just win back the initiative.[18]

The subscription lists are open for three days, from 10am on Monday 27 November until 10am on the Thursday. For Stonehouse, pride, idealism and his financial future are at stake. Although he's the unpaid chairman, he's a shareholder and this could be the solution to his perpetual money problems. By the evening of Tuesday, applications for £300,000 have arrived, but it's still a long way short of the half million pounds needed for a successful share issue – and even further from the £620,000 Stonehouse boasted about before the weekend. Some of the companies and individuals he contacted after the *Sunday Times* article have stayed loyal, including his Epacs client Plessey and the Crown Agents, but there is nothing from Welsh financier Julian Hodge. As for the Bengalis, a measly £15,000 has trickled in.[19]

As Stonehouse approaches the end of 1972 and his third year as businessman extraordinaire, the pressure is equal to his final years in office when he balanced a high-profile ministerial career with a double life as a Czech agent. Stonehouse needs £200,000 in hard cash to push the issue over the line and the mercurial twister looks for a solution. It's illegal for a company to lend money directly or indirectly for the purchase of its own shares, but the office chat is that many small-scale banks do exactly that. Failure is not an option for a man who has only a casual regard for the truth and, armed with the belief that in the City everyone does it, he can now see a way out.[20]

In a direct breach of company law, Stonehouse uses his existing companies, alongside four new ones, to subscribe for shares on money lent by BBT. Stonehouse lays a complex trail of multiple loans between outside banks, the companies and himself, but at the end of the line, it all comes back to BBT.

It takes a lot of legwork and, as late as the morning of Thursday 30 November, company secretary Philip Bingham – a 22-year-old Cambridge graduate who also serves as Stonehouse's PA – and assistant manager John Broad are scurrying round London in black taxis, dispatching and collecting completed application forms and cheques. At the same time, Stonehouse has one eye on the fallout: he knows this will have to be concealed from the auditors by any means.

One of the taxis goes to the offices of Banque Belge, a founder member of the City's prestigious Association of Foreign Banks. BBT general manager Keith White tells the Belgians that a client, Ronvale, wants to subscribe for BBT shares. It won't have the required £100,000 until the Monday morning and he wants Banque Belge to help out. What he doesn't say is that Ronvale is one of the shell companies Stonehouse acquired just a week earlier for the purpose of investing in BBT.

Banque Belge innocently think it is a standard inter-banking transaction. They agree to buy £100,000 of shares, sell them to Ronvale after the weekend and then, as they routinely and legitimately do for other clients, hold them for Ronvale only as a nominee. Their completed form, together with a cheque for £100,000, is soon on its way back to Dover Street. Stonehouse will shortly be able to brag that the highly respected Banque Belge is his largest institutional shareholder when he issues the list of subscribers to the City.[21]

In the hour after the 10am Thursday deadline, the cheques are added up and the forms cross-checked. At 11am, the board convene. Stonehouse, Kazi Ahmed, John McGrath, Keith White and the very green company secretary Philip Bingham are all present. Bingham reports applications totalling £651,140 and Stonehouse declares the issue a success. That only £312,000 of the £651,140 raised comes from genuine third parties – of which only £50,000 comes from 287 Bengalis – is neither here nor there to Stonehouse or his supine board. All have been handpicked by him, all are in awe of him and none have the independence to call it out. Rules, regulations and indeed the law are to be shamelessly broken in the hope that the business will be able rapidly to make enough money to put everything right.[22]

More than half – 52 per cent – of the 'successful' issue comes from Stonehouse and connected parties using money illegally provided by BBT itself. The board approves loans totalling £265,000 to Stonehouse and associates, guaranteed by Stonehouse, McGrath, White and Ahmed. The approvals take only as long to agree as it takes to read them. None of the guarantors are worth anything like the amount they have guaranteed and no one at BBT makes any attempt to verify their worth. BBT is lending money to buy its own shares in breach of Section 54 of the 1948 Companies Act and its own articles of association. The twister is back in business.[23]

NO ONE ARGUES WITH
MR STONEHOUSE

As 1972 becomes 1973, John Stonehouse has plenty of new year resolutions to choose from. He could finally clean up his act and finish his relationship with Sheila Buckley, becoming the family man he presents to the world. Yet his relationship with her is so much more than an affair now. She's his secretary, his closest confidante and his lover. They arrive at Dover Street together in the morning, they lunch together – they share practically every moment. He won't give that up and he won't let Buckley give it up either.[1] Whenever she wavers, he tells her he can't possibly live without her. He doesn't know what he'd do if she left him. It's a scenario with which the long-suffering Barbara is only too familiar.

Then there are the Czechs. He hasn't taken money from them since 1968 – and the Cold War is easing following last year's Nixon–Brezhnev nuclear arms deal – yet they remain a threat. They think that Stonehouse is as likely to tell officials what he did rather than be blackmailed into further collusion, but they'd be wrong. He has convinced himself of his innocence; his Labour colleagues are terrible human beings for entertaining the rumours. And yet he's not up for trying to prove it. So there's nothing to be done there either.

As for his political career, Wilson has reunited Labour under a centre-left agenda and looks to be a threat to Heath's thirty-seat majority, but Stonehouse isn't part of potential cabinet plans. Politics is still limited to Wednesbury and membership of parliament. He must keep his constituents happy by showing his face in the West Midlands and speaking in the House. But he already does that, so no resolutions there either.

Which leaves BBT. He needs the bank to make some money to pay down the loans to the directors and regularise the accounts. It was only ever intended to be a short-term arrangement to get the share issue away and this is where his focus must be in 1973. He and his family are still feeling the financial impact of his Co-op campaign expenditure nearly a decade earlier. They need the bank to be a success and he owns nearly 50 per cent of it through his various companies. If he plays his cards right, he could become a very wealthy man. The Barber Boom is in full swing. A relaxation of credit controls has stimulated property investment, cranes soar above town centres and house prices rise by 50 per cent. In this environment, BBT can get down to some lucrative banking business. Now that's the kind of resolution Stonehouse can really embrace.[2]

On Tuesday 2 January, the first working day of 1973, West End shoppers flock into the January sales on Oxford Street. Just south in Mayfair, Stonehouse is at his desk studying the first month's banking records. There are only 350 customer accounts, mainly small gestures from friends, family and business associates, and the only significant loans are to directors and their associates. The biggest is to Stonehouse's own company, Ronvale, and he looks for the ledger card straight away. There it is, £100,000, marked 'Purchase of BBT shares'.[3]

The accountants Dixon Wilson will be back in in July 1973 and if they discover that BBT has lent money for the purchase of its own shares, the Department of Trade will have to be told. Then there would be no question of getting the banking certificate it needs to call itself a bank. There could even be criminal charges.

Stonehouse can't allow that. Although he thinks it is common practice for companies to lend money to buy their own shares, he evidently knows it is illegal. He reaches for the intercom and buzzes angrily. 'You are to have your staff retype the cards without these words on,' he barks at assistant general manager John Broad. Still hiding his status as an undischarged and undisclosed bankrupt, Broad jumps to it. He tells ledger clerk Vera Kemp to fix it, but she throws up her hands in horror. Fifteen years in banking and she has never heard of anything so outrageous. It is just not done to retype ledger cards.

She hurries upstairs to the first floor where Broad and general manager Keith White have their offices and says: 'It is not allowed to retype ledger cards.' She is told, 'Mr Stonehouse's instructions.' She knows how things work at BBT and shrugs. 'Who am I to argue with Mr Stonehouse?' After all, no one else does. But before she leaves, she adds: 'Of course, it will be shown wrong on the backing sheet and there is no way to alter the backing sheet without retyping the whole day's work.' She is told, 'Don't worry about the backing sheet'.

Back downstairs, she types 'Sanctioned Overdraft Facility' into the accounting machine. It spews out a new card and she watches the old one being torn up. Upstairs in his office, Stonehouse is still angry. He looks at the other ledger cards and gets even more cross. The loans to White, McGrath and Bingham also read 'Purchase of BBT shares' and Kemp is ordered to alter those as well.[4]

But as soon as one problem is fixed at Dover Street, in late January a more worrying one appears – and it comes in the shape of Inspector Grant from Scotland Yard's Fraud Squad. The Department of Trade want to investigate the alleged false statements in the Bengali handbill, as reported by Anthony Mascarenhas in the *Sunday Times*. Stonehouse is amazed that they want to follow up on such a scurrilous story, but he talks to Grant nevertheless. Despite his best efforts, Grant can't pin anything on BBT. The matter is closed, but it adds to Stonehouse's obsession that unsubstantiated rumours are ruining his public standing.[5]

Come February, Stonehouse is also fretting that the big Ronvale loan will attract the attention of the auditors. He decides that a further cover-up is necessary and distributes the shares to friends and family. He starts with his impressionable nephew Michael Hayes, soon to qualify as a Winchester solicitor. The young man is easy prey for the smooth salesman. Habitually charming but with an underlying hint of menace, Stonehouse says that he plans to sell some BBT shares but fears this will worry other shareholders. Could he transfer some shares to his nephew as a nominee before he sells them? It will only be for a short time, he assures Hayes; BBT will lend him the money and Stonehouse will cover the costs and risk. Not wanting to disappoint his famous uncle, Hayes agrees to take £25,000 of shares.

Stonehouse also phones his sister Elizabeth in Southampton. She works for a firm of shipping agents who do business with Connoisseurs of Claret. Stonehouse explains what he has done and asks if she will do the same. The family and business connections are valuable to her and, on 1 March, she agrees to hold £20,000 of BBT shares as a nominee. No risk, no cost.

Stonehouse then approaches a cousin, John Harris, who in November had bought £500 of shares for himself and £500 for his two daughters. The story changes slightly, but it's the same deal. He invents a client who wants to buy BBT shares but wishes to remain anonymous. Will Harris hold them on the client's behalf, no risk, no reward? Harris is happy to hold £15,000 of shares as a nominee and, on 17 April, BBT lends him the money.

Barbara Stonehouse's interior design company IDD takes £5,000 of shares, a subsidiary of Connoisseurs takes £15,000, and another property development company part-owned by Stonehouse takes £15,000. Everything is financed by BBT and everyone is told that they are not at risk, that it is just a paper transaction.

This leaves only £5,000 of the Ronvale holding to be dispersed and Stonehouse is able to find a genuine buyer of some standing. Sir Charles Forte is a recent contact (following an introduction from Sir Charles Hardie) and the genial Italian is one of the most admired businessmen in Britain. Having started out with a pre-war milk bar on the Strand before being interned on the Isle of Man during the war, he is now chief executive of Trust Houses Forte, a hospitality business that stretches from London's Café Royal to motorway service stations. He declines Stonehouse's invitation to join the board, but agrees to buy £5,000 worth of shares. It's not a big deal for such a wealthy man but for Stonehouse signing up Forte is a real coup.[6]

Tidying up done, Stonehouse has a banking business to develop if he is to make his fortune. Economists fear that the Barber Boom has got out of hand, stoking inflation and an import bill that the country can't afford. But Prime Minister Heath insists that there will be 'no going back, no loss of nerve'. Some property developers are still gung-ho, including Zeawood, a long-standing client of general manager White. Between January and April 1973, BBT lends Zeawood £127,000, mainly for the purchase and development of the Lynwood Arms, a hotel in Horsham, Sussex. It's the kind of loan BBT wants to make many times over, but wiser developers see the property market cooling. Accordingly, it's the only genuine deal of any size that BBT does in the half-year.

As BBT prepares for the auditors' visit at the beginning of July, the stakes are high. The accounts have been drawn up on Stonehouse's say-so by his brow-beaten staff and this is the first time that anyone from outside the company has seen them. A probing audit would reveal what he has been up to and it's a tense period as the dreaded day arrives.

Dixon Wilson, however, think they are auditing a small business chaired by an eminent friend of their senior partner, one that has been trading for only seven months. It looks like a routine job and they send along only an audit manager and an articled clerk. They are at Dover Street for just two weeks, but that's two weeks too long for Stonehouse as he nervously awaits their final report.[7]

It comes from Dixon Wilson partner Marius Gray at the board's audit meeting on Friday 13 July. It is an unusually full turn-out for a board that has been meeting more in name than reality. McGrath attends despite a heart attack six months earlier, Stonehouse and White are there as usual, so too is company secretary Bingham. But Ahmed is once again too busy to attend.[8]

On such a formal occasion, Stonehouse must not put a foot wrong. Gray, forty years old and from an academic family, has a quietly reassuring manner. There is not much to discuss. There have been very few transactions and BBT has lent out little more than half a million pounds. As Gray speaks, it seems that the auditors have failed to spot that most of that has been illegally used to buy shares in the bank. Stonehouse breathes more easily, but Gray is not quite finished.

He settles his half-moon spectacles onto the bridge of his nose and turns to the long list of loans to directors. He says that these are 'material' and insists that they be disclosed. The atmosphere changes instantly. The board are about to apply to the Department of Trade for the much sought after banking certificate and this is not the moment to alarm the regulator.[9]

Stonehouse can't say as much openly and finds other reasons to object. He protests on the grounds that disclosure will put off customers, but Gray thinks that being transparent with customers is exactly why the loans should be disclosed. The more Stonehouse blusters, the more suspicious Gray becomes. By the end of the meeting, he has made up his mind that BBT is not quite what it seems.[10]

Sir Charles Hardie must be told at once. Gray heads back to Dixon Wilson at 55 Basinghall Street, takes the lift to the first floor, hurries past the uniformed commissionaire and goes to see the senior partner. Gray tells him that he is 'totally dissatisfied with everything' about BBT, and Sir Charles, who could famously solve a problem in no more than fifteen minutes, agrees to take charge while Gray is on holiday. Before Gray goes away, on 17 July he writes to the BBT board setting out his concerns and enclosing a list of the outstanding loans which he wants them to discuss with their solicitors.[11]

Stonehouse is alarmed when he receives Gray's letter. Disclosure risks Department of Trade attention; refusal risks the disgrace of a qualified audit opinion. The former jeopardises approval of the cherished banking certificate and might trigger a full inquiry into a company that has a lot to hide, while the latter might trigger another malicious *Sunday Times* investigation. When company secretary Bingham raises Gray's letter, Stonehouse, still smarting from the first *Sunday Times* piece – and, as usual, telling himself with one side of his brain that he's done nothing wrong while knowing with the other half that he has – stamps his foot. He says that he is not having any of it and Bingham should get that clear. It's the kind of outburst that makes people reluctant to tell him bad news or to stand up to him in any way.

Stonehouse discusses the letter with Eric Levine & Co, his new solicitor since March following an introduction from White. The replacement of a respected firm like Stanleys with a smaller, eponymous firm so soon after a share issue is extremely unusual and Eric Levine is in no doubt what his new client wants. He agrees that disclosure might not be necessary and, working late into the night, puts that in writing, copied to Dixon Wilson.

Sir Charles is still not fully engaged. He doesn't look at the BBT files, keeps no record of the meeting with Gray and doesn't question the management. Instead, he calls Edward Sibley of Dixon Wilson's own solicitors, the City firm Berwin Leighton. Staring out over the Thames from his office on London Bridge, Sibley listens carefully. He asks for the files to be sent over and they confirm his instincts. He bluntly tells Sir Charles that the loans have to be disclosed and drafts a letter for him to send. Sir Charles can't ignore that advice. He strengthens the letter and it arrives at BBT at 2.30pm on 26 July. A flurry of letters and phone calls leads to Levine calling Sibley on 1 August to try to resolve the matter. Neither man will budge and a meeting is arranged for 10.30am on 2 August at Levine's Mayfair office.[12]

Stonehouse scrambles around to hide more of the loans. One is a £30,000 loan to Kazi Ahmed's company, which is simply reassigned to a Miss Olwen Black. She is Sheila Buckley's sister and payment is washed through Buckley's National Westminster account. Ahmed is abroad on business when this is happening, but when he returns to Dover Street on 1 August, he meekly signs all the forms and Buckley herself witnesses his signature.

The following day is the showdown in Mayfair. Stonehouse

and White are accompanied by Broad and Bingham, while Sir Charles takes along Sibley. Everyone knows that it is very rare for a company's solicitors to be confronted by the senior partner of its auditors and his solicitor in a serious dispute over the accounts. But Stonehouse has been in bigger fights than this in politics and plans his strategy carefully. He will isolate Sibley, lean on Hardie and count on the support of Levine.

He has a formidable opponent. Sibley says not only are the directors' guarantees flimsy and the loans material, but they were made to facilitate their own share purchases and not in the ordinary course of business. They are therefore in breach of Section 54 of the 1948 Companies Act and this is a very serious offence. He is adamant that they should be disclosed, but Levine pulls a rabbit out of the hat. Taking each loan separately, he says, none is material and the directors' report need not refer to them.[13]

It is scarcely believable and puts Sir Charles in a tight spot. If he accepts Sibley's advice, he will be bringing disgrace on a former government minister, a serving MP and privy counsellor, a man he still considers trustworthy and one he himself has brought into the firm. If he listens to Levine, he is ignoring not just his solicitor but one of his most trusted partners and putting his own reputation and that of his firm on the line. It is the devil's dilemma.

Fortunately for Stonehouse, Sibley has to leave the meeting for another appointment and, with the lawyer no longer staring him down, Sir Charles weakens. Provided that the loans are repaid, he agrees to sign the accounts. He is taking a risk and he knows it, but it is not even the biggest mistake he is making. Extraordinarily, despite Sibley's strong steer, he fails to consider whether BBT's loans to directors were illegally used to finance the purchase of its own shares.

Stonehouse and his board can scarcely believe their good

fortune. All they need to do now is to repay the loans and they use their old tricks to do that. Various Stonehouse companies are inserted into the chain and BBT disappears so far down the paper trail that it is virtually invisible. Not that Dixon Wilson look very far. The senior partner has spoken and they merely check that the directors' loans have been cleared and don't enquire where the money has come from. On 6 August 1973, they sign an unqualified audit report and the BBT board breathe a sigh of relief. Stonehouse has pulled it off again.[14]

I 3

THE UNACCEPTABLE
FACE OF CAPITALISM

On 11 October 1973, a select group of BBT's investors and customers troop across the ancient floor of Westminster Hall. It was the centre of the English legal system for seven centuries and it is where Churchill had lain in state. They walk under the 14th-century rafters, past where King Charles I stood trial for treason, up the stone steps and turn left to the Central Lobby. The place exudes solidity and that's exactly the image Stonehouse wants to convey. With the auditors off his back and an application for the banking certificate lodged the previous Friday, it is time to get on with building the bank. And for a serving MP eager to impress his business associates, where better than the House of Commons?[1]

Downstairs in a private dining room, each guest is given a green carnation for their buttonhole as they take in the view across the Thames. Property prices are easing off after the explosive growth of 1972, the Yom Kippur War is raging in the Middle East and the rising oil price is a talking point, but the stock market isn't panicking and neither are the guests.

They include James Charlton. Stonehouse has known 'Jim' since 1967 when he was minister of aviation and Charlton was company secretary of British Aircraft Corporation. He loves his English gentlemanly demeanour and the fact he used to be a barrister. Like Stonehouse, Charlton is now working in the import-export business and has just approached BBT for a loan to finance the sale of some Romanian tractors. He is not the only one to be impressed by the many dignitaries at the dinner, including Bank of England officials whose presence is taken to be a clear sign of approval.[2]

But the Old Lady of Threadneedle Street soon has more to deal with than attend nice dinners at the House of Commons. On 31 October, the Arab oil-producing states announce a 20 per cent cut in oil exports, the oil price surges and stock markets tumble. In November, Britain's railway workers and miners join power workers in industrial action.

The country grinds to a halt and Ted Heath declares a state of emergency, conserving petrol and electricity. Confidence collapses and property prices plummet. Many small banks have lent wildly to speculative property companies, recycling loans from the bigger banks. When the bubble bursts, the big banks want their money back and the fringe banks rush round to Threadneedle Street for help.

Jim Keogh is the man they need to see and, on 29 November, he organises a lifeboat fund to rescue one of the biggest, London & County Securities. He will need to do the same many times over during the next few months as, one by one, Britain's secondary banks run out of money.

But as other banks flee the market, Stonehouse steps in. Ever the optimist, he thinks that their retreat gives BBT an opportunity to make its decisive move. On 5 November, BBT lends a further £129,000 to Zeawood, its only large client, for further property development, this time in Balham in south London.

So sure is he that the other banks are running scared without good cause, and so desperate is he for BBT to trade its way out of its illegal jam, the bullish Stonehouse plans to raise more money from shareholders to expand. There is an unexpected obstacle from the usually compliant Eric Levine & Co, who want the auditors to conduct a review of trading first, but when Stonehouse resists, Levine backs down. When this news reaches Dixon Wilson, Marius Gray sends off another letter to Stonehouse: 'My firm has made no examination of the Trust's accounts since that date,' he warns. 'We are therefore quite unable to comment on either the present financial position or the prospects of the Company.'

Stonehouse ignores this and presses on with the fundraising. This time he draws on one of his few successful companies, Global Imex, which started in January 1972 as another export business. Andrew Scott, an experienced Lonrho executive, became managing director in April that year and the combination of Stonehouse's contacts and Scott's know-how produced profits of £19,000.

Scott is glad to be out of Lonrho. A year after he left, his former CEO Tiny Rowland survived a High Court case in which he was accused of running Lonrho as a corrupt personal fiefdom. Ted Heath immediately described the case as revealing an 'unacceptable face of capitalism' and the phrase is instantly taken up by the press as a catchphrase for dubious business practices.

Forty-nine-year-old Scott is determined to avoid getting mixed up in anything like that and is one of the few directors at any of Stonehouse's companies ready to stand up to him. He soon realises that most of Global's capital is tied up in BBT and other Stonehouse companies on the chairman's instruction. He can see no commercial benefit from the arrangement and when Stonehouse recommends that Global invests a further £30,000, he is appalled. Stonehouse assures Scott that the Department of Trade are about to approve the banking licence and BBT's shares will now appreciate very quickly. If so, Scott archly remarks, he would like to see Global repaid.[3]

The banking certificate duly arrives on 10 December. The Department of Trade and the Bank of England have cheerfully waved it through on trust. Jim Keogh later summed up the latter's attitude: 'If ever you found a chap out in a lie, he was finished forever. You assumed that nobody would be so stupid.'

But that's not how Scott sees things. A close relationship with BBT was not in the plan he had signed up for and he for one has spotted Stonehouse's conflict of interest. On 12 December, he writes to Stonehouse. 'Bearing in mind that you may wish to be impartial – as you are also chairman of British Bangladesh Trust Limited – I think you may find it helpful to have my views.' He says that Global would have to borrow money at a very high interest rate to find the £30,000 Stonehouse wants, a move Scott calls 'commercially unsound'.

Global's board consists of Stonehouse, McGrath and Scott, all of whom are shareholders. A board meeting is held the next day at 26 Dover Street. McGrath is in a Brighton nursing home still recovering from his heart attack, leaving Stonehouse and Scott as the only directors present, together with the company secretary, Sheila Buckley. And even Buckley isn't exactly onside at the moment. The pair had an enormous fall-out over Stonehouse's silver wedding anniversary party that Barbara had arranged with great fanfare last month. 'It's totally hypocritical,' shouted Buckley, throwing her sherry glass at him. 'Almost obscene!'[4]

Stonehouse reports that the National Westminster Bank has lent Global £30,000 on his personal guarantee and proposes that Global invests it in BBT. Scott is furious. Only recently did the board agree not to take out overdrafts backed by personal guarantees and his letter has been completely ignored. He votes against the proposal, tying the directors' vote. But the chairman has a casting vote and Buckley records the outcome: 'It was agreed that Global Imex Limited subscribe for the Rights Issue shares in the amount of £30,000, the Managing Director dissenting.'

For Scott, it's a big issue, but for Stonehouse, it's just another brick in the wall. Similar decisions are taken all over his empire and the fundraising is declared a success. But when everything is tallied up, he, his companies and nominees provide half of the £340,884 raised. It is a rerun of the 1972 funding, smashing through the 10 per cent directors' limit and with BBT illegally funding the purchase of its own shares. Once again, a Stonehouse company sticks out as the largest investor. This time it's not Ronvale but Epacs that holds £185,000 of BBT shares. He needs to hide that before the books are closed off on 31 December. By now, he knows what to do: family and friends beware.[5]

On 14 December, he approaches Jim Charlton and asks if he will hold £25,000 worth of £10 shares in BBT as a nominee. In Charlton's world, as in Keogh's, you either trust someone or you don't. The impressive Commons dinner still fresh in his mind, he replies, 'I would be very happy to be responsible for the 2,500 shares'. He does not immediately have £25,000 available and BBT lends him the money.

Stonehouse twists a few more arms, but Christmas gets in the way and, on New Year's Eve, he still needs £50,000 to cover up Epacs' holding. It's essential to do it before the books close and time's running out. He calls on his family, this time phoning his 23-year-old daughter Jane, who is now an artist living down the road in Fulham. He tells her the bank is in a bit of trouble. People who were going to buy shares have not come forward and he needs some other people to act as nominees. There would be no financial reward or risk to them – does she know of anyone who might help? She is not at all interested in money, but is close to her father and agrees to invite some friends to a meeting early that evening.

She starts with Susan Hill, a childhood friend. After leaving school, Hill had worked as a model and occasional shop assistant, but in December 1973 she is living on benefits with a small child. It is not often she gets invited to meetings these days, let alone one hosted by a privy counsellor, and she is pleased to accept.

Jane then moves on to Leslie Nowicki, a successful architect and interior designer who had once employed her and who has also been a Christmas guest at the Stonehouse family home. He had declined Stonehouse's earlier suggestions to deposit money with BBT, but when Jane and her smooth-talking father invite him to the New Year's Eve gathering, he is too embarrassed to say no. His accountant and solicitor advise him strongly not to be involved, but he thinks it would be discourteous not to show up.[6]

When Hill, Nowicki and a few other friends of Jane's meet at Dover Street, Stonehouse explains that he wants to retain control of the bank without appearing as the holder of too many shares. He says that his friends have already helped as much as they can and asks for volunteers to act as nominees with funds provided by BBT. Again, no risk, no reward – just helping a friend.

The meeting breaks up into small groups discussing what they have just heard. Jane tries to explain to Nowicki, but it is clear to him that she has no idea what is going on. Nowicki says, 'It looks like a bit of a cheat', to which Jane replies, 'But my father was a minister who would never cheat or do anything wrong.' Nowicki quizzes one of the BBT people. 'If Stonehouse is going to be run over by a bus, would I be liable for the payment of the money I am signing for?' 'Oh no,' comes the reply. 'It's only a paper type of thing.'

Nowicki agrees to take £30,000 worth of BBT shares as nominee and Hill takes £20,000, both financed by BBT loans. They are presented there and then with pre-typed letters signed by Stonehouse and White, but Nowicki is still uneasy. He can see that Hill is out of her depth and insists on letters of indemnity for them both. Stonehouse whips out his pen and writes them on the spot.

At midnight, Big Ben chimes in the start of the three-day week, forced on Prime Minister Heath by the striking miners. Electricity is rationed and Stonehouse needs to make the most of the daylight hours and what he sees as a massive investment opportunity. On Wednesday 2 January, the first working day of 1974, he calls White into his office. He proposes that BBT diversifies from property lending into the stock market. Shares are at a seven-year low, he tells White, and a 1920s-style crash is extremely unlikely. Four months should do it: buy now and sell in the spring.

This is too much even for White. It's not the kind of business that BBT's shareholders are expecting. It's high risk and Stonehouse is just an amateur investor. White demands a full board discussion, but Stonehouse doesn't let him finish: 'Shares have dropped considerably,' he declaims. 'And if they continue to drop and we buy,' counters White, 'we are going to lose a lot of money.' Stonehouse is insistent. 'Share prices are going to go up.'[7]

Resistance from the usually compliant White is a surprise, but Stonehouse regards the company as his own and needs to get some cash to regularise the BBT accounts before the auditors come back in July. He simply ignores his general manager. The following morning, he has breakfast with City stockbroker Tony Rudd in the Victorian dining room of Brown's Hotel in Albemarle Street. It's just round the corner from Dover

Street, as well as being on Rudd's route into the City from his Kensington home. As they tuck into their scrambled eggs, Stonehouse asks Rudd whether he would be willing to open loan accounts for three BBT companies. That shouldn't be a problem, replies Rudd, who already handles Stonehouse's small personal investments.

Stonehouse mentions some shares he likes, Rudd doesn't object and Stonehouse says he wants to go ahead. As the breakfast plates are cleared away, Stonehouse suddenly adds: 'Would you put all the money in?' Rudd is considered an enterprising character in the City, but Stonehouse is asking for a loan of £500,000. He swallows hard. 'It might be a little bit beyond us,' he says and they settle for a loan of £100,000 instead. Stonehouse puts all of that into the market immediately and deposits £35,000 as security. White is outraged when he finds out and says he is going to raise the matter at the next board meeting. But before he has the opportunity to do so, he, like McGrath before him, has a heart attack and is admitted to hospital.[8]

Having placed his bet, or at least part of it, Stonehouse turns his attention back to Global where managing director Andrew Scott is still resisting the proposed investment in BBT. There is a board meeting on 4 January 1974 and Stonehouse summons the convalescing McGrath up from Brighton. Scott once again attacks the plan, but McGrath's presence means that this time there is no need for the chairman's casting vote. Stonehouse and McGrath formally endorse the investment; 'the Managing Director dissenting,' Buckley again records. Stonehouse won't even let him see the company's bank statements and Scott hands in his notice. He has been with the company less than two years.[9]

Stonehouse still does not blink at the resistance from White and Scott, his two most senior executive directors. There is no outward sign of doubt and, as the stock market falls steadily throughout January, he doubles up, telling Rowe Rudd to invest a further £116,000 of BBT money and lodging another £38,000 as a deposit. He's in it deep now: this is double or quits.[10]

What does make him blink is a headline on the front page of *The Times* on Friday 25 January 1974: 'Defector reveals MPs' part in spy ring'. It doesn't take Stonehouse long to realise that the defector in question – photographed on a visit to the paper's newsroom – is the man whose allegations got him called into Number 10 in the summer of 1969 and hammered the final nail into the coffin of his political career. Now that Josef Frolík's background within Czech intelligence has been confirmed by Whitehall, he tells *The Times* how he gave the CIA the names of three British MPs he knew were in thrall to the Czechs in the 1960s. One of course was Will Owen, tried and acquitted; the other two were recruited by Lt Captain Václav Táborský during the 1950s. The party at Donald Chesworth's flat is not mentioned, and Frolík says when he unmasked the three MPs in 1969, 'their usefulness was finished'.[11]

A fortnight later, Heath calls a general election and Stonehouse turns his attention to the good people of Wednesbury. The winter has been grim with power cuts and candles on the cheerless evenings. The 'Who Governs Britain?' general election on Thursday 28 February is a contest between Heath's 'Firm Action for a Fair Britain' and Harold Wilson's 'Let's Work Together' manifestos. The pundits favour Heath and finally Stonehouse gets some good news: the stock market rises in the hope of another Conservative government.

Stonehouse's constituency has been renamed Walsall North following electoral boundary changes and, as soon as the election is called, he is on the campaign trail. On 11 February, he stuns a rally in Walsall when he says that the striking miners should go back to work. It's taken as a rebuke to Wilson and an endorsement of Heath. His political colours are changing. Stock market gains, it would appear, are now more important to Stonehouse than political favour. Pundits call him an embarrassment to his party, but they don't know the half of it.[12]

Confident of a Conservative victory, the stock market rises further during February and Stonehouse makes back all the money lost in January. He is exultant. He thinks his money worries will soon be over when the stock market soars on a Heath victory. The last poll before election day shows a clear Tory lead and the first editions on the day the country goes to the polls carry headlines predicting a comfortable Heath majority. It is Stonehouse's chance to make even more money and on election day, when he is not knocking on doors in Walsall, he is making phone calls to Rowe Rudd investing a further £18,288.[13]

Early results on election night show Labour taking the north of England and the Midlands, and the Tories mopping up the south. Stonehouse romps home in Walsall North and is pictured celebrating joyously with wife Barbara. But he really needs a Tory government if his gamble is to pay off. As the night wears on, it's clear that Heath's 'Who Governs Britain?' question has backfired. When all the results are declared, Labour is in possession of four more seats than the Tories.[14]

But all is not yet lost for Stonehouse's stock market punt. If Heath can persuade the fourteen-seat Liberals to support him, he can form a coalition government. Stonehouse follows the news reports anxiously over the weekend. On the Sunday, Liberal leader Jeremy Thorpe spends two hours with Heath in Number 10, but his party won't stand for an alliance with the Tories. At 6.30pm the following day, Heath heads to Buckingham Palace to resign.

Wilson forms a minority government and although Stonehouse puts on a hopeful front, the shadow cast by his behaviour in 1969 is long. He knows he won't get a call. But that's the least of his worries. Far-left-winger Michael Foot is minister for employment and his fellow radical Tony Benn is minister for industry. They scare the stock market by telling journalists to expect state intervention in industry. Chancellor Denis Healey threatens to squeeze property speculators 'until the pips squeak' and everyone knows that the rich – property speculators or not – are his real target.

The stock market's pre-election rally is reversed, wiping 20 per cent off Stonehouse's share portfolios. His big play has failed. At the end of March, shares drop to their lowest level since October 1962, Stonehouse's quarter of a million pounds bet has lost 25 per cent and he is personally liable if Rowe Rudd call in the money he owes. He has used BBT money without board permission and this becomes another thing to conceal from Dixon Wilson.

From his hospital bed, White watches the plunging stock market in despair, if not in surprise. When he is out of danger but still in hospital, he receives an unexpected visitor. His deputy Broad appears with a paper bag containing the BBT directors' attendance register. Broad says that Stonehouse wants White to sign them. He refuses, saying he hasn't attended the meetings and doesn't know what took place there. Broad is friendly enough: 'I knew bloody well you wouldn't sign it.'

A fortnight later, White receives another visitor. This time it is Stonehouse, arriving without warning, bearing the minute book and a bunch of grapes. 'I would like you to sign these minutes,' he says. 'Look, John, I cannot sign them,' says White. 'You will either sign them or give me your resignation,' threatens Stonehouse.

'Well, I am not signing your minutes,' White replies.

He is discharged from hospital in early April and on the afternoon of the 10th, Stonehouse calls at his home. 'Either you will sign the minute book or you will sign this,' Stonehouse says, and offers White a typed document that is his resignation letter. 'I hereby formally resign as general manager of British Bangladesh Trust Limited and all other related directorships as from 1st July 1974.' Stonehouse says that if he resigns, the other directors will formally write to him committing to repurchase all his BBT shares and pay him £250 per month from 1 July until the end of December. White agrees and his resignation is recorded. He attends no further board meetings and receives no such letter.

At the end of the month, architect Leslie Nowicki gets his BBT bank statement and sees that he is being charged interest on his £30,000 loan. He has been told that he won't have to pay it, but he thinks back to the advice of both his solicitor and his accountant, and those doubts return. He has been unsuccessfully pressing Stonehouse to cancel the deal for some weeks and now asks Jane Stonehouse to intervene. Her father can't put it off any longer and at the end of April, he closes Nowicki's BBT account through a series of fictitious transfers. But the closing statement is plain enough: 'Re Disposal of Shares'.[15]

May brings a glimmer of hope. The stock market has now fallen 50 per cent from its peak, investors are starting to say that the bear market is over and there is a brief rally. Stonehouse feels a little better and steps up his efforts to attract business for his export companies. He is a one-man band and the trips mount up: Cyprus and North Yemen, Cairo and Beirut, Zürich and Brussels, New York and Los Angeles. He travels to Romania with Jim Charlton, who has business interests there, to see if they can get in on a deal exporting its cement to Nigeria. The West African nation is rebuilding following the civil war and is in desperate need of construction materials. It's a complex deal with many parties, but if they can get in on this export from Romania to Lagos, it will be the answer to his financial woes. It's an audacious move, but as usual Stonehouse exudes confidence.[16]

His return to Heathrow brings an unwelcome surprise: on Sunday 19 May at 11.17am, a car bomb exploded in the Heathrow car park where he had left his Rover. He returns to find it destroyed in the blast. Stonehouse tells police he has no reason to believe himself to be any sort of target, but back on Sancroft Street in Kennington, he discovers that another bomb was found at the NAAFI headquarters close to his house at 11.20 on the Sunday evening. It's concluded that they are both the work of the IRA's mainland bombing campaign. Barbara remembers some threatening anonymous phone calls back in 1959 and explores insuring her husband's life.[17]

The stock market recovery is short-lived. A rash of finance and property companies collapse, stock exchange members bail out failing brokers and Jim Keogh's lifeboat is frequently called into action. At the end of May, the *Financial Times* warns that 'something nasty is about to happen' and the stock market hits new lows. Stonehouse realises that there is no hope of a recovery before Dixon Wilson are back in June for the annual audit.

BBT's stock market losses have blown a hole in the balance sheet and, to someone for whom the accounts are just an irritation, the solution is obvious: pretend that BBT is holding the shares for someone else. Various bogus transactions are invented to transfer the shares to third parties, including a 'Miss S. E. Black', Buckley's maiden name. Unfalteringly compliant, Buckley signs the paperwork as Black. Company secretary Bingham comments that she is doing so in her own handwriting.

With White out of the way, Stonehouse needs some new directors on the board. He persuades Jim Charlton and – a real feather in his cap – eminent shareholder Sir Charles Forte to become directors. They attend their first board meeting on 7 June, a stage-managed affair at which BBT is renamed London Capital Group. Forte does not attend another board meeting until 27 November.[18]

14

BECOMING JOE MARKHAM

It is early July 1974 and Dixon Wilson are back in Dover Street. The mood has changed since the 1973 audit. The worst banking crisis in living memory is in full swing, emergency Bank of England bailouts are becoming routine for fringe banks and Dixon Wilson are asking BBT the questions they should have asked a year earlier. Stonehouse's heart sinks every time he sees them in the building.

He thought the big Romania–Nigeria cement deal was the ticket out of trouble, but Lloyds has categorically refused an overdraft to finance it. The 'everyone else is doing it' excuse doesn't feel so good right now. He's scared of the phone and night times are worse. He is not sleeping well, waking up covered in sweat. McGrath and White, men of his age, are not long out of coronary care. He's so busy that he's forgetting to turn up to meetings he has called, and so anxious that Dr Maurice Miller MP, unofficial GP to many members, prescribes him drugs in the House of Commons.[1]

But despite the addictive sedatives, Stonehouse still can't relax. He wishes he could start his life all over again and it's then that he remembers the Jackal: 'It is possible. The point is getting away with it.' The movie of Frederick Forsyth's *The Day of the Jackal* was a big hit in the summer of 1973, but naturally he'd already read the book. A year later, he gets an idea.[2]

Friday 12 July 1974 is a typical morning in the medical

records office at the Manor Hospital in Walsall. Rows of medical secretaries work their way through piles of buff folders, typing up the doctors' notes, occasionally drawing a sombre black cross on the cover when a file needs to be closed. Derek Perks, the patient services officer, one of the few men in the room, is called to the phone. John Stonehouse MP wants him and they don't get to talk to many celebrities down in the patient services department. Perks tries to zone out the clatter of typewriters and listens carefully.

Stonehouse says that he has funds available to be distributed to young widows in the area and he is interested in obtaining the identities of males in their forties who have died in the hospital in recent months. He tells Perks there is some urgency as he is visiting his constituency the next day and gives him his London telephone number.

It wouldn't be good to disappoint a local MP, especially one who has campaigned for local hospitals, and Perks goes straight along to hospital records. There he searches the long ranks of grey filing cabinets for recent death certificate stubs and finds details of five males between the ages of thirty and sixty. He calls London. 'Mr Stonehouse's secretary,' replies a female voice. Perks is put straight through to the MP.

Stonehouse gets out his pen and takes down the details. Everything must be accurate and you don't get to be patient services officer by being sloppy: that's just the one 'l' in Mildoon. It's an interesting interlude in an ordinary life and Perks doesn't expect to hear anything more of it.[3]

Back in the West Midlands, on the afternoon of Saturday 13 July, Stonehouse knocks on the door of a red brick semi-detached house at 23 Lichfield Road in Brownhills. He introduces himself as an MP and tells Jean Markham, three months a widow, that he is doing a survey on the taxes on widows' pensions. She doesn't recognise him and asks for his credentials. He is surprised – he's often recognised on the streets in and around Walsall – but produces his wallet and shows some ID. Satisfied, she invites him in and introduces him to her mother-in-law, who is visiting that day. Stonehouse doesn't want any witnesses to this conversation and asks to speak to her alone.

He needs to reassure the prickly Mrs Markham and runs through some questions about her widows' pension. But what he really needs to find out is if they'd ever been overseas. Joe had never been abroad – he worked as a foundry worker locally – and never had a passport. Stonehouse asks if she is happy with the doctor's treatment of her husband. Jean and Joe Markham have got to know Dr Gelling well over the years, particularly during Joe's recent heart trouble. She doesn't see what this has to do with widows' pensions and sharply tells Stonehouse that Dr Gelling is satisfactory in every respect. Stonehouse sees she is annoyed and takes the conversation back to pensions. As he leaves, he thinks it wise to ask if Mrs Markham knows any other widows. She names a Mrs Dorsett. Stonehouse doesn't want the widows he visits talking to each other and so that's one woman he won't be calling on.[4]

The same afternoon, the door of Elsie Mildoon's mid-terrace shop on the Walsall Road swings open. It is a typical newsagent in a working-class area. A few unsold dailies, the *Tit-Bits* and *Reveille* weeklies, sweets, pop, ice creams and cigarettes are all crammed into the tiny shop. The tall good-looking man who comes in doesn't look like a normal customer. Top shelf? No, not him. Then she remembers where she has seen that face before: the election posters.

Stonehouse says he has seen her husband's death announcement in the local *Express & Star* newspaper just three weeks ago and offers his condolences. He says he has a motion going through the House of Commons on single parenthood and knows she has one child. He wants to ask her some questions but, learning from the encounter with Jean Markham, assures her that she need not answer if she finds them difficult. Although surprised by the details, she is glad of some advice on how to look after young Nigel. She is a nice enough woman and he tells her to contact him or his secretary if she needs any financial advice. When it comes to asking whether Mildoon had ever been overseas, she tells him they had been on holiday to Austria in the spring of 1971.[5]

Stonehouse now has what he needs on Joseph Arthur Markham and Donald Clive Mildoon. He orders the men's birth certificates under the names S. J. Lewis and H. Humphries, using a different West Midlands solicitor for each, and will pick them up personally from the General Register Office for Births, Marriages and Deaths when he is back in London.[6]

BBT's second annual audit meeting is held on 17 July. Part-qualified auditor Michael Jarvis, about to take his final accountancy exams, has been added to the audit team and before they leave Basinghall Street, he briefs Marius Gray. The auditors have discovered that more than half of BBT's total loan book is accounted for by just ten dubious loans. This concentration is far too risky and they decide that a provision against default will have to be made. But that is not all. Jarvis has noticed that letters to one of those customers, 'Miss S. E. Black', go to Buckley's home address and he tells Gray that 'Miss Black' may be a pseudonym for Stonehouse's secretary.

Gray hasn't forgotten how BBT wriggled away last year and he's not going to let it happen again. He opens by declaring that he is 'only prepared to discuss one aspect of the accounts and that is a provision for bad debts'. He goes through all the big loans demanding to know what security the bank holds against each. The directors are vague, Stonehouse won't look at him and complains about the length of time the audit is taking. It is the first time he has avoided eye contact and it convinces Gray that there is something very seriously wrong.[7]

Gray's attitude adds to Stonehouse's anxiety. There are rumours in the City of further trouble in the finance and property sectors, Wall Street is unsettled by moves to impeach President Richard Nixon after the Watergate break-in and the stock market takes a precipitous tumble in the second half of July. His brokers Rowe Rudd press him to cut his losses but he can't afford to do that.

With his auditors and his brokers on his tail, he has a better plan. On 18 July, he makes his way over to Holborn. It is twenty years since he was walking these streets on his way to lectures at the London School of Economics, but youthful idealism has given way to a severe midlife crisis and he is getting desperate.

At St Catherine's House, an imposing Edwardian edifice at the junction of Kingsway and Aldwych, stands the General Register Office. Stonehouse pushes through the doors, finds the Public Search Room and presents receipts for the two birth certificate applications. To staff he's just another middle-aged man who might be doing a family history and no one notices him. Being unobtrusive is the art of going undercover and it is one that the naturally extrovert Stonehouse is rapidly learning.[8]

While Stonehouse is collecting the rudiments of his new life, Gray is briefing Sir Charles Hardie on the wreckage of his old. He lays it on the line and this time Hardie listens. Before Gray packs his bags for his summer holiday – true to type, the accountant is a creature of habit – he writes a strong letter to Stonehouse insisting BBT makes a provision against bad debts.

Stonehouse, Charlton and McGrath discuss the letter at a

board meeting on 19 July. A provision would wipe out BBT's reserves and send it into the Bank of England's lifeboat, revealing all the previous year's fabrications. But Gray's absence gives Stonehouse one last chance to call on the old pals' act and he writes an evasive and misleading letter to Hardie.[9]

Creating the Markham and Mildoon personae offers Stonehouse a welcome escape from BBT's problems. He closes his office door and fills in passport application forms for Markham, using the same hand he employed for correspondence with his Czech handler Holan. He invents an address – 30 Eccleston Square, London SW1 – and next of kin – Elsie Meah, 55 Old Elm Street, Manchester. Just like the Lewis persona who applied for the birth certificates, this bears no relation to any reality – Stonehouse's or Joseph Markham's.[10]

Now for the passport photographs. He'll be using that passport when the real John Stonehouse is still in the news and it must not look at all like him. Stonehouse slicks back his hair, takes off his tie and arranges the oversized 1970s collars of his shirt over the lapels of a dark sports jacket. Then on with the glasses: dramatic big black frames that dominate the face. Forsyth would be proud of him.

Stonehouse finds a busy back-street photographer. He joins the queue and when it's his turn he beams crazily into the camera holding several different poses. He's delighted with the results. They are perfect. He looks like the village idiot and he is confident that no one will ever connect such a bumpkin with the Rt Hon. John Stonehouse, MP.

He needs a witness for each of the Markham photographs. He wants a witness who no one will challenge and thinks of poor Neil McBride, a Scottish politician just out of hospital and not expected to live long. He turns over two of the photos and on the back of each carefully writes in a neat hand, 'I certify that this is a true likeness of Mr Joseph A Markham. Neil McBride.' On the accompanying form, he gives McBride's occupation, 'Member of Parliament'.[11]

Markham is his first new identity and he needs somewhere to stay. Victoria is Stonehouse's beat, but he doesn't want to be bumping into people he knows. He finds an area just south of Victoria Station where the Westminster crowd rarely venture. On St George's Drive, there is a white period terrace mainly given over to cheap hotels. Tucked away in the middle at Number 39, the five-storey Astoria Hotel looks suitably anonymous. Stonehouse climbs the four steps, rings the door bell and waits under the stone portico for someone to answer.

Irish manager Margaret Reilly, in her mid-forties, makes her way up from the basement where she lives with her husband. Stonehouse explains that he comes up from the country on business regularly and is looking for a single room, one night a week, usually a Wednesday. She shows him one of the rooms and explains the house rules. Breakfast is served between 8am and 9am, and they require a deposit in advance. Stonehouse has had his fair share of one-nighters in cheap hotels and this one is fine. He says that he will be back in touch soon.[12]

Stonehouse is going to need money and he's not going to rob a bank, at least not in the conventional way. He needs to find a bank where his signature is not known and that's not easy. His various companies bank with Lloyds, Coutts, Barclays, Midland, Clydesdale, Grindlays, National Westminster, Hambros and First National City Bank. But Midland don't know him that well and, in his walks around Victoria, he has seen a Midland Bank on the corner of Rochester Row and Vauxhall Bridge Road. This, the Rochester Row branch, is handily placed near the Astoria and, on 22 July, Stonehouse calls in to open an account. The bank want to see employment records and references before he can open a current account, but Stonehouse has cash he wants to pay in immediately and opens a deposit account on the spot. He gives his name as Joseph Arthur Markham, a self-employed clerk of 39 St George's Drive and says he will be in touch later to open the current account.[13]

Nothing must be too obvious. He is going to have a lot of money to deposit and needs to spread it around. Rushing through Waterloo Station, he spies a post office. As postmaster general, he had never liked plans to open a National Girobank in every major post office, but it will serve his purposes now. Thousands of people pass through Waterloo every day and he will never be noticed. He opens an account at the station's post office and, before long, he's writing to them on Markham-headed notepaper.[14]

The same day, Stonehouse the MP puts in an appearance. With Wilson's Labour government struggling to get legislation through the evenly divided House, a general election could be called at any moment and the member for Walsall North knows that it's as well to keep up one's profile. The previous Saturday, Turkish forces invaded Cyprus and Stonehouse pops up in the House with a question for Foreign Secretary James Callaghan, but his mind is really elsewhere.[15]

The next day, he meets Hardie who, like Gray, insists that provision be made against various property loans. He also demands to know the borrowers' identities, their connection with BBT and the value of their assets. Stonehouse has no answers and Hardie puts everything in writing in a letter to the board.[16]

On 24 July, Stonehouse takes a walk along the Strand. Midway between the Savoy Hotel and the Vaudeville Theatre, Stanley Gibbons's famous emporium is considered the home of stamp collecting. The former postmaster general has a collection that might be valuable and he asks Stanley Gibbons director William White to sell them either by private treaty or auction.

White advises that auction is the way to go and Stonehouse says he wants to avoid publicity if possible. They agree that the stamps will be offered at three auctions in New York in the autumn under the vendor's code name Ajax.[17]

The letter from their auditor's senior partner gives the BBT board no choice but to comply – or, at least, to appear to comply. On the last day of July, they reluctantly agree to the provision and give partial information on borrowers. But they dare not come clean on the most serious offence, instead brazenly declaring that 'the advances have not been made for the purpose of acquiring shares in the holding company'.[18]

One deception follows another for BBT and its chairman. On 1 August, the day after the board meeting, Stonehouse takes Markham's form to the passport office in Petty France, just up the road from his flat. Stonehouse joins the queue and Martin Christie, a 21-year-old civil service clerical officer midway through a three-month stint as a passport-examining officer, calls him forward. He matches the details on the form with the birth certificate and checks that Neil McBride's signature on the back of the photo is the same as that on the form. It's the height of summer and Christie is dealing with 100 applications a day. This one is nothing special and he tells Stonehouse to go over to the cashier and pay his £5 fee. Next please.[19]

At 10am on 5 August, Stonehouse goes back to the Passport Office, taking the receipt for his £5 fee. James Mitchell, a middle-ranking civil servant in his fifties, is on the desk. He confirms that Stonehouse's receipt matches the file and produces the dark blue, leather-bound British passport numbered 785965A. He wishes Stonehouse a pleasant holiday and calls forward the next person in the queue.[20]

Now that the board are playing ball, or at least pretending to, Hardie summons Stonehouse and Charlton back to Basinghall

Street. He is not satisfied with their partial explanation and takes them through a schedule of loans one by one. Stonehouse claims never to have heard of some of the borrowers. 'Surely you don't make advances of £30,000 to people you don't know the identity of?' says Hardie. 'Well, I will have to find out who it is,' mumbles Stonehouse. Hardie reminds Stonehouse that it is for Dixon Wilson to take a dispassionate view and after his visitors have departed, he tells the audit team to chase everything down.

Dixon Wilson partner Albert 'Claud' Stokes is the man for that job. Forensic analysis is his speciality and, on 9 August, he writes to Stonehouse telling him that he will be doing a full review of BBT. It means scrutiny of all the company's records, a terrifying prospect for a company with so much to hide. Stonehouse pleads with Hardie to call it off but he refuses. Stonehouse contemplates how BBT's newest director, a man introduced by Sir Charles Hardie, could help – but Sir Charles Forte understands audit impartiality full well and he too declines to intervene. With neither Sir Charles willing to help, Stonehouse gives up on the auditors' questions and puts all his energies into his contingency plan.[21]

Markham is going to need an office and Stonehouse looks up the names of local business services companies who offer registered office addresses, postal collection, telephone answering and message taking. He finds one just round the corner from his bona fide Mayfair business address: at 243 Regent Street. Number 243, he finds, lies within the huge and ornate Regent House, which takes up an entire block between Princes Street and Hanover Street. Nestled deep inside above the shops are the offices of many companies, including one Management Business Services.

Stonehouse makes his way there and sets up a business office address with the women in the front office, giving the name of Joseph Arthur Markham and a profession: export consultant. He is allocated a registration number by manager Edward Cox, given a Regent Street telephone number where messages will be taken. Neither Cox nor the ladies in the office realise that he is in fact John Stonehouse the MP. It's all going swimmingly and, while he's in Markham mode, he orders a driving licence in that name, care of 243 Regent Street. The parallel identity is ready to relieve him of the horrors of his daily life.[22]

15

CASHING OUT

On 12 August, John Stonehouse is happy to be driving the familiar route out of London to Heathrow for a flight overseas. He is heading to New York for some meetings before taking a red-eye to Los Angeles to meet Harry Wetzel, a businessman he's known since 1967 and his minister of technology days. He now considers Wetzel a personal friend.[1]

Wetzel is a top executive with the Garrett Corporation, a big US engineering company who own shares in British Aircraft Corporation. It is one of industry minister Tony Wedgwood Benn's targets for nationalisation and Garrett needs advice on what to do with them. Stonehouse is there to persuade Wetzel that a serving Labour MP and former minister for aviation is the very man to give it.

They differ in their politics – Wetzel is a dedicated Republican – but they have a common interest in wine; the American has a vineyard in Sonoma County. It proves to be an easy sell and, on the morning of 15 August, Stonehouse walks away from Garrett with a $25,000 consultancy contract. Better than that, Wetzel has agreed to pay half up front and Stonehouse has a Bank of America cheque for $12,500 in his pocket.[2]

He is booked onto another red-eye back to London, but when he gets to Los Angeles International, he's got just enough time to cash the cheque before he leaves. He sees a Bank of

America money centre on South Sepulveda Boulevard opposite the airport and crosses the highway. It's a sweltering California morning and the air conditioning inside the bank is an instant relief, but soon Stonehouse feels hot under the collar. He wants his $12,500 in cash, but the clerk points out that the cheque is made out to Epacs. Also, cheques have to be paid into a bank account and cleared before any money can change hands.

Stonehouse makes a fuss and she calls over her supervisor, Peggy Bierke. 'We can give you a foreign draft in lieu of your cheque,' says Bierke. Stonehouse brightens: bank drafts can be exchanged for cash. 'I would like the draft payable to myself,' Stonehouse says, and pushes his luck in asking to get part of it on the spot as cash. Not so fast. Bierke says the draft has to be to the same person and for exactly the same amount as the cheque. She suggests he returns to the Garrett Corporation and asks for a new cheque in his name. He says he has no time for that as his plane leaves soon, but a Bank of America banker's draft is better than a Garrett cheque and he settles for that.[3]

He lands at Heathrow on 14 August and goes straight to the office. He tells his assistant Philip Gay that a fee of £5,000 will be payable by Garrett on completion of the consultancy, but makes no mention of the $12,500 advance from the American. He now needs to switch the banker's draft from Epacs to himself, but that's no problem as, although she has resigned as a director, the ever-loyal and willing Sheila Buckley is still Epacs' company secretary and an authorised signatory. She makes the draft over to Stonehouse and he takes it along to his own bank, Lloyds in St James's Street, where he pays it into his personal account.[4]

Stonehouse is now fantasising about his escape the whole time, as the nightmare of a failed business adds to the worries of a failed political career and rumours of espionage and fraud. But with every step towards a new persona, this fantasy becomes closer to reality and he thinks about those he will be leaving behind. It will be hard on Barbara and the children, so the least he can do is to make financial provision for them.

On 20 August, David Miles, a life insurance consultant with Royal Insurance, is called to reception at the Dover Street office. A tall good-looking man in his forties, evidently annoyed that he has been left waiting for a short while, tells Miles that he wants to arrange life cover of £30,000 for a seven-year term. He produces a completed application form in the name of John Stonehouse and gives his occupation as member of parliament. Miles checks the form and conversationally asks 'to whom are we indebted for the introduction?' Stonehouse haughtily says that he knows several directors of the Royal. There are similar policies with Canada Life, Yorkshire General, Norwich Union and Phoenix Life.[5]

With Barbara's position taken care of, it's time to think of himself. He's going to need all the Garrett money when he becomes Joe Markham so, on 21 August, Stonehouse returns to St James's Street and withdraws £5,100 in cash. He puts the notes in his briefcase and takes a cab to Rochester Row where he pays the money straight into the Markham account.[6]

At 7pm that evening, he arrives at the Astoria to spend his first night there as Markham. He has pre-booked it by phone and, when he arrives, Reilly notices that he is carrying only a briefcase for his overnight stay. It's a Wednesday, just as he had said it would be. He pays his £3 deposit and is given the key to room number seven, together with a front door key.

He is up early the next morning and slips out to a nearby newsagent to buy the papers. He reads them in his room before coming down to breakfast just before 9am. He grabs a cup of tea before paying the remaining 50 pence room charge and dashing off to work. Before he goes, he says to Reilly, 'I hope you don't mind. I will be getting some mail here. Will you hold it for me?' She agrees but he strikes her as being above the type that normally stays at the Astoria and she wonders what he is really up to. After he leaves, she lets herself into room seven. She wants to see whether the bed has been slept in. It has.[7]

Back in the real world, the forensic auditor Albert 'Claud' Stokes is sifting through the evidence in Dover Street. He is looking for a smoking gun and thinks he has found one in 'Miss Black', the BBT client with the same address as Buckley. He writes to her asking for confirmation that she owes BBT £70,851. This one loan represents 10 per cent of BBT's loan book and is the equivalent of three quarters of a million pounds in 2022.[8]

On 22 August, 'Miss Black' replies, confirming that she owns the shares as a nominee for another client of the bank. 'Claud' is in his element. He phones her home address and is given her office number, which is none other than BBT's switchboard. Stokes calls, Buckley picks up and Stokes asks to be put through to Miss Black. Buckley says that no one of that name works there and offers a call with Bingham. Bingham phones Stokes right back and repeats that no one of that name works there. Stokes says he has reasons to think otherwise and terminates the call.[9]

By 28 August, Dixon Wilson have the picture. They can't trust anything that BBT say, but they need to go through due process before they inform the Department of Trade. They send a formal Audit Review Note to BBT asking further questions about the loans to Black and the directors, as well as the identity of certain director-connected companies. Stonehouse has no option but to table the note at the next day's BBT board meeting.[10]

That evening is the second Markham stay at the Astoria. The Audit Review Note is a terrifying catalogue of everything that has been going on. Stonehouse can fib his way through the board meeting, but he is running out of time. He needs a Markham credit card for the lifestyle he's planning and spends the evening hunched uncomfortably over the dressing table in his room filling out an American Express application form. He uses the St George's Drive and Regent Street addresses, and gives Midland and the J. A. Markham Export Consultancy as referees.[11]

At the board meeting on 29 August, attended by all the directors apart from Sir Charles Forte, Stonehouse puts on one last show. He says he is confident in the company's prospects and proud of its achievements. In due course, the auditors will be receiving a written response to their Audit Review Note. In the meantime, it's business as usual.[12]

It is now only a matter of time. BBT shares will soon be worthless and Stonehouse has talked several friends and relatives, as well as the unfortunate Susan Hill, into holding them. He never intended them to lose money and on 30 August devises a plan to get them off the hook. He will simply transfer all their shares to a new holding company and, provided that all the paperwork is in place, the nominees will be freed of any obligation.[13]

He needs another name to go on the new company's letterhead and who better than his old friend Jim Charlton? Stonehouse spins a yarn of negotiations with banks in Miami and Beirut wanting to buy BBT shares at a fancy price. He says it will make things easier if all the shares are put in one place. Charlton is an old-fashioned businessman who takes everything on trust and he agrees to serve on the board of the new holding company, Dover Street Nominees.

On 3 September, Stonehouse personally drafts a letter to his friends and relatives informing them of plans that will 'liquidate your facility with this Bank and your other liabilities in connection with your security that we hold'. BBT staff insist that the nominees sign the appropriate forms and Stonehouse scurries around securing their signatures over the next few days. There is just one signature he is unable to collect: that of Jane Stonehouse's friend Susan Hill.[14]

Stonehouse is in action as Markham again as he makes his way along Threadneedle Street, past the Bank of England where this whole mess started and onto the Bank of New South Wales at Number 29. He tells the branch accountant Arthur Jones he is considering emigrating to Australia. He presents a letter on Markham-headed notepaper giving his occupation as export consultant and shows his Markham passport. He tells Jones that he has not finally made up his mind but, if he goes, it will be to Melbourne in November. He will have about £14,000 to open a current account and wants to be ready.[15]

This is but a brief respite from Stonehouse's reality. His brokers Rowe Rudd have been pressing him to cut his stock market losses throughout the summer. Stonehouse puts them off with stories that he knows the chairman of this or that company and is adamant that everything will come right. But by the end of August, the stock market is in free fall and Stonehouse owes Rowe Rudd £136,505. He can't delay any longer and, on 4 September, reluctantly tells them to sell everything, even though he's sure the market is going to go up. They acknowledge the instruction on the understanding 'that your cash flow will be extremely strong end November and that you expect any debit balance to be comfortably settled by then'. That certainly puts an end date on it.[16]

John Stonehouse might have been forced out of the stock

market, but Joe Markham hasn't. He's damned if he's going to miss out on the rally he feels certain is just round the corner. No sooner has he told Rowe Rudd to cut Stonehouse's losses than he is on the phone again as Joe Markham calling James Robson, bank manager of the Rochester Row Midland. It is the first time they have spoken and Markham says he wants to buy some shares. Over the past few weeks, he's paid more than £10,000 in cash into the Midland – a pound in 1974 is equivalent to around £10 in 2022 – and Robson can see that the account is in credit. Although deposit account customers aren't usually given such a facility, Markham seems to be a wealthy, trustworthy man and Robson agrees to let him deal. Over the next few days, Markham invests about £10,000 in British Leyland and GEC, and his secretary occasionally calls Robson: 'This is Mr Markham's secretary. Mr Markham for you'.[17]

The night spent at the Astoria slaving over an American Express application pays off. When Amex take up the reference on 10 September, branch staff see that Markham now has the manager's permission to buy and sell shares in addition to his deposit account. 'We have no reason to suppose that he is not suitable for your purposes,' they tell Amex. The J. A. Markham Export Consultancy confirm that Markham has been working there since 13 April 1963 on an annual salary of £14,500 and Amex issue the card.[18]

Despite the time away from Barbara, Stonehouse successfully maintains the charade of being a good husband. She's baffled by the fact that he now carries two briefcases, but she doesn't dwell on it. He seems in a much better mood now that the audit is over and, on 9 September, he takes her to the Farnborough Air Show. It is part corporate jolly, part trade fair and the former aviation minister is a regular. All the top aerospace companies are there, there's a spectacular flying display and in one of the hospitality suites he and Barbara bump into Alfred Gundry. Gundry is the manager of the St James's Street branch of Lloyds who three months earlier had turned Epacs down for a £50,000 overdraft. Noticing that Gundry is rather taken with Barbara, Stonehouse resolves to try the bank again.[19]

Before he can do that, politics – his main profession just four years ago – gets in the way. On 18 September, Prime Minister Wilson calls a snap general election for 10 October. He had been running the first minority government since 1929 and the first-ever government in which a combination of the winning and third-placed parties had no majority.

Labour's chief whip Bob Mellish has eased through some bits of legislation, but as Wilson told US president Gerald Ford, recently installed in the White House following Nixon's post-Watergate resignation, 'the twin problems of a high rate of inflation and the prospect of rising unemployment present us with an economic situation in which it is desirable that there should be a government with a clear majority'. Stonehouse will have to go through the motions in Walsall North, but his mind is elsewhere.[20]

On 19 September, he takes a plane to Zürich where he picks up a rental car and cruises through the mountains to Mauren, a village near Vaduz, capital city of Liechtenstein. He is there to see Herr Oswald Bühler, the lawyer who has been handling Stonehouse business since 1971. Over the years, Stonehouse has sent £20,000 to Liechtenstein. As usual, Stonehouse has phoned him in advance to warn him of the visit. Bühler is ready with the 97,000 Swiss francs (£14,000) in cash which Stonehouse has requested. They have a cup of coffee, Stonehouse puts the money into his briefcase and heads back to Zürich. There he opens three accounts in the name of Joseph Arthur Markham with the Swiss Bank Corporation, and one at the Swiss Credit

Bank. He stays in Zürich overnight, empties several other accounts and pays £20,000 into the Markham Swiss accounts.[21]

If Stonehouse needs any more encouragement to execute his plan, the latest issue of *Private Eye* is it. The Diplomatic Bag column claims that two Labour MPs are under investigation by the Special Branch for connections with the Czech embassy. 'The Czech embassy,' it says, 'covers espionage and dirty tricks for the whole Soviet bloc, allocates £20,000 a month for "gifts", "retainers" and "consultancies"' to politicians 'who might prove useful.'[22]

On 23 September, Stonehouse has his appointment with Lloyds Bank manager Gundry. Brandishing the Epacs accounts, he asks for a short-term overdraft of £10,000 to hire some part-time consultancy staff in connection with four contracts he expects to win in the US. He tells Gundry that the commission on each will be $25,000. Gundry, who has indeed been impressed by Barbara, agrees the overdraft on Stonehouse's personal guarantee. Stonehouse goes into the branch a few days later and signs that personally, and they arrange to have lunch together.[23]

It's one bank after another now. He opens a Markham account at the Bank of New South Wales in mid-September and, on the 24th, asks Jones for an introduction to the Stock Exchange branch of the Bank of New South Wales on Collins Street in Melbourne. Exchange control is still in operation – not that it has prevented Stonehouse from filling several Swiss bank accounts – and he completes Exchange Control Form 1E. It's where Stonehouse's money will eventually be going, but £10,000 of this is currently invested in the stock market through the Rochester Row Midland. The election call unsettles the London market and US secretary of state Henry Kissinger warns that the world is heading for a

The ideal couple. John Stonehouse and wife Barbara, in the spring of 1957. He has just won his seat in Wednesbury, later renamed Walsall North.

A politician's wife and working woman. Barbara at home in Canonbury, Islington, in early 1959.

The rising star. John Stonehouse outside the Labour Party Conference in Blackpool, the year before Harold Wilson took power in 1964.

The look that says it all. With PM Harold Wilson in 1969,
just before he is confronted with espionage allegations.

The Postmaster General. Posing in front of one of the Post Office's
satellite dishes in Goonhilly, Cornwall, and with the Queen in the
late 1960s – but the dream of leading her government is over.

Seasonal Greetings and All Good Wishes

Dcary Kolona: daughters of Kolon. Vlado
Koudelka, Stonehouse's first handler,
annotates Agent Kolon's Christmas card.

Sucked in. A young Koudelka, whose rotation
at the Czech Embassy in London saw the
recruitment of John Stonehouse.

Out for lunch with Robert Husak.
Stonehouse's third handler is dogged in his
pursuit of his prize minister.

The ultimate defector. Karel Pravec fails
to keep Agent Twister in line in 1970, and
exposes him in 1980.

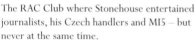

Sir Charles Forte, founder of the hospitality group Trust House Forte, was one of the many victims of Stonehouse's scams.

The RAC Club where Stonehouse entertained journalists, his Czech handlers and MI5 — but never at the same time.

Edward Eveleigh, the trial judge. But the final judgement on the so-called Stonehouse companies comes after the Old Bailey . . .

. . . when Michael Sherrard and Ian Hay Davison meet Stonehouse — again. This time it's not Melbourne, Australia, but Wormwood Scrubs.

That'll do nicely, sir. The Markham and
Stonehouse credit cards.

The copy of Markham's birth certificate that
Stonehouse used to get his fake passport.

The many faces of John Stonehouse. Posing
as Joseph Markham for his passport snaps.

The legendary Fontainebleau hotel in Miami Beach,
from where John Stonehouse staged his disappearance.

The *Mirror*'s multi-page 'dossier' on Stonehouse includes a comic strip
that summarises the entire scandal. This is an excerpt.

The Christmas Eve *Mirror*. Reporters in Melbourne for the Ashes get hold of the story.

The ever-stoic Barbara Stonehouse joins her runaway husband in Australia.

Etheridge gets his man. Finally back on British soil, accompanied by the Fraud Squad's detective chief superintendent.

Sheila Buckley leaving committal hearings, autumn 1975, briefcase in hand.

Outcast at the Labour Party Conference, Blackpool, September 1975.

Looking the other way. The three prime ministers who covered up John Stonehouse's relationship with Czech Security Services officers – proxies for Soviet Russia.

general depression. The Markham £10,000 is already showing a small loss and Stonehouse can't risk losing any more. On 30 September, he tells Robson to sell the lot.[24]

The October election campaign never really gets going. The issues have only been aired in February and public interest is low. But Stonehouse knows how to do this and when the results are in, the *Birmingham Daily Post* reports that in 'safe Labour territory' at Walsall North 'Mr John Stonehouse won a massive majority of 15,885 over his Conservative opponent'. Labour gain eighteen seats, mainly from the Conservatives and now have a majority of forty-two over them. But the Liberals, Ulster Unionists and Scottish and Welsh Nationalists are unusually strong and the government's overall majority is only three – and that's assuming all 319 Labour MPs are present to vote.[25]

PART FOUR

The Great Escape

16

WHAT THEY DIDN'T KNOW

Monday 14 October is the beginning of Wilson's fourth administration, but the anxious wait for a call from Number 10 is now a distant memory for John Stonehouse, backbench MP for Walsall North. Instead he goes to Dover Street and finds a letter from brokers Rowe Rudd. They have sold his reckless punt with BBT money at a loss of £117,287 and want him to settle up. It spells financial ruin and Stonehouse needs to become Markham very soon.[1]

Two days later, Stonehouse as Markham, as always with just a briefcase, is greeted at the Astoria Hotel by Mrs Reilly, keeper of the Markham post since the summer, for the last time. It is early evening as he collects his room and front door keys, and any remaining letters, before leaving again. The next morning, he arrives back at the hotel, morning papers already under his arm, just as breakfast is finishing. He gulps down some tea before leaving the breakfast room, settling the bill and saying goodbye to Reilly.

On his way to Dover Street, he passes Rochester Row. The funds from the Markham stock market dabble have now been cleared and the Midland are of no more use to him. He closes the account and sends a total of £14,100 across London to the City branch of the Bank of New South Wales.[2]

The following Saturday, 19 October, he dons the thick-rimmed glasses and goes into Pan American's offices on

Piccadilly. He asks to book an evening flight from London to New York for two days' time, one he has no intention of taking. Jane Grubb, the ticket agent, asks if it will be a return. 'No,' he tells her, 'I'm flying on to Sydney.' He says he wants an open-ended ticket from New York to Sydney, via Houston and Mexico, and shows no surprise at the cost of nearly £500. Grubb checks his face against his passport: same glasses, same man. Markham hands over his American Express card, pays and leaves with a transatlantic flight booked for Monday and the rest of the trip open for a year.[3]

Instead of taking the flight to New York, on Monday Stonehouse hauls a conspicuously large metal-coated shipping trunk onto the back seat of the family car. He drives the short distance across Mayfair from Dover Street to 24–25 Binney Street and rings the bell for Clowhurst Limited, a shipping agent. The company's director Garry Wakefield is immediately taken by how very well dressed this fortysomething English gentlemen looks. 'Can you arrange to ship a trunk?' Stonehouse asks Wakefield. Together they get the hefty trunk out of the back seat of the car and manoeuvre it up a flight of stairs to the offices proper.

'It's going to Melbourne, Australia,' says Stonehouse. 'I'm emigrating.' He gives his name as Mr J. A. Markham and states his contact address as 243 Regent Street, London W1. Stonehouse fills out the customs declaration and completes the consignment note, then writes Wakefield a Bank of New South Wales cheque for £37.69. Wakefield produces the paperwork in triplicate, but notices that Mr Markham forgets to take his copy.[4]

The following day, Arthur Jones calls the Regent Street number from the Bank of New South Wales's Threadneedle Street branch. He wants to confirm the transfer of £14,100 to the Collins Street, Melbourne branch and asks to speak to Mr

Markham. A woman asks which company Markham works for and Jones just says he's an export consultant. She puts him through to another woman who identifies herself as Mr Markham's secretary, but declines to say whether Markham has left yet for Australia.[5]

Stonehouse is considering Sheila Buckley's future a great deal now. The next day, Wednesday, he writes to Stanley Gibbons informing them that she is the owner of the stamps they have arranged to sell for 'Ajax' in New York between 1 and 14 November. He gives her address as that of her parents: 31 Harvel Crescent, Abbey Wood, London SE2.[6]

He plans to give up the lease on his flat in Victoria where Buckley has been living and she needs somewhere to stay. On the 24th, Stonehouse and Buckley head north to Highfield House on Fitzjohn's Avenue in Hampstead, an imposing five-storey Victorian confection. They climb the hotel's steps and receptionist Mariella Zandstra opens the front door. She thinks it strange that they don't have any luggage but the older man is quick to explain. 'I'm going away,' he says, 'and I would like my wife to stay somewhere while I'm away.' Zandstra gets the impression he is heading overseas, but she doesn't ask questions. Instead she shows them both around the hotel, and they compare the weekly rates against the daily ones. She explains that some rooms have their own cooking facilities.

They follow Zandstra upstairs to Room 20. The door opens onto a dark and gloomy room equipped with a kitchen sink and a gas hob that sits atop a fridge. There's a desk with a phone, ashtray and a small bed. They'll take it, but neither gives any indication of how long for. They put down a deposit of £20 for the first week and, that Sunday, Buckley moves in on her own. Mariella Zandstra never meets the tall man with the dark-rimmed glasses again.[7]

Back at Dover Street, Buckley gradually gives up more of her official duties. Although Stonehouse appears to dominate her, many of the staff there see her as a shrewd, tough fighter and no one mistakes this for a loss of influence. Before Philip Gay replaces her as an authorised signatory on the myriad business accounts, Buckley unquestioningly signs multiple cheques amounting to tens of thousands of pounds for Stonehouse to cash.[8]

His new life as Joe Markham is building up a head of steam. On 29 October, at the Bank of New South Wales in Threadneedle Street, Arthur Jones receives a call from a woman identifying herself as Markham's secretary. She is following up on their conversation of a few days before. She tells him that Markham left for Australia on 25 October. In fact, 'Markham' is still in London, but his trunk isn't. It is now safely in Container 241487, and has left Tilbury Docks, heading for Melbourne.[9]

On the last day of October, at the Bank of New South Wales's Collins Street branch in Melbourne, accountant Peter Street sits behind his desk looking at an Overseas Remitting Warrant for the value of AUS$24,982.38. It's come from his opposite number in London, instructing him to open a savings account in the name of J. A. Markham. This is routine business. He issues a passbook for account no. 077661, credits the account and looks forward to the weekend and next week's Melbourne Cup public holiday.[10]

Meanwhile John Stonehouse, member of parliament, is back on Piccadilly buying more flights, this time from National Airlines. He buys a flight to Miami for Wednesday 6 November, then another on to LA on the Friday where he has arranged to meet Harry Wetzel, returning to London on the same day. He also asks ticket agent Sally Richard to book two nights' accommodation in Miami Beach. 'Either the Fontainebleau or Eden Roc,' he says. He proffers his Diners Club card and Richard is taken by the name on it: Rt Hon. John Stonehouse. She explains the hotel reservation will have to be confirmed at a later date and Stonehouse gives her details of his secretary and business number.[11]

Before he leaves for the States, Stonehouse has one more overseas trip to make. On Friday 1 November, he catches an early flight to Zürich. First stop is the Swiss Bank Corporation on Paradeplatz, where he makes a deposit of 199,150 Swiss francs — £30,000 — into bank account no. 332917 in the name of Joseph Arthur Markham. He makes further deposits at other banks, taking the total stashed away in Switzerland to £50,000. By 4pm, he's completed his to-do list and returns to the airport for his 5pm flight back to London.[12]

After a fitful weekend performing for his family as if nothing is afoot, on Monday 4 November John Stonehouse MP for Walsall North goes to the House of Commons for what he intends to be the last time. He heads to his small room above the members' tea room and settles down to write a speech, trying to block out the voice of the Tory member next door. He knows, as a member of the Privy Council, he has a decent chance of being called to speak in the debate on the Queen's Speech and he's going to make it one to remember.[13]

Downstairs, he grabs a cup of tea and takes the corridor that leads him through the swing doors to the Members' Lobby. It's a route he's taken countless times before; past the journalists and fellow MPs, some of whom he greets. He collects his Order Paper and makes his way into the chamber, past the statues of the great parliamentarians Winston Churchill and David Lloyd George which flank the entrance.

Wilson isn't in the chamber today, but Stonehouse spots

foreign secretary James Callaghan, who he regarded as an ally during the 1969 Post Office strike, and then a man he remembers less fondly, Tony Benn, whose wild talk of nationalisation had scuppered his recent stock market punt. When his turn comes, Stonehouse takes a measure of revenge, denouncing Labour policy on the economy and finishing off with a withering comment on the state of the nation: 'This is the time when the kidding has to stop. For too long we have fooled ourselves and have tried to fool others that Britain would somehow muddle through,' he says, seemingly unaware of the startling parallels with his own life. 'It is a failure to adjust to our new situation in the world, which does not owe us a living and is making it extremely difficult for us to earn one.'[14]

It's 6.30pm and dark by the time Stonehouse finishes what only he knows is his swansong. He leaves Westminster feeling relieved. It's something else from his old life he's managed to draw a line under. Everything is in place. He's shut down the Regent Street business address for Markham, he's transferred funds to his Swiss and Melbourne accounts, he's got Buckley ensconced in her Hampstead bedsit. He's got an unused open ticket to Sydney, the Markham passport and the Mildoon birth certificate up his sleeve too.[15]

Early on Wednesday morning, Stonehouse arrives at Terminal 3 at Heathrow Airport in his new Rover 3500. He won't be driving it again and, after parking, exchanges banter with the check-in lady about his choice of novel, Le Carré's *Tinker, Tailor, Soldier, Spy*. He says that it's hardgoing and that he prefers the work of Frederick Forsyth. If only she knew that carefully secreted in this man's briefcase is a second passport in the name of a dead man – a trick he learned from that very same author.

As National Airlines' DC-10 flight to Miami departs,

Stonehouse looks out of the window down at Britain for the last time. He feels safe. He literally has a passport to a whole new life and he can be Joe Markham the entire time now, not just for snatches here and there. He thinks of it as a rebirth.[16]

CAN I GET A WITNESS?

Stonehouse's arrival in Miami on 6 November goes without a hitch. He finds his way to the Hertz office, hires a Chrysler and drives across the causeway to Miami Beach. He's heading for the disappointingly charmless Fontainebleau, but he's pleased enough with his suite and its sweeping view of the ocean. Stonehouse puts in a call to his contacts at the Southeast First National Bank of Miami and arranges to see them the next day about buying into BBT, now renamed London Capital Group. Tomorrow will be his last lunch as John Stonehouse, unless the Southeast First National Bank offer a financial lifeline. What he would do then, no one knows.

He pushes that possibility to one side and concentrates on his exit strategy. He sees that the Eden Roc Hotel next door, his other option for this trip, is in fact shut down for refurbishment. This presents itself as an unexpected opportunity and he hides a spare set of clothes at the deserted hotel.

Then Stonehouse gets into his rented Chrysler and drives back to Miami Airport. There he buys a new suitcase and a full set of clothes, and stores them in a left-luggage locker. Using the seemingly random name of George Lewis, he buys a ticket to Houston, where he plans to switch to his open-ended Markham ticket and fly on to Mexico. He's already got Markham's Mexican visa safely tucked inside that passport and from there he'll get the Qantas flight to Sydney.[1]

After a good night's sleep, he gets into his Chrysler and drives into Miami Beach to meet John Odgers, vice president international, at the Southeast National Bank. Odgers listens politely to Stonehouse's proposition of a takeover, but bankers everywhere know about the problems of London fringe banks and most think the UK economy is a basket case. Odgers knows BBT won't get touched by any bank in the world. He tries to set Stonehouse up with some of his colleagues, who in turn direct him to a subsidiary in Luxembourg. Odgers and Stonehouse go through the motions of a business lunch, but even Stonehouse knows he's getting the brush-off. He returns to the Fontainebleau and his escape plan.[2]

Back in his room, Stonehouse prepares the scene. Passport, traveller's cheques, credit cards and money are locked in his combination case. Clothes are in the wardrobe – except for his trunks, trousers and sports shirt, which he changes into. Stonehouse gives his room key to the porters so it will be hanging there clearly on its numbered peg. He signs the checklist for guests at the entrance to the beach club, strips down to his trunks, leaves his clothes on the beach and enters the sea. The strong ocean swimmer heads straight out into the Atlantic and towards the horizon.[3]

When Stonehouse swims back to the shore, instead of the Fontainebleau beach area, he heads to the Eden Roc. He puts on his fresh clothes and hails a taxi on Collins Avenue. 'Airport please,' says Stonehouse. Once there, he retrieves his new suitcase and clothes from the locker, and boards the plane to Houston as Lewis. As it's an internal flight, no documents are needed and he will be hard to trace – especially as he will soon be on his way from Houston to Sydney via Mexico on his Markham ticket.

Then the first obstacle: there are flight delays. In Mexico

City, he misses his connection to Sydney by a whisker, and there isn't another one for days. He checks into an airport hotel as Markham, paying with the Markham Amex. He plans to fly to Los Angeles where there are more connecting flights, but the delay unsettles him. He decides that he should treat this as a dummy run and learn from it for the real thing.[4]

In Los Angeles, he meets Wetzel and calls Barbara, telling her he should be back in time for the Cenotaph Remembrance Sunday service in Walsall, a tradition they both like to uphold. But he realises he needs to know whether he has been registered as missing if this is to work, so he flies east back to the Fontainebleau to collect his things. Not a single soul has noticed that John Stonehouse hasn't been there the entire time.

Then he receives some big news that might mean he doesn't have to escape after all. He has been working with a contact in north London, Sylvester Okereke, on a cement order from Nigeria that would be so large as to be transformational for both of them. Okereke tells him that the deal is close and asks Stonehouse to meet William Asturrizaga of Whiting Construction, who want to supply the cement, and J. David Shaver, a Miami broker who's offering to finance it. American cement is a dangerous game – the Mafia are big in the US construction industry – but it's too lucrative a deal to resist and Stonehouse meets both men.[5]

By now it's late Sunday afternoon – and still no one has noticed that he was ever missing. He goes to the beach to find his clothes but they have been taken. Helen Fleming, the secretary in the Cabana Club kiosk, sympathises, and tells him to try lost property. He shrugs his shoulders at this advice and walks away, but his mind is whirring. These people are hopeless. If he is going to disappear, he will need to get someone to see him go. His death needs a witness.[6]

He gets the red-eye from Miami to London and arrives on the morning of 11 November. Nothing has changed. Life is exactly as he left it, including Barbara. She is sorry they didn't attend Remembrance Sunday in Walsall together, but recognises that her husband has a whole raft of business interests to deal with and there's a wedding anniversary dinner to look forward to on Thursday. She thinks everything is normal, but within the week he is once again plotting to abandon her.[7]

A few days at BBT reveal that everything is still in a mess. Several weeks have now passed since Stonehouse promised the board a rebuttal of the Audit Review Note, but the losses on his unauthorised stock market gamble with BBT's money will have to be recognised in the accounts. He's also still in love with Buckley, and no nearer to ending his marriage to Barbara. And he knows from *Private Eye*'s Czech embassy hint that the Frolík defector story is far from over. Escape is indeed the only solution and this time he will do it properly. That means a return to Miami Beach, a return to the bank who had all but rejected him and a return to the Eden Roc with a stash of spare clothes for Markham. And a witness.

Stonehouse badgers James Charlton to accompany him to Miami to meet the Southeast First National Bank. He has persuaded Charlton to go along with a revaluation of BBT/LCG shares and if they can pull off a sale of the bank, it will be the deal to end all deals. But the board still haven't replied to Dixon Wilson's Audit Review Note and Charlton thinks that it may be inappropriate to approach another bank until those problems are solved. Eventually Charlton gives in: he'll go to Miami with Stonehouse as long as he can fly on to New York, where he has other business to do.[8]

By 14 November, Stonehouse can't resist going to the

Commons again, even though he thought he had delivered his farewell speech ten days ago. The leader of the House, Ted Short, Stonehouse's predecessor as postmaster general and, not that either know it, a fellow recipient of an StB codename, is presenting business for the following week. Stonehouse doesn't intend to be around for long, but it's important no one suspects that and he asks Short for a future speaking slot. Short promises to do his best to fit him in before Christmas.[9]

Across London, Stonehouse's Nigerian cement associate Okereke meets with William Asturrizaga. They come to an agreement that Asturrizaga will supply American cement at $64 per metric ton and a bridging loan from the financier Shaver will definitely be needed. Okereke writes to Stonehouse at the Vandon Court address to that end, saying he hopes Stonehouse's upcoming trip to Miami and his meeting with Shaver is successful. Okereke signs the letter, stamps the pro-forma and thinks nothing more of it. Stonehouse thinks that paying 'inducements' to agents and dealing with these kind of characters is all part of the international business merry-go-round, but he's playing a dangerous game. Bribery, usually hidden to the outside world, is rampant in the early 1970s. The address they have for Whiting Construction doesn't even exist — and little do he or Okereke know it yet, but Shaver is already dead.[10]

Private Eye's issue of Friday 15 November doesn't pick up on this particular aspect of Stonehouse's business life, but it does put the boot solidly into BBT/LCG. With two columns on the Business News page, the magazine reveals that BBT rents its offices from Epacs and that Keith White is suing Stonehouse for the equivalent of a year's wages. They also identify the long relationship with McGrath dating back to the mid-1960s, alleging that Stonehouse recommended him for the BAA job and observing that McGrath joined the Post Office board when Stonehouse was postmaster general. According to the *Eye,* Stonehouse's involvement in War on Want one minute blurred into the BBT Bengali handbill debacle the next. Stonehouse is livid and speaks to a solicitor about suing the magazine for defamation.[11]

The following Monday, Stonehouse heads for British Airways at 75–81 Regent Street, just up from Piccadilly Circus. Stonehouse wants flights to Miami for tomorrow, economy class. Ticket agent Anthony Sait sells him a single in his name for the next day, and a return ticket for Mr James Charlton, via New York, open for a year. Stonehouse uses his American Express credit card to pay for both, and after Sait has received the necessary go-ahead from American Express, the transaction goes through and Stonehouse gets his tickets. It's the kind of thing Sait deals with every hour of every day and he thinks little of it.[12]

In Harlesden in north London, Okereke hears good news from the Nigerian government. They have finally sent him the order for 250,000 tons of cement, a deal that could be worth nearly £60 million over the next five years. That evening, Okereke keeps an appointment with an associate in Teddington – Nigel Newman, a shipping broker with connections in Nigeria. He and Newman are going to discuss getting the cement to Nigeria and he leaves his housemate a note saying he'll be back around 9pm.[13]

They meet at the Tide End Cottage on Ferry Road and have a couple of drinks and a friendly enough chat, which is surprising as just a week earlier Okereke had written to Newman asking for money owed. Seemingly, it's been resolved. They don't hang around long at the pub; just a couple of drinks and they're on their way. It's a rainy and windy night, not really the time to be going back to Rum Tum, Newman's houseboat. Tide End Cottage barmaid Maureen Rose is the last person apart from Newman to see Okereke alive.[14]

The next day, Stonehouse and Charlton travel from London to the Fontainebleau. Stonehouse has become a past master at hiding his true feelings, but these next two days will be the ultimate test. The following morning at the beach club and the long swim to alarm Charlton is all part of a careful plan, as is the meeting at the Southeast First National Bank of Miami. It goes as expected; a meeting for the sake of a meeting. This waste of time for everyone concerned ends with a convivial expensed business lunch to disguise the inconvenient truth that absolutely no one wants to invest in BBT.

Back in the Fontainebleau, Charlton rests and reads in his room, believing his surprisingly upbeat colleague is swimming and shopping. But, just along the corridor, Stonehouse is once again setting the scene. He lays his belongings out carefully: credit card and watch on the table, passport and family photos by the bed, clothes casually strewn as if by a man who is just popping out for a swim.

Around 4.15pm, he goes down to the beach club. 'Hello, I'm here again,' he says to Helen Fleming, the secretary in the kiosk there. He asks her to look after his clothes which she thinks odd, with so many lifeguards and attendants, but agrees. Stonehouse makes more small talk as he hands over his check shirt, trousers and sandals, and Fleming thinks what a good mood this man is in. He walks down onto the beach in his blue-grey trunks and, when Fleming finishes her shift at 5.30pm, his clothes are still on the shelf in her kiosk.[15]

This time, instead of entering the ocean, he sneaks straight next door to the deserted Eden Roc Hotel where, for the second time in as many weeks, he has a spare set of clothes waiting for him. He pulls them on and makes his way to Miami Airport, where he picks up Markham's luggage from a locker, just as he had done ten days before.

18

ON THE RUN

Stonehouse takes the six-hour flight from Miami to San Francisco and touches down just as the city is getting dark. Believing he has missed an international connection to Sydney, he decides to stay the night. He takes a taxi into the city itself, and to his mind he puts the world to rights with the local taxi driver. The driver might see things differently after the Englishman ribs him over Watergate.

Stonehouse is on Markham credit by way of the Amex and asks to be taken to the best hotel in town. They soon pull up at the Fairmont on Nob Hill and Stonehouse finds himself in the finest suite of the entire hotel by way of an upgrade. It has its own bar and card table, and if you listen hard enough, you can almost hear Tony Bennett singing 'I Left My Heart in San Francisco' in the bar downstairs. Stonehouse marvels at the hi-tech remote controls in both the sitting room and the bedroom, and concludes that Joe Markham has fallen on his feet.

But the hotel isn't enough to hold his interest. He wants to explore. Stonehouse wanders downhill all the way until he hits the Tenderloin red-light district. He decides to try out one of the strip bars, telling himself it's purely 'out of interest'. The pressures on the men rich enough to live at the top of Nob Hill, he muses, are what makes them seek refuge in this seedy experience.[1]

As Stonehouse makes his way back to his luxury suite at

the end of his evening out in the flesh pots of San Francisco, his secretary and lover Sheila Buckley wakes up in her bedsit in Highfield House in Hampstead. Her boss may have disappeared – John McGrath has been in touch with the news – but she still needs to attend to business at Dover Street. There, she meticulously removes key pages from her shorthand notebook.[2]

The next day, Stonehouse decides he is still not ready for the final leg of his journey to Melbourne. He opts to go to Hawaii first, where he seeks out another luxury hotel in the name of Markham. This time he plumps for a Sheraton and checks into Room 1706. It's not any old Sheraton hotel in the city of Honolulu though. Like his last hotel, this one occupies a prime spot at another internationally renowned location – Waikiki Beach.[3]

There's barely enough time to unpack before he decides to phone Buckley. He works out how to make an international call from his room – dial 80 – and the Hawaiian Telephone Exchange pick up. 'London, England, 435 1976 please,' he tells the operator. The phone rings downstairs at Highfield House. It's nearly midnight to Stonehouse's early afternoon. The hotel receptionist answers to an operator: 'A call from the United States coming through.' Room 20 gets buzzed and Buckley leaves her room for the phone on the landing. She is ecstatic to hear from Stonehouse; she had a sixth sense he was alive. She asks if she should tell his family but he insists they are not told. 'John's dead,' he says. 'He had to die.'[4] And he promises to call again soon. Buckley worries that if she tells anyone he's still alive, he'll kill himself.[5]

Just after he hangs up, Stonehouse makes a dash to the banks before they close. He has some hard cash – sterling and dollars – and he needs it transferred into a banker's draft for Australia. He takes himself down to the nearest branch of the Bank of Hawaii and waits his turn at one of the windows. Kathleen Elia greets him. 'What is your exchange rate for pounds sterling to US dollars?' enquires Stonehouse. The reply is not to his liking. He thinks on. 'Would a better rate apply to larger amounts of sterling?' Elia goes off to check with her boss. 'Yes,' she says, 'a better rate might be possible if you bring the money in.'

Stonehouse goes back to his room and gets the cash. He's ready to haggle. Elia's final offer is 2.275 dollars to the pound and Stonehouse accepts. He asks for a banker's draft in the name of Lewis Jones, staying at the Royal Hawaiian Hotel – just that bit more upmarket than the high-rise Sheraton – made out to J. A. Markham, Bank of New South Wales. Elia doesn't require any identification from Mr Jones and issues the draft.

Four nights later, on 25 November, Stonehouse checks out of his hotel with the Markham Amex – but not before phoning Buckley again. It's another $15 call, but money is no problem with a Markham deposit account of £14,000 waiting in Melbourne and a bank draft for a further £6,000 in his luggage. From his base of Room 1706, Sheraton Waikiki Beach, Stonehouse has spent a relaxing five days swimming in the Pacific and touring the island of Oahu. Now it's time to be Joe Markham, resident of Melbourne, Australia.[6]

On 25 November, Stonehouse crosses the international date line and while he is in the air, Buckley makes her way from north London to west London. She has accepted a dinner invitation from Caroline Gay, Philip's wife, at the Gays' family home in Fulham. While her husband is away in Miami dealing with Stonehouse's disappearance, Caroline Gay could do with some company and thinks Buckley might feel the same. She has long suspected that Buckley is more than just his secretary, and feels sorry for her. Barbara is getting all the sympathy at this time of Stonehouse's disappearance, thinks Gay. Maybe Sheila could do with some too.

After dinner, they sit and talk. Buckley, who has spoken to Stonehouse the day before, repeatedly insists that everyone should just accept that he is dead. Caroline Gay is surprised by this, and by the fact that she doesn't seem as upset as she expected. They get on to talking about Stonehouse's children: Buckley is very fond of teenager Mathew, she says, but less so Stonehouse's two grown-up daughters. Maybe at some point in the future she will meet Mathew again, she says, and explain everything to him. Her host isn't quite sure what she means.

As the evening draws on, Gay gently asks Buckley what she intends to do after it is 'all over'. Buckley says she thinks she wants to go and work abroad. Gay makes what she thinks could be some helpful suggestions – how about the United Nations, for example? – but Buckley isn't sold on any of them. 'I'll probably go to Australia,' she tells Gay. 'I have friends over there.' Shortly after midnight, Buckley makes her way back to her Hampstead bedsit.[7]

As Stonehouse waits in Sydney Airport's transit area for an internal flight to his final destination of Tullamarine Airport in Melbourne, he grabs all the American and British newspapers he can get his hands on. He's been missing for an entire week now and constantly wonders if his disappearance is news. But in the selection he finds, there is nothing on either his disappearance or death. Joe Markham needs to know the man whose body he occupied is accepted as dead or at least missing, he tells himself.

On touchdown on Australia's south coast, Stonehouse as Markham enters the country without a hitch. He has an X-ray ready to prove his alter ego doesn't have TB, but the immigration staff aren't the slightest bit interested. The Markham passport – Number 7859658 – gets its entry stamp and Stonehouse takes a cab into the city.

There he checks into another Sheraton hotel, this time on Spring Street downtown, and wastes no time in going to the local branch of the Bank of New South Wales on Collins Street. He's delighted to find out that the £14,000 he asked to be moved from his London Markham account has been successfully transferred. He opens a fresh current account to sit alongside his savings and pays in the banker's draft from Hawaii.

But before long Stonehouse worries that the identity of Markham isn't enough to give him the distance from his old life and identity. The links between Stonehouse and Markham's travels are too obvious. Thank goodness for Donald Clive Mildoon! Stonehouse predicted that just one ill-gotten birth certificate in the name of a dead man wouldn't be enough, and he's proved himself right. He decides it's time to put plan B into operation. Markham needs to disappear from Australia and Clive Mildoon needs to take over.

He withdraws A$22,000 from Markham's Bank of New South Wales account and opens a new account in the name of Mildoon a few doors down at the Bank of New Zealand. The cashier confuses his new identity with that of a Kiwi politician named Muldoon. Stonehouse has to control himself; it is neither the time nor the place for his anecdote about his meeting with larger-than-life Robert Muldoon when he was on ministerial business in New Zealand in the late 1960s.

Stonehouse checks out of the Sheraton and goes in search of a cheaper hotel. Something more akin to Highfield House in Hampstead or the Astoria in Victoria would do nicely. The Regal, in the beach suburb of St Kilda, is the answer. Now in another city and another red-light district, Stonehouse books a room and dumps his few belongings. It's time to take to the air again. You can take the man out of the ministry of aviation . . .

No, Stonehouse can't settle in Australia yet. He has unfinished business to attend to and Europe beckons. He's going to fly to Copenhagen. That's a neutral enough city, he thinks. He needs to see the press and he needs to try to see Buckley again. At first she's resistant, but if she won't come to Denmark, he'll say he has to go to London. He's sure that will make her get on a plane.[8]

A master of the skies like Stonehouse knows that there is a direct flight from Bangkok to Copenhagen on SAS's Trans-Asian Express. But he'll have to get to Bangkok via Singapore, where, economising at last, he spends a night in a low-rent hotel before taking off for Denmark.

It's the early evening of 29 November when he lands at Copenhagen's island airport and the cold winter air feels good. The transfer to the mainland is quick and the Grand Hotel in Copenhagen is surprisingly busy. Manager Ole Andresen has been forced to step in on reception due to staff shortages and, at around 10pm, he gets a walk-in. He's a tall man in his late forties asking for a single room. He offers up his name as Markham, and says he's British. Andresen gets him to sign the hotel register and allocates him Room 357, one of the cheaper ones. Stonehouse takes the key, goes up for the night and Andresen gets on with the ringing phones and waiting guests.

The next morning, Stonehouse's first priority is to catch up on the English papers. He puts on a pair of corduroy trousers and his jacket, and goes out in search of international newspapers. Finally he finds a seller of *The Times, Daily Mirror, Daily Mail* and *Daily Express*. They are full of stories about him. Shocked, he goes on to scour the city for old copies of British papers languishing on unattended shelves.[9]

With every page he sees a different angle. First of all, he's robbed Bangladeshi immigrants of a million pounds. The Reverend Michael Scott appears to be behind this allegation. Stonehouse remembers Scott from their Africa days, a man he thinks so blinded by his cause that he's pre-programmed to believe people of colour before a white man. Next, he reads his wife's version of events in the *Daily Mirror*. She firmly believes that her husband is dead and is forced to deny that their marriage was on the rocks.

Then he sees that the FBI is involved in the manhunt for him in Miami because the local police are baffled. He sees that his nephew and solicitor Michael Hayes is trying to defend his uncle as fellow MPs circle for answers. The publicity and tone are nothing short of disastrous for Stonehouse, yet he manages to convince himself it's just the work of muck-raking journalists. He's done an honourable thing; saved his family and colleagues the ongoing embarrassment of his presence.

He reads more. It takes some nerve as his photograph is in every British paper he buys, but the Markham heavy black glasses give him an element of safety. As his week in Copenhagen passes, he follows every development. He sees that his colleague Bill Molloy is telling the press that he has enemies everywhere and fears he may have met a sticky end at the hands of the Mafia after a deal gone wrong. They've found out that the country house Barbara was renovating in Pitton in Wiltshire has been put up for sale. There are stories about MPs scouring parliamentary procedure to get a clearer idea of what to do about the missing MP.[10]

By midweek, he gets twitchy. He thinks about the possibility of going to the UK via a ferry to Harwich, then dismisses it. When he passes Bennett Travel Bureau on the Copenhagen thoroughfare of Rådhuspladsen, he can't resist going in. He asks about availability of flights to Melbourne – for that day. It's too risky here, he should go back to safety.

The travel consultant tells him the cheapest way to fly is via Singapore with Aeroflot at 15.00. Stonehouse gets as far as watching an order form being made out, with a connecting British Airways flight from Singapore to Melbourne, then realises he has to go and get cash or traveller's cheques. When he returns, he's changed his mind. He actually wants to fly that Sunday, 8 December, instead. The consultant tells him to come back for the ticket later that afternoon, but he doesn't return to pay until the next day.

Stonehouse has a spring in his step when he finally does so. It is Wednesday 4 December and he has spoken to Buckley. She's going to make the dash for Copenhagen and is at the Hampstead Travel Agency on Heath Street. Now it's her turn to take on a new identity.

Using the name Mrs E. Morgan, she enquires about a one-way flight to Copenhagen that Friday. Her preference is for an evening flight, but the 18.25 SAS flight is already full. She thinks about it and then tells the agent she'll take the 14.30 British Airways flight instead. She well knows you can only buy tickets for other people if you pay with a credit card and so settles the £60 bill with Sheila Buckley's Access credit card. Stonehouse calls her that evening to check she's still coming – she is – and on Friday 6 December, Buckley boards the 14.30 Heathrow flight to Copenhagen in her own name.[11]

It's early evening when she arrives and they take in the city together. That night they celebrate their reunion with a meal at the Shanghai Restaurant. It's a classic menu: chow mein, chop suey and fried rice. But the day after next they must part again. It's too risky for Buckley to stay any longer, and Stonehouse needs to get out of Europe.

The next day after lunch, Stonehouse goes to the downtown SAS office on Hammerichsgade and – muddling Buckley's alias and her real identity – buys a ticket for London in the name of Miss S. Morgan. This flight is on Markham and his now trusty Amex credit card. Buckley will be leaving at 16.15 hours. Come tomorrow, the tryst is over. Stonehouse reveals to Buckley that he will adopt the name of Clive Mildoon once he returns to Melbourne and asks her to write to him in that name, c/o Bank of New Zealand, Collins Street, Melbourne. She agrees. Buckley gets a plane back to London and Stonehouse returns to Australia, via Moscow and New Delhi and then a flight to Melbourne from Singapore.[12]

On the morning of 10 December, while Stonehouse is in the air, Buckley, now back in London, gets an unexpected call from Barbara. The *Daily Mirror* and *Daily Express* are asking her about a flat in Vandon Court, and why her husband's secretary has been living there. Barbara tried to track Buckley down at the weekend, but of course she was nowhere to be found. Stonehouse's wife is finding it hard to believe that his latest lover is Sheila Buckley. His other women were intellectuals; all highly intelligent. Buckley doesn't seem on the same level. Barbara summons her to a friend's place in Knightsbridge. Buckley obliges and when she arrives, Barbara – who she notes is looking as intimidatingly elegant as ever – offers her a glass of sherry. These two women have known each other for years. Now, just two days after spending the weekend with a man whose grieving wife believes him to be dead, Buckley sits with Barbara, and doesn't tell her he's alive.[13]

The two women drink, and a brutal conversation emerges as Barbara tries to get to the bottom of Vandon Court. 'Were you having an affair with him?' she demands. Buckley begins to cry. 'I've been in love with John for a long time,' she says.

She decides not to use the terms 'mistress' or 'affair', but she knows Barbara gets it. She thinks Buckley seems terrified, but then she is only slightly older than their daughter Jane.

'Don't think you're the only woman in his life,' Barbara says. 'He's had hundreds of affairs.' Affairs that she has tolerated for the greater good of family life for most of her marriage. While she was in labour back in 1951, Barbara tells Buckley, her husband was off on an overseas trip with a Swedish girlfriend. He even got a colleague to send Barbara letters from where he purported to be while she was left to have their daughter all on her own. Then she details another sexual liaison of her husband's that happened while she was on holiday with him.[14]

Buckley does the maths and realises she was also sleeping with Stonehouse at the time. Barbara confides that she's worried she will come under police suspicion as a result of the five insurance policies that have been taken out. Buckley is furious at the stupidity in taking out so many at once, but her mind is elsewhere. She is reeling at the news that her lover has been cheating on her too. Is there nothing straightforward about this man?[15]

Yet when Betty Boothroyd, MP for West Bromwich, throws Buckley a lifeline, she refuses to take it. 'I can get you a job with another member of parliament,' offers Boothroyd, still astonished that Stonehouse said she had agreed to a fake pairing via a note on her desk. Buckley looks at her squarely in the eyes. 'No, thank you,' she says. 'I was only valuable to John.'[16] Even when faced with the harshest reality, Buckley remains in thrall to this master manipulator.

19

A NEW LIFE IN THE SUN

John Stonehouse is not the only middle-aged man whose disappearance in the middle of November 1974 is a mystery. Nigel Newman has reported to the police that Sylvester Okereke slipped and fell from his boat on the night of the 18th. Newman says he tried to rescue him, but Okereke was swept away and a body has not been found.

The Nigerian High Commission are asking the Home Office to investigate and one of Okereke's friends in London, Dr Edith McCarthy, has started her own probe into his disappearance. She believes that as a swimmer of Olympic standards, Okereke didn't accidentally fall into the Thames and drown. It's a theory shared by one of Okereke's London business associates, Bernard Broadway. Broadway claims that Stonehouse owed Okereke money for early groundwork on a cement deal that never materialised.[1]

If true, that money is now in a bank account on the other side of the world, and within Stonehouse's grasp as he arrives back in Australia from Denmark on 11 December. He gets through immigration as Markham once more without a problem, picks up a cab at the rank and asks the driver to take him to the Regal Hotel in St Kilda. As Stonehouse flicks through a local newspaper in the back seat, he sees an advert for 'executive apartments' in the centre of the city. They take his fancy and he makes a diversion to Flinders Street to see for himself.

He likes the look of the building – there's a pool in the central quad – and he takes Flat 411. Within a couple of hours, retired British businessman Clive Mildoon pays the owners Rod and Joan Wilcocks a deposit plus a month's rent of A$230, saying he'll move in in the next day or so. Not only is Stonehouse dead, so too now is Markham.

The Wilcocks are quite taken by their new tenant and comment that he's 'almost aristocratic' with his cut-glass accent and fine clothes and luggage. A couple of days later, Stonehouse gets his new flat kitted out. Life is looking up for him, but not so for the women he has left behind.[2]

His wife, his mother and his children still have no idea what has happened to him, nor what the future holds. The latest news from Miami is of a Mafia-style concrete coffin discovered in Fort Lauderdale. Stonehouse had been in that city just a few days before to meet J. David Shaver and police are checking to see if the body is that of the missing MP. Barbara is also making enquiries of the insurance companies. Her name is on policies and although she fears it will lead to speculation that she is involved in his death, she needs the money.

As for Buckley, she's still going into the Dover Street offices and living through the aftermath. McGrath is belatedly crawling all over the books and not far behind him are Scotland Yard's Fraud Squad and the Department of Trade. Buckley suspects McGrath has brought them in.[3]

Buckley also thinks she might be pregnant. Barbara's revelations play on a loop as she considers the possibility of having Stonehouse's baby. As Clive Mildoon settles into his new executive apartment, Buckley drafts the first of her letters to him, c/o Bank of New Zealand, Melbourne. As well as using her pet name for him, Dums, she invents a code that she hopes only he will understand, referring to him by the name George, just as Stonehouse had on his dummy run as George Lewis.[4]

But her first letter is no time for subtleties. If her loyalty remains unchallenged in public, in private it's quite a different matter. 'I have heard the most dreadful things about George from his former wife,' she writes. 'Everything he's ever told me clashes with what she says. He's had hundreds of affairs. He had one affair with a girl while they were on holiday. This is at the time George and S were "married" and I had his solemn word about other women. I asked many times for him to leave me alone and in peace, but he always convinced me in the end that he couldn't do without me.' She has discovered from Barbara that Stonehouse's liberal use of emotional blackmail is not unique to her. 'You can imagine my shock to discover that he had said the same thing to his Mrs for nearly thirty years.' Buckley checks out of her room at Highfield House earlier than anticipated and moves to her sister's up the road in Belsize Park.[5]

While Buckley is mired in doubt, Stonehouse has got a new life to build in Melbourne. He goes downstairs every morning and collects *The Age* and *The Sun*, then returns to his room. He listens to the Australian Broadcasting Corporation's output on his new radio. His neighbours hear Mahler and Bach wafting from his flat. During the day he pops out frequently, usually to post letters to his offshore bank accounts. He's trying to get his Markham money out of Zürich and applying for some credit in the process.[6]

Buckley writes again and this time she's more forgiving and starts referring to herself in the third person. 'Oswald came through but no news on all the other yet,' she writes of Bühler in Liechtenstein. She says she is being driven to distraction by the unresolved nature of the plot. Why is her boss and boyfriend still just missing, rather than assumed dead? The Department of Trade investigators are crawling over everything, she tells him, and the insurance issue is now front-page news. She can't believe he has been so stupid as to draw attention to himself: 'Fancy taking out that lot!' she chides. She asks him to reply care of her sister's place.[7]

He slots the letter-writing into his busy schedule of sunbathing and watching TV in the communal lounge two or three evenings a week. That is, until he discovers the Melbourne chess club, where he can allow his mind to be distracted for hours at a time. Never though, the Wilcocks notice, does he have any visitors.[8]

The urbane Englishman Clive Mildoon seeks out some local jazz on his first Saturday evening in town, and sits in the bar listening, while nursing a schooner of Foster's. The live music prompts him to join the jazz club, which in turn leads to invitations. Before he knows it, Clive has got new friends. There are barbecues and bring-your-own house parties and fundraising for Boxing Day's Australian Jazz Convention. Stonehouse even buys the requisite T-shirt to wear on the big day. Clive is a joiner and a socialite, and Stonehouse loves him. So much, in fact, that he gets business cards made up with 'Donald Clive Mildoon, Export Consultant' in embossed writing at the top.[9]

What he doesn't know is that bank clerks on Collins Street, Melbourne, talk to each other. In opening two separate bank accounts in two separate names, at branches just a stone's throw from one another, Stonehouse made his first false move. The clerks think they might be looking at a bank fraud and tell the police about the Englishman with the dual identity. Detective Sergeant John Coffey has already been in to see Peter Street, the accountant at the Bank of New South Wales who opened the Markham account just over a month ago. Now he's waiting to catch sight of the man in question.[10]

At last Buckley gets some good news. She's not pregnant after all – the timing was terrible – and, on 17 December, she writes telling Stonehouse the news that Wilson has denied the spy story in the Commons. The way she puts it is that 'Uncle Harry' has just spoken to his 'big family' and is 'standing by George completely, a true friend'. That's certainly one interpretation of their relationship. 'She loves him more than life,' concludes her gushing third-person letter, her earlier anger all but dissipated.[11]

Buckley might not have been quite so gushing had she known that Stonehouse won't be the first to read it. Detective Sergeant Coffey of Victoria State Police knows all about Clive Mildoon's letters. He's at the Bank of New Zealand getting them steamed open and photocopied as soon as they arrive. He and his colleagues are also following Stonehouse round the city and photographing him reading them. One of Coffey's officers has got so close he's read the addresses on the letters Stonehouse is posting. One of the envelopes read 'Miss Black'. Even though they think the Englishman might be the missing aristocrat Lord Lucan, the fact that they've realised he goes by the names of Markham and Mildoon puts them one step ahead of their London counterparts.[12]

Before Buckley's letter can reach Stonehouse via Melbourne Police, on 18 December news of Stonehouse's past as a Czech informant makes the front-page of *The Age*. The article 'Missing MP a spy: defector' is accompanied by a clear headshot of Stonehouse. He panics and wonders whether he will now be recognised.[13]

But he doesn't know that while he is out buying the papers, someone else is in his flat. Coffey and his senior colleague

Detective Senior Sergeant Morris don't have a warrant, but they are old-school cops and they have a look regardless. As they pick around Stonehouse's belongings, they unearth a simple but conclusive clue: a book of Fontainebleau-branded matches. That Saturday, Coffey gets a message and visual likeness from Interpol in London and it's game on.[14]

The British police are closing in too and, on 23 December, Scotland Yard sends Detective Chief Inspector Barbara Tilley to Dover Street to interview Buckley. Tilley starts off by asking a seemingly practical question: 'Do you know the combination of his briefcase?' 'I think it's either 130 or 131,' Buckley says. She then takes the initiative and tries to throw Tilley off the trail. She tells the detective that her boss was a very good swimmer and obsessed with keeping fit, but in recent weeks had not appeared too well and had become a little 'paunchy'. On one occasion, she had found him lying down and taking a rest, which was unusual; he seemed 'preoccupied recently' too. He had also complained of pain in his right arm, says Buckley. Tilley knows that heart attacks, like the one that prematurely killed Stonehouse's own father, as well as the real Joseph Markham, are widely known to be pre-empted by pain in the left arm.

The detective chief inspector then makes it clear that the enquiry is a missing persons one only, that they are working on the assumption Stonehouse is alive. Without prompting, Buckley blurts out: 'He's dead'. This definitive statement takes Tilley by surprise. Afterwards, she reflects that Buckley didn't seem either upset or distressed at the apparent demise of John Stonehouse.[15]

With his photograph now in the Australian papers, Stonehouse ups his disguise. The dark-rimmed sight glasses of Markham are no more. Now he is never without dark glasses and a hat that comes right down past his ears, even when watching TV in the communal room at the executive flats.[16]

Victoria State Police now know for sure the man they are tracking isn't missing aristocrat Lord Lucan. They are both male and white with posh English accents, but Stonehouse is two inches shorter. Although Detective Senior Sergeant Hugh Morris would like more evidence before he makes his move, he doesn't want to give the suspect the time to commit any offences in Melbourne. The local police are still recovering from letting train robber Ronnie Biggs slip through the net in 1970 and this one must not get away. They put a rotating team of ten officers on his tail and stake him out from one of the flats in the same block.[17]

On Christmas Eve, Stonehouse takes the twenty-minute trip from the hubbub of City Terminus on Flinders Street down to the 1920s seaside resort of St Kilda. On the way, he collects another love letter from Buckley from the bank before heading back to the Regal Hotel in St Kilda to get Markham's post. It's the Astoria on St George's Drive all over again: one man pretending to be another as he collects his mail. Except this time it's Mildoon posing as Markham.

Hugh Morris and sergeants Coffey and Clarkson trail Stonehouse all the way down to the end of the line and watch on as he goes into the Regal for his letters. It's unusual for fraud squad officers to carry guns, but then this is an unusual case. Morris has been on the force for nineteen years and while this man is not the big international criminal he first hoped for, Stonehouse is a decent catch and they don't want to lose him.

Stonehouse collects his post as planned and makes his way back across Fitzroy Street, dodging traffic and trams, to the station opposite. He buys his ticket and gets onto the waiting train. Then they pounce. Morris is first in the carriage, quickly joined by his colleagues. The three plain clothes officers pull Stonehouse back off the train and onto the platform. It's all so fast he has no idea who they are or what is happening. Coffey looks him in the eye. 'Are you Joseph Arthur Markham?' he asks. 'No,' replies Stonehouse.[18]

20

THE GAME'S UP

'We believe that you are in possession of a passport in the name of Joseph Arthur Markham,' says Coffey. 'Who are *you*?' asks Stonehouse. The police identify themselves, read him his rights and search him right there in the ticket hall. Stonehouse isn't carrying a weapon; just some post addressed to a dead man. 'You are being apprehended on suspicion of being an illegal immigrant,' says Morris and asks him to roll up his trousers in search of an identifying scar on the inside of the right knee. It's not even 11am.

The police take Stonehouse out of the train station and put him into a waiting car. They drive back to the state police head-quarters along the wide St Kilda Road, across the Yarra River and into Melbourne city centre. They pass Clive Mildoon's executive apartment block and the trappings of his new life. Stonehouse doesn't say a word. He thinks Markham has let down the newborn Mildoon, but knows the game is up.

They arrive at a huge statement of a police headquarters on Russell Street that wouldn't look out of place in Manhattan. Stonehouse is led to a room in the fraud department. Coffey and Morris attempt to interview him, but he refuses to talk, let alone answer questions. They make sympathetic noises and tell Stonehouse that they have been bugging him and are recording the interview. He doesn't make a fuss or seem surprised.

They need him to open up, so decide to change tack, offering him an insight into their month-long investigation. 'Y'know, the reason we checked your scar was to make sure you weren't that other pom Lord Lucan,' they say, with a grin. After nearly an hour of the two officers talking at him, Stonehouse finally cracks: he admits who he really is and the floodgates open.

'It was an article in the *Sunday Times* that started it all,' Stonehouse tells the police. 'I was being blackmailed . . . People were using my political position to blackmail me. I was disillusioned and under pressure . . . There were so many tensions.' Then the trademark pomposity makes an appearance: 'I must advise you that if I make an application to the proper authorities, it might well be possible for me to remain in Australia.'

Morris and Coffey give Stonehouse the chance to phone his wife, and he rings Barbara, not Buckley. He knows she'll be at Faulkners Down House with the children for Christmas. It's 4am in the UK. 'Hello darling,' says Stonehouse breezily, as if he spoke to her that morning. 'I'm with the Melbourne police who have been very helpful and I'm in good heart. They've picked up on the false identity here and kept me under watch and eventually twigged who I was. You will realise from all this I've been deceiving you and I'm sorry about that. But in a sense I'm glad it's all over.'[1]

Barbara has just been interviewed by the BBC current affairs doyen Robin Day about why her husband must be dead. 'It is wonderful to hear your voice again,' he goes on. 'I'm so sorry to have caused you so much worry.' Her husband sounds like a naughty little boy who has been found out. 'I decided to drop out of my own identity in Miami. They all wanted me to be the scapegoat on everything. Come out as soon as you can,' he tells her, 'and bring Sheila.' Despite this outrageous final demand of her husband's, there's no doubt in her mind: she must pack and fly to Melbourne.[2]

Now that Stonehouse has admitted his real identity, Morris and Coffey can leave him at the station to await the national Commonwealth Police. They go off to his small flat in Flinders Street to gather some of his possessions as evidence. Tucked inside one of his combination-lock briefcases, they find both the Markham and Mildoon birth certificates Stonehouse obtained in the summer, along with the Markham passport.[3]

The Australian press has got wind of the story and have gathered outside the police headquarters on Coffey and Morris's return. British journalists are in town to cover the Test cricket and they're quick on the uptake too. If they turn this around fast enough, they can take advantage of the eleven-hour time difference and file for the Christmas Eve editions of the UK papers. Word is the police are giving a press conference at 3pm.[4]

These same journalists are jamming phone lines into the British consulate asking for comment. The state police have informed Ivor Vincent, the consul general, and he thinks someone ought to go and visit Stonehouse. But he's told in his first exchange with the night desk in London to stay put; this one is going to get political and they don't want the press to get wind of any official visit. The line at the moment has to be: 'We know no more than what the Victorian police have told us and cannot comment.'[5]

Morris, somewhat dishevelled after the morning's action, emerges to speak to the press pack. He tells them Stonehouse was under surveillance for a number of days and was relieved 'once his real identity became common knowledge'. Morris goes on: 'He told us of tensions and pressures which caused him to do what he did. He mentioned blackmail. A *Sunday Times* article. His wife was relieved to hear from him and he was happy to speak to his wife.' 'How much money does he have available to him in Australia do you know?' asks an Australian reporter. 'He has quite a good deal of money available to him,' says Morris. Then his boss, a chief superintendent, appears. He adds, without prompting, that Stonehouse's mental health is good. 'He's not being charged with any offence. He's being held as a suspected illegal immigrant.'[6]

At 5.30pm, Detective Inspector John Sullivan arrives in Russell Street. He's from the Commonwealth Police, and originally from England. Sullivan is in possession of Morris and Coffey's haul from Stonehouse's flat and sharing the same mother country doesn't mean he's about to give him an easy ride. He finds Stonehouse and says he's taking him to the Commonwealth Police headquarters on Mackenzie Street. They make a sneaky exit out of the back door to avoid the reporters. The police briefing hasn't satisfied them. In fact, it's interested them even more; now they want the man himself.[7]

This time there are no tape recorders in the interview room; Sullivan is a detective who makes notes the old-fashioned way. Stonehouse answers all of the simple questions. Name, date of birth, profession. Sullivan ups the pace, but Stonehouse doesn't miss a beat. Was Markham a relation? 'No relation, the man is deceased.' How did you obtain this passport? 'By presenting a birth certificate to the Passport Office in London.' And how did you obtain the birth certificate? 'By making an application at Somerset House in London.' And how did you know he was dead? 'Through making enquiries at hospitals. I asked about persons who may have died in my age-group.' Why did you do this? 'To establish a new identity and come to Australia.' Why? 'I was the subject of blackmail. I thought I had to escape.'

Sullivan has no idea about the business fraud Stonehouse is running away from, the Czech spying career, nor the Mafia cement trades. And Stonehouse isn't about to offer them up. Instead, he's back on the smear campaign by Harold Evans's

Sunday Times. He tells Sullivan about the sheer injustice of it, and how it ruined his altruistic efforts to help the Bengali community at that community's invitation. 'I had to put all my personal resources into it to save the institution,' he says. 'Certain individuals put me under extreme pressure. I felt it would be much better if I moved myself on and spared my colleagues the embarrassment.'

Sullivan is acutely aware there hasn't been a solicitor present during any of this. He needs to put this right and offers Stonehouse a recommendation: another British ex-pat, Mr Jim Patterson. Sullivan knows Patterson as a lawyer of some repute having represented Charmian Biggs when her train-robbing husband Ronnie was on the run.[8]

Patterson turns up at Mackenzie Street at 7pm. He's a laconic former copper originally from Liverpool, who swapped the north-west of England for Australia after the war and briefly joined the Melbourne Police before retraining as a criminal solicitor. Now any trace of a Scouse accent is barely detectable. He and Stonehouse talk easily and establish a rapport.[9]

Back in their homeland of England, it's still dark. On Harvel Crescent, in the south-east London suburb of Abbey Wood, the phone rings in Sheila Buckley's childhood home and wakes her, and her parents. 'Hello?' says Buckley, who's home for Christmas. Barbara Stonehouse is on the line. Barbara tells Buckley what she has known all along: the man they both love is alive. Buckley does a good job of playing dumb before being thrown into negotiations about her role in the aftermath. 'Will you promise not to go to Australia?' Barbara pleads. 'At least in the immediate future.' Reluctantly, a half-asleep Buckley agrees. For now, the very fact that Stonehouse asked his wife to bring her to him is assurance enough.[10]

Meanwhile, the Foreign Office is also receiving messages

about Stonehouse, all copied to the Home Office and Number 10. As the prime minister's staff wake up and head for Downing Street, an oblivious Harold Wilson is on a train speeding west. The flash telegrams from Australia come thick and fast: 'Will there be a request to hold Mr Stonehouse pending charges or extradition proceedings?' 'What was the nature and origin of the Interpol message?' 'Is there any message for the consul-general to deliver?'

Ivor Vincent dispatches one of his officials, Eric Manvell, to see Stonehouse. They are under strict instructions to behave in line with normal practice for a UK citizen facing charges. There must be no special treatment. Stonehouse is not best pleased to see Manvell, but there is one thing this diplomat can do for him. He wants to send a message to Wilson. He has every faith that the prime minister will completely understand.[11]

Stonehouse is given paper and a pen, and gets to work. 'Please convey my regrets that I have created this problem,' he writes. 'My wish was to release myself from the incredible pressures being put on me, particularly in my business activities and various attempts at blackmail.' He hits his stride; the orator is alive and well. 'I considered, clearly wrongly, that the best action I could take was to create a new identity and live a new life away from these pressures. This can be summed up as a brainstorm or mental breakdown. I can only apologise to you and all the others who have been troubled by this business. Again, thank you for your kind statement in the House.' It's a message to which Wilson will never reply.[12]

By 9pm, Stonehouse is ready to be transferred to the Immigration Detention Centre via his flat to get some belongings. Most of the media are still gathered outside the state police station on Russell Street, but at least one canny Australian photographer has headed over to the Commonwealth Police headquarters on Mackenzie Street. With newly acquired representation Jim Patterson at his side, Stonehouse emerges to flashing bulbs. He looks positively dapper: tie and jacket, matching handkerchief neatly tucked in, one hand in his trouser pocket, the other one carrying his briefcase. It's almost as though he knew the cameras would be there.

Stonehouse is received into custody at Melbourne's Immigration Detention Centre, Maribyrnong, by Constable Alan Plant. The centre is made up of a collection of brick buildings with green tin roofs, and the perimeter boasts 2.5 metre fences topped with barbed wire. Plant thinks, all things considered, this British member of parliament seems calm and composed. Stonehouse gives up his belongings – including his washbag and his Gillette razor, macabrely pondering how hard it would be to slit your wrists with a modern safety razor. In 1959, he was declared an illegal immigrant in Africa. Fifteen years on, he's locked up in Australia for exactly the same offence.[13]

As his old protégé drifts off down under, Wilson wakes up at Penzance railway station in Cornwall. The prime minister and his wife Mary get off the London sleeper train and are one step closer to their second home on the Isles of Scilly. They're heading there for Christmas, and it can't come soon enough. The last few days have been a tiring end to a gruelling year.

Chief whip Bob Mellish threatened to resign again and he needed more persuasion than usual to stay put. The Australian prime minister Gough Whitlam is in town and had to be wined and dined over the weekend and it was heavy going. And just last night was the Number 10 staff Christmas party. It was nearly 10pm before they could leave for Paddington.[14]

Wilson can't be reached while he's on the train or during the crossing to the island, but his home here, Lowenva, is kitted out with secure phone lines. With the usual Russian 'fishing' trawlers listening offshore, it's a wise precaution. There's a teleprinter, duty clerk and detective in the Customs House, and another police officer in a guest house near Lowenva to complete Wilson's holiday detail.

While Mary unpacks the groceries that have been delivered to their modest bungalow – it's communist bloc chic – her husband catches up on overnight developments. My word: Stonehouse has been arrested in Australia! Wilson suspected he wasn't dead but this is nothing short of sensational. Just a week ago he was forced to stand in the Commons and deny the man was a spy!

Now the country's biggest-selling paper the *Daily Mirror* has got 'Stonehouse Found Alive!' splashed across its Christmas Eve front page – '2am News: Australian police are holding missing MP' – and it's clear from the clatter of the teleprinter that Number 10 is in overdrive. To think, ten years ago, the Wilsons had gifted Stonehouse a holiday in this very bungalow. He weighs up the risks. Stonehouse was a minister only five years ago and Wilson knows he's a master of self-serving press leaks and manipulation. He doubts that the MP is going to go quietly and thoughts of a quick by-election give way to damage limitation.[15]

Wilson needs to keep Stonehouse in custody. It will be a sensitive issue with the Australians, who resent any interference from Britain, as he learned all too recently from Whitlam. He asks his staff to find out whether the Department of Trade fraud investigation into the Stonehouse companies is serious enough for the government to oppose bail, and Wilson wants the Foreign Office involved.[16]

Just as he expected, the story moves fast. The Home Office tells the press that no question of extradition has arisen and any alleged offences are a matter for the Australian authorities. The Australians say they want more information on crimes he might have committed in the UK. Then Number 10 makes its boldest step of all: Wilson's press chief Joe Haines releases the full text of Stonehouse's personal message to the PM. They're hanging one of their own out to dry.[17]

PART FIVE

To Catch a Thief

2 1

MERRY CHRISTMAS

The early hours of Christmas Eve are frantic at Faulkners Down House. Barbara is still in shock and the phone is ringing off the hook. While Rupert Murdoch is using his local contacts to get the inside scoop down under, Barbara is the big catch in Britain. Beaverbrook's *Daily Express* are quick off the mark and Barbara agrees to fly to Australia with them for a fee of £4,000. The rest of Fleet Street wildly exaggerates this to be £35,000 plus expenses. She makes sure that everything is ready for a festive lunch she won't now be cooking, packs a suitcase and is driven from Hampshire to Gatwick where she gets on a plane with *Express* reporter Paul Hopkins.[1]

The journey takes more than thirty-five hours, during which time Barbara is confronted with the inescapable realisation that her husband was willing to walk out of her life for ever, to abandon his family. Every moment of what she thought of as a happy marriage is called into question. Maybe it was her fault. Maybe his natural instinct is to live as a bachelor. Maybe she's been living in a fool's paradise of her own making. She reflects on how she'd allowed him other women all these years; how she'd acquiesced because she thought them necessary to his ego; how she accepted it as long as he was discreet, as long as no one, especially the children, found out; and how she'd been desperate to keep this family unit intact after her own father abandoned her as five-year-old. But now this rejection, this terrible, total rejection, makes her consider the very real possibility of divorce.[2]

While Barbara is in the air, the Foreign Office makes it known that it's keen for her to be met at Tullamarine Airport in Melbourne. Foreign secretary James Callaghan has taken a personal interest and wants her to be offered every assistance. Her connecting flight from Sydney will get her there at 10.25am on Boxing Day, local diplomats are told. They also ask the Commonwealth Police to let her see her husband on arrival.[3]

But she's not ready yet. After catching the TN493 from Sydney to Melbourne, and being met by a member of the Melbourne consul general's staff, Barbara is dropped off at Noah's Palm Lake Motor Inn. The *Daily Express* are doing it in style. The luxurious four-storey motel is fringed with palm trees round a heated swimming pool, but Barbara is in no state to enjoy the facilities. She retreats inside, telling everyone she has a migraine. The press chase her down the corridors bombarding her with questions, but even they stop short when she gets to her room.[4]

Barbara's husband is also in temporary accommodation, albeit of a less luxurious kind. He's had a rough night's sleep and that's not ideal for a man due to stand in front of a magistrate the next morning. While Barbara is unpacking at the Palm Lake, DI John Sullivan is escorting Stonehouse from Maribyrnong to a grand Gothic building downtown, the Melbourne City Court. A huge scrum of newspaper reporters and TV crews are already there. 'Have you heard from Mr Wilson? Can you tell us any more about the pressures you were under?' Some of them push telegrams and messages into his hands. 'Not even Frank Sinatra got this treatment,' quips Sullivan. The detectives encircle Stonehouse so they can get into the courthouse, and send a cameraman flying in the process.[5]

Inside the courthouse, Stonehouse finds stipendiary magistrate John McArdle waiting for him. He is being charged under Section 38 of the Immigration Act; there are no criminal charges, just passport violation counts. McArdle allows Stonehouse to make a statement from the witness box and the irrepressible MP takes full advantage.[6]

'I am not a criminal in the accepted sense of the word,' he begins. 'It is only my wish to do what hundreds of thousands have done before me – to come to Australia and establish a new life here in a free community. I was subject to blackmail by certain individuals; I felt I had to escape.

'In the past two days, I have received more understanding and sympathy in Australia than I have in England in the last two years. I came to hate England for what was being done to me.' But the rhetoric has little impact on McArdle's decision. After less than an hour, the magistrate decides that Stonehouse must return to detention for another week while the immigration minister decides what to do.[7]

Back in the press ruck, Stonehouse reiterates that he is being treated very well and is grateful for the reception he has received. 'I am very happy,' he says of the detention centre. 'It's not entirely up to the Hilton standard, but it's getting that way.' 'Have you been in touch with the minister for immigration, Mr Stonehouse?' He ducks the question and repeats the line that he's very pleased with how the Australian authorities have treated him. Stonehouse is taken back to Maribyrnong through the courtroom garage and waves to photographers. 'Bye, bye,' he shouts. 'Thanks a lot.'[8]

As Stonehouse is escorted away, his new counsel Jim Patterson briefs the press. He starts off by confirming that Stonehouse will make a move to stay in Australia. No, Patterson doesn't know the specifics of the blackmail yet.

Then the press weigh in. After a tip-off that Stonehouse picked up mail from the Bank of New Zealand, the press are sure someone knew he was alive. 'Do you know as a matter of fact that his wife didn't know?' 'That's an impossible question to answer,' says Patterson. 'How would I know that?' They keep pushing. 'As far as I'm aware, his wife knew nothing about it.' 'Who were the letters from then?' For this, Patterson doesn't have an answer.[9]

Back in detention, Stonehouse reads the telegrams. There is nothing from his Labour Party colleagues, he notes bitterly, but the man who gave the go-ahead to that damaging article about his business is after him: 'Glad to see you are alive and kicking. Will you write an article for the *Sunday Times*?' asks Harold Evans. 'Two years too late,' thinks Stonehouse. And besides, there's another old contact who can help him a lot more than Harold Evans: Australia's immigration minister, Clyde Cameron.[10]

In 1967, while Australia's Labor Party were in opposition, Cameron had met the visiting UK minister for technology and, over the years, the two centre-left politicians remained in touch. Now Cameron is in a position to help and, surprisingly, personally phoned Stonehouse over Christmas from his Adelaide home. From detention, Stonehouse writes a long and emotional letter to him explaining his actions, leaving Patterson to write the formal plea. But Cameron is not the only person Stonehouse needs to get onside. Now the press are asking Barbara about 'the other woman' who sent the letters and Barbara is, by her own admission, 'hopping mad'.[11]

At the Palm Lake, she prepares to meet her husband for the first time since 19 November. Since then he's been dead then alive, missing then found, a family man then a love rat, a blackmail victim then a spy. Somehow she finds it in herself to get ready. She covers her distress with some oversized sunglasses and goes out the front of the motel to the waiting car. As always, she looks like the model wife.

She takes presents of T. E. Lawrence's *Seven Pillars of Wisdom* and Stonehouse's favourite cigars, but the reunion is awkward. All her instincts are against this meeting. She doesn't know if she loves him or hates him. She demands an explanation and Stonehouse repeats his story of intolerable pressures leading to mental breakdown. Eventually he breaks down in tears, and Barbara holds him in her arms. There's no way round it: despite his terrible behaviour, she still loves this man. She also thinks he needs to see a doctor.[12]

Back in Hampshire, as they clear up after Christmas, the Stonehouse children await a call from their parents. But the only people who want to speak to them are the press, who are now stood ten deep outside their house. The children are more concerned about how their mother must be feeling. It was incredible to see her so overjoyed to hear from their father, but the reality of his extraordinary behaviour must now be faced. They discuss his mental state and decide that there has been a gradual change in him. The complexities of his businesses have made him tense and he has found it increasingly hard to relax. They put this down to the unique pressures public figures face, exemplified by press banging away at the front door.[13]

It is a classic holiday season news story. Buckley in particular is a target for the media. She may have promised Barbara she wouldn't fly to Australia, but she never said anything about talking to the press. Even though they already have Barbara sewn up, the *Daily Express* chases after Buckley and, on Boxing Day, she too goes on the record with them. She insists that she knew nothing of his plans and that their relationship was purely professional. 'Tell him if he wants me to, I am willing to work for him in Australia,' she says. 'If he sets up business there, I wouldn't mind working for John because I have a number of good friends in Australia.'[14]

The following day, she welcomes ITN News into her parents' home in Abbey Wood. The camera crew and reporter frame her in front of the family's Christmas tree with its gaudy baubles and tinsel. 'If Mr Stonehouse was on the end of a telephone line to you now, what would you say to him?' asks the reporter. 'I would merely send him my very best wishes' – Buckley smiles coyly – 'and generally tell him that he has my loyalty.' Then the smile widens slightly. 'And if there's anything I can do for him, I shall do it.'[15]

She won't give ITN a comment on the blackmail allegations – 'I know he was under pressure from some people, and I would rather not comment anymore on that at this stage as I feel sure Mr Stonehouse will enlarge on this for you' – but after months of having to keep everything secret, she can't contain herself for long. 'I do know why he was blackmailed,' she tells the papers. 'It was nothing to do with his personal, political or private life. I believe it was something to do with a business deal. It was a business affair.' And then later: 'They turned on him and threatened to expose him in some way.' This is the nearest anyone has got to pinning down Stonehouse's amorphous 'blackmail' claim.[16]

Another ITN News crew pulls up at Faulkners Down House the day after. Jane and Mathew Stonehouse have given in and are waiting by the fireplace to be interviewed. Jane sits nervously in an armchair, denimed legs crossed under her. She looks the same age as the woman who viewers heard discussing Stonehouse the night before, and like her, has dark, centrally parted, poker-straight hair. Mathew, only 14, sits awkwardly in front of his sister on a stool.

'Do you feel betrayed by your father?' asks the female reporter. 'No, no, no I don't. And nor does Julia or Mathew. It's very difficult to explain to anybody. We know our father quite well, not as well as we thought obviously or otherwise we'd have known he was going to do this, but . . . We can understand what he did and we can forgive what he did. I mean after all he is alive and that is relief enough. What we went through in those five weeks of agony and hell. So no, no, we don't feel betrayed.' The devotion this man engenders, even after walking out on his own children with no intention of ever seeing them again, is nothing short of astonishing.

The reporter goes on to ask the question that everyone wants answered: 'Do you think your mother knew where he was in the five weeks when he disappeared?' Jane gasps, looks appalled and then darkly amused. 'Absolutely not,' she says emphatically. 'Of course not, no. All you have to do is ask our friends who saw us in those weeks.' Then, as had Buckley, Jane is given the opportunity of sending a message to Stonehouse. 'Daddy, we wish you all the peace and all the happiness in the world and if there's anything we can do, we'll do it.'[17]

But there's not much they can do right now and Stonehouse spends Friday 27 December waiting for Clyde Cameron's decision. Barbara visits him in his brick hut, this time in a tabloid-friendly yellow and white gingham blouse and a green trouser suit, and is visiting him again the next day when Cameron shows his hand – or at least some of it.

Cameron is known for his contrarian views and will make up his own mind, not do what UK diplomats tell him. He announces that although Stonehouse had presented a passport in a name other than his own on entry, British MPs are entitled to enter Australia without an entry permit, a privilege he himself confirmed when he took office. Stonehouse has committed no offence in Australia and, using his 'ministerial discretion', Cameron says Stonehouse can be released from custody on condition that he reports to the Immigration Department in Melbourne once a week. But the tough former sheep shearer is no more swayed by his friend's blandishments than those of the diplomats and he really wants more time to consider the case. He quietly lets it be known that he's 'not pleased' at the subterfuge that Stonehouse used to enter Australia and that deportation is still an option.[18]

Stonehouse is free to go for now, but the press are in a throng outside. Sullivan suggests that they leave the detention centre in the middle of the night when all but the most dedicated reporters will have given up. At 2am on Sunday 29 December, Barbara leaves first, then a police car pulls across the road and blocks off any press pursuit. Once she is safely out of the way, Stonehouse is driven off in a separate car.[19]

Later that morning, Patterson faces the press and, in answer to a question, confirms the Stonehouses are not together 'at the moment'. What he means, he says, taking deep puffs on a cigarette, is that with the press trailing Barbara, and her husband wanting to rest and compose himself, they're not physically together. His impression, however, is that they are a very loving and affectionate couple.[20]

They need somewhere to hide and an old school friend of Stonehouse's, Griff Bartlett, now a Melbourne architect, lives just fifty kilometres away in Yellingbo, a village in the middle of a vast nature reserve. The two men who formed the left-wing Citizens of Tomorrow group in Southampton as teenagers are now reunited in Bartlett's sprawling mock Tudor mansion, a safe haven from the eyes of the world. Stonehouse goes straight there and Barbara joins the next day.[21]

There is a cyclone ripping through the Northern Territory on a scale that sees Gough Whitlam rush back from London, but it can't knock the Stonehouses out of the headlines and the editorials seize on Cameron's statement. The generally pro-Labor Melbourne daily *The Age* is incredulous: 'Are we really to believe that people can perpetrate abuses of immigration procedures, use fake passports and assumed names and pay no penalty? Is the passport system only to apply to those ordinary citizens who have no reason to try to circumvent it? As a member of parliament, a former minister and a public figure, Mr Stonehouse enjoys certain privileges and rights in this country. He also bears a heavy responsibility to uphold the law.' If Cameron knows something we don't, says the paper, we should be told.[22]

Cameron would really like the British to take the matter out of his hands with an extradition request, but he's getting no lead from London. The leader of the House of Commons, Ted Short, says he expects Stonehouse to do the right thing and resign as an MP, but Whitehall's best legal minds are scratching their heads. Scotland Yard tells the director of public prosecutions (DPP) that urgent enquiries are proceeding and an application for extradition could be made within ten days, but the DPP isn't convinced there's enough evidence. As a result, the Foreign Office informs the Australian attorney general that any extradition request is going to take a long time and can't be made public yet. They want the Australians to deport him and the two sides are far apart.[23]

With Wilson in the Scillies, Number 10 is operating with a skeleton staff over the holiday and the prime minister's private secretary, Robin Butler, is the man on duty. On the 27th, he cyphers Wilson in the Scillies with the news that Stonehouse has been released from prison and that Barbara has asked the consul general in Melbourne to retrieve her husband's original passport from Miami.[24]

Three days later, Butler reports that a month-long Department of Trade investigation into BBT/London Capital Group will soon have to be made public, news that is likely to cause a run on the bank. He tells Wilson that 'the company has enough cash to meet the claims of small depositors (about £60,000) provided that the Crown Agents do not withdraw their £350,000'. Another fringe bank failure at this particular time, let alone one connected with his own party, is the last thing Wilson needs. Fortunately, the Crown Agents have just been given an £85 million bailout to keep them afloat and will do as they are told. On New Year's Eve, when the appointment of Department of Trade inspectors is announced, they leave their money where it is.[25]

Wilson is getting twitchy. He always preferred the idea of the Scillies to actually being there, calling Number 10 regularly, sometimes from a pay phone to avoid disturbing Mary, and often cutting short his holiday and returning to London alone. This year runs true to form. There are secret meetings in Belfast with the IRA, hopes that their Christmas truce will be extended, and Church leaders from Northern Ireland are travelling to London for talks. It is the Wilsons' wedding anniversary and they're not due to travel back until 2 January, but Wilson wants to meet the churchmen and they cut short the holiday by a day. Back in Number 10 on New Year's Day, he's told of the latest Stonehouse developments. His passport is en route from Miami to the Australian police and there's a real risk Stonehouse will get hold of it and be free to travel to a country without an extradition treaty.[26]

FLIGHT RISK

Thursday 2 January 1975 marks the Stonehouses' fifth day with their friends, the Bartletts. They have fallen into a pleasant routine, the men playing chess and the women chatting on the veranda. The Stonehouses' relationship goes back to something approaching normal on their long, daily walks in the woods together and it's almost possible to imagine that none of this ever happened. But that evening Barbara is watching television when she is called to the door. It's the *Daily Mail*. She tells reporter Peter Birkett in no uncertain terms that 'John is thinking out his position and will not see anyone at the moment'. Then she adds: 'And I'm flabbergasted that you have traced us here. I cannot believe it.'[1]

Once the *Daily Mail* calls, there is no point in hiding. The next day, they leave the Bartletts and Stonehouse reports to the Immigration Department in Melbourne at 8am, as he is required to do every week. Patterson has given up on his attempts to secure an out-of-town check-in, but Stonehouse simply tells the authorities that he wants to visit friends in Sydney. He and Barbara are well on the way by the time the Immigration Department realise he's gone. In a panic, they bring in the police. The hunt is on as Patterson refuses to tell them anything.[2]

The police try to get the registration number of their car, and airports and ports are told to be on the alert for a couple who could be travelling under aliases. Cameron senses the risk to his own reputation and authorises Stonehouse's arrest if he tries to leave Australia. Told by Patterson that he is a wanted man, Stonehouse telephones the police from a call box in the city of Albury only three hours' drive north of Melbourne and confirms that they are indeed going to Sydney. No you're not, say the police. They warn him that he will be arrested if he leaves Melbourne again without permission and order him to return. The couple are back in Melbourne on 5 January and, finally, Barbara and Patterson can get Stonehouse in front of a doctor.[3]

Doctor G. Gibney is a psychiatrist who practises at 428 St Kilda Road, the exact road that Coffey and co. drove him up nearly two weeks ago. Gibney listens to Stonehouse, hears Barbara's take and diagnoses 'reactive depression'. Stonehouse claims it started in 1971 when he 'campaigned to assist Bangladesh' and culminated in his decision to establish a new identity. 'I decided to kill off Stonehouse,' he explains to Gibney. 'I wanted to die, but not physically.' You could, Gibney concedes, consider it suicide, from a psychiatric point of view.[4]

The British and Australian authorities know nothing of this assessment and are on a 'deport versus extradite' collision course. In the first full working week of the new year, they get together in the Melbourne offices of the Australian attorney general to sort things out. The attorney general's first secretary – John Ballard, an experienced British lawyer before he emigrated to Australia – chairs the meeting. Cameron's Immigration Department is represented by another official, and a senior British diplomat flies down from Canberra. The Commonwealth Police and the Victoria State Police, already criticised for departmental rivalries, are also present, while, swapping a chilly British winter for the warmth of an Australian summer, are two recent arrivals from London: DCS Kenneth

Etheridge, deputy head of Scotland Yard's Fraud Squad, and his sidekick DCI David Bretton.

Etheridge – 'a good thief catcher', according to his boss – is a London copper of the old school. Having survived an official investigation into his links with a Soho nightclub owner, he has just put away John Poulson, a corrupt property developer with political connections, for five years and now he's after another big fish.[5]

The Australian police, suddenly united, ask what Etheridge is doing on their patch. He's careful in his reply, explaining that he's not there to interview Stonehouse but to trace a series of bank transfers between Stonehouse's many Australian and Swiss bank accounts. A sum of £350,000 belonging to the Crown Agents is at risk and there's likely to be much more. It will take the Department of Trade and Scotland Yard between six months and a year to complete their enquiries.

It would be stretching Cameron's powers to restrict Stonehouse's movements without charge for that long. The Australians want the British to take the matter out of his hands and apply for extradition, but Etheridge explains that the only charge the police are certain of landing at this stage is passport forgery. This has never previously been used in an extradition case; besides, there's an even more important reason not to extradite just yet. Under extradition law, whatever Stonehouse is extradited for, would be the extent of any future indictments: charges for prior alleged offences could not be added once he is back in Britain. That means it's going to be a long wait and Etheridge is concerned that, like Ronnie Biggs, Stonehouse might escape to a country without a formal extradition agreement.

After a long discussion, the Immigration Department finally agrees to encourage Cameron to urge Stonehouse to return to the UK voluntarily. If Stonehouse refuses, this might open the way to deportation, but no one present is in any doubt that this would be a very difficult political decision for Cameron and the Australian government. Ballard reports back to Cameron that there is a very weak case for deportation. The minister agrees but hints that the situation would change if the House of Commons were to expel Stonehouse.[6]

That's not an option that appeals to Wilson's fragile Labour government. It risks politicising the whole affair and the prime minister has an alternative suggestion. Adding his own words to an official note, he tells leader of the House Ted Short that the best outcome would be for Stonehouse to resign. 'Is there anything to be said for a communication to him from you or the chief whip, urging him to make such an application at a very early date in order that his constituents may not be effectively disenfranchised for what might be an indefinite period of time, in terms which would make it clear to him that, wherever his future prospects may lie, they do not now lie in a parliamentary or political career in this country?'[7]

While the authorities deliberate, the Stonehouses are at breaking point. The media are doorstepping them again in Melbourne and the couple want to get out of town properly this time. With police permission, they fly to Sydney using the name Taylor, but their travel plans have been leaked and on landing they are once again swamped by journalists – to the point that it's impossible even to retrieve their luggage. Stonehouse looks confused and distressed, and Barbara tells the BBC's Bob Friend that she wishes they would all 'desist', saying her husband needs psychiatric treatment. She and Dr Gibney have convinced him to get this when he returns to Melbourne.[8]

Once they finally emerge from the scrum at Sydney Airport,

and under Commonwealth Police surveillance, the couple buy a car. Dodging the press, they move from hotel to hotel, ending up at Noah's Newcastle Motor Inn, a beachfront hotel north of Sydney, on Sunday 12 January. It's been a fraught weekend playing cat and mouse with the press pack and, in the middle of Sunday night, Stonehouse gets up and writes a letter on motel notepaper to Ted Short.

'I have consulted a leading Australian psychiatrist with regard to my breakdown and following these consultations I now appreciate that the long traumas I suffered were caused by a deep disillusionment with the state of English society and the complete frustration of the ideals I have pursued in my political and business life.' He says he plans to retire from public life and live in Australia, and asks the leader of the House to 'set in motion the formalities required for my resignation as the member for Walsall North'. The letter complete, he returns to his motel bed and tries to find sleep.[9]

The following morning, the couple begin a long drive south. The police escort them for the first thirty miles and then, confident that they are safely on the way, leave their Melbourne colleagues to resume surveillance nearer the city. Melbourne, however, is not where Stonehouse is going, at least not just yet.

Conveniently, Herbert 'Tommy' Tucker, the diplomat allocated to him by the High Commission as his personal 'information counsellor', is listed in the Canberra telephone book. Stonehouse phones him at home, requesting an urgent meeting in the car park of a Canberra motel. He tells Tucker not to mention the proposed meeting to anyone yet and asks how he will recognise the diplomat. They find each other easily enough and with Barbara watching from the car, Stonehouse gives Tucker a signed copy of his letter to Short and asks that it be sent in the next day's diplomatic bag. As he drives away, he tells Tucker, who he believes is a member of the secret service, that he hopes never to see him again.[10]

Stonehouse stops at a call box to update Patterson on what he has done. Far from pleased, Patterson nearly drops the phone in shock. They need to meet in the morning as a matter of urgency, says Patterson, but it's too late to stop what's been put in motion. Short receives the letter by cypher and at 20.45 London time on 13 January, the British government issues a press release wholeheartedly welcoming Stonehouse's intention to resign.[11]

Short swiftly replies to Stonehouse, telling him how to go about it. He then observes: 'I am sure, if I may say so, that you have taken the right decision, in your own interest as well as that of your constituents; and that is certainly the unanimous view of press comment on your decision.' For their part, the Australians at last see a way out of this tiresome affair. The Immigration Department requests confirmation of his resignation since a change in his status 'will be an important factor in Mr Cameron's decision on [the] future of Mr Stonehouse'.

But if everyone else is relieved, Stonehouse can't believe what he's done. Patterson is right. If he resigns, he'll surrender his rights as a British MP, and lose the only leverage he has to remain in Australia and avoid deportation. Then the solution comes to him. He'll just say that he's changed his mind. He calls a developing contact at the *Daily Telegraph*, Ian Ward, and, before long, Stonehouse's volte-face is the lead story, leaving the British and the Australian authorities firmly back at square one.[12]

Britain's man on the ground, Melbourne consul general Ivor Vincent, is a former British Indian Army officer and ex-ambassador to Nicaragua, now on his last posting before retiring. It's not turning out to be the easy last tour he was expecting and he calls Stonehouse late in the evening of 15 January, enquiring whether he has seen Short's reply. Stonehouse, who is now on his own as Barbara has gone back to the UK, confirms that he has no intention of making any decisions just yet.[13]

When Vincent suggests that MPs might consider expelling him if he were to revoke the resignation, Stonehouse launches a tirade against the UK and says again he will absolutely not be rushed into a decision. Later that evening in another call, Patterson firmly tells Vincent that he won't advise his client to resign as it risks him being detained again. Stonehouse, he says, is in a highly excited and nervous state of mind and is in no fit psychological state to take such a decision.[14]

Vincent reports this to London where the Commons is back after the Christmas recess and Number 10 can see this getting difficult. On the 15th, Wilson's principal private secretary Robert Armstrong drafts a message for Vincent to deliver personally to Stonehouse 'with the authority of ministers'. With opinion in the House turning against the sitting member for Walsall North, Vincent is ordered to point out 'that it is probably in Mr Stonehouse's own interest, as well as being certainly the more dignified course, for him to effect his resignation rather than have his resignation forced upon him'.[15]

Delivering that message is easier said than done. Neither Stonehouse nor Patterson will come to the phone and when Vincent knocks on his door, Stonehouse leaves the house and drives off angrily. It is the following evening before they finally have a phone call. Stonehouse dictates a reply to London saying that Patterson has advised him not to resign while he studies the legal position and he won't make a decision until he receives that advice.[16]

While that conversation is taking place, Wilson's cabinet

meet. The second item on the agenda is 'Mr John Stonehouse'. Stonehouse has his sympathisers round the table who detect mental illness – including surprisingly Roy Jenkins, Anthony Wedgwood Benn and Barbara Castle – but for others, like Bob Mellish, faking his own death is inexcusable. The prime minister sums up. The matter should not be determined by the strength of feeling against Stonehouse on the government's benches, but by whether he has treated the House with contempt and abused his privileges. The leader of the House should consult the speaker and the leader of the opposition and if Stonehouse has not relinquished his seat by next Monday, a select committee should be set up to consider his continued membership of the House.[17]

On Friday 17th, Stonehouse holds an informal dinner for the press in a Melbourne hotel and tells them what Dr Gibney has told him. It's supposed to be off the record, but it's soon all over the papers. He grants the BBC's Bob Friend a sit-down interview and claims his position is tantamount to sick leave. He says he is on a fact-finding tour of his 'inner self' and the overall situation is something he's only just beginning to understand after seeing Gibney and having had a period of 'rest and relaxation'. There is no doubt that Stonehouse is suffering in the wake of his discovery, but what he can't prove is that he was mentally ill beforehand – although that doesn't stop him trying. He hopes people will understand that the 'trauma took place over a long period of time and in that period when there were two personalities in parallel, one isn't behaving rationally about everything . . . That must be borne in mind by anyone who tries to make an assessment of my situation.'[18]

Etheridge of Scotland Yard is someone charged with doing just that and, when London wakes up, he tells Vincent that Stonehouse is trying to negotiate a contract with a British newspaper and has withdrawn A$8,000 from a Swiss bank account. If he is not careful, Vincent will lose both the media war and his man, and that's not the way he wants his career to end. He persuades Stonehouse and Patterson to come to his official residence, a detached house in the suburb of Toorak. Vincent hints that the Australian government's attitude might be hardening, which shakes Stonehouse. Patterson reiterates that his client is emotionally disturbed and needs a long rest. After two hours, they leave.[19]

Yet Vincent senses Stonehouse is 'not wholly negative' to his blandishments and the very next day he invites him to stay overnight at his house. Stonehouse accepts, but a comment in the previous day's *Daily Mail* has upset him. He says that in no circumstances will he return to Britain of his own free will. If he goes, it will be in handcuffs. He plans to remain a member of the House of Commons and submit questions to the House about Scotland Yard's activities. He wishes to settle in Australia and has written to Cameron appealing for special treatment, providing a report from Gibney to back up his claims. For Vincent, the overnight stay couldn't have gone much worse.[20]

The Immigration Department tells the British High Commission in Canberra what is in both the letter to Cameron and Gibney's report. The High Commission pass this straight on to the Foreign Office in London, reminding them that 'Mr Stonehouse, of course, should not find out that we know the contents'. Gibney is reported as having spent five hours with Stonehouse, concluding that Stonehouse is suffering from 'significant depression' which requires 'ongoing' psychiatric care and perhaps treatment in hospital in future.

But High Commission official J. B. Hay is less convinced. He has no doubt what Stonehouse is up to. 'Such is Mr Stonehouse's desire to remain in Australia, however, that I would have expected him to use any device to try to soften Mr Cameron's heart – even to the extent of producing evidence of severe mental disturbance rather than the sort of depression which is an everyday part of all too many people's lives.'[21]

On 28 January, the House of Commons debates a motion to set up a select committee 'to consider the position of Mr John Stonehouse as member for Walsall North'. Short argues that the collective wisdom of a select committee is 'much the fairest way of establishing the full facts of what has happened and of finding the right course to take'. Opposition leader Ted Heath surprises many with a compassionate summing-up: 'This House understands full well the weaknesses and frailties of our fellow human beings. Above all, we understand the consequences of strain and conflicts in individual personalities in this House.' The motion is carried 237–30.[22]

On 29 January, the action shifts to south-west England, specifically the Devon Motel on the Exeter bypass. DCS Etheridge has issued a summons to Sheila Buckley, who has been staying with an aunt in Cornwall since New Year. She has heard from Barbara, who is back in the UK for a while. She says her husband is in turmoil, threatening suicide. Buckley is distraught at this news, but makes her way to the rendezvous with Etheridge nevertheless.[23]

Out of the tourist season, the extended Georgian manor house that comprises the Devon Motel is a quiet location for the interview. Etheridge is accompanied by his boss, Deputy Assistant Commissioner James Crane, and WPC Shields is there to take the notes. After the drop-in at Dover Street last month, the interview is Buckley's first formal meeting with the police and it extends over two days. Had she known it was to be so long, Buckley thinks, she would have gone with a solicitor. In the event, she tells Etheridge she's quite willing to help but insists, 'I am not willing to discuss my personal affairs'.[24]

That proves to be difficult. Etheridge begins with the letters she sent to Stonehouse in Melbourne. 'Referring to the letter Exhibit JHC/3. The letter is addressed to My Dear Dums. Was that your pet name for Mr Stonehouse?' 'That is my nickname for Mr Stonehouse,' she confirms. 'The letters are written intending to convey a message to Mr Stonehouse personally and when I refer to my friend, my boyfriend, my fella or George I am in fact referring to Mr Stonehouse.' She explains more about the code she had used in the letters. 'Harry' is the prime minister. 'The Scottish thing' is Scotland Yard. 'Industry' is the Department of Trade. 'Mr Rags' is the press. 'Royal' is the insurance companies. 'Co-operation India Association' is the CIA.

Etheridge takes her through several company cheques payable for cash and to Stonehouse. She confirms that they carry her signatures. 'Were you authorised to draw cheques on the account in favour of Epacs Ltd?' he asks. 'Yes, my name has been on the mandate since 1970 and still is today as far as I know.' But when she is asked the reason for the transactions, she says she has 'no specific knowledge of what this money was for. I suggest you ask Mr Stonehouse.' As for why she resigned as a director of Epacs on 19 August 1974, she says it was at Stonehouse's suggestion following pressure from Sir Charles Hardie.

Etheridge questions her about the insurance policies. She says she was aware of a medical on one policy, that is all. He turns up the heat. 'From what you have told me, you knew that Mr Stonehouse was not dead and you were aware of a number of insurance policies in existence on his life. We suspect that, in relation to these insurances, a criminal offence has been committed and in view of your close and personal involvement with Mr Stonehouse, I feel that it is my duty to caution you before any more questions are put to you.

'You do not have to say anything unless you wish to do so but what you say may be given in evidence.' Etheridge tells Buckley he wants to see her again and that in due course the facts will be submitted to the director of public prosecutions. 'Do you really think I would be prosecuted?' asks Buckley. 'I can't see how I'm involved.' Etheridge does nothing to reassure her. 'You were a director of a company, at all times authorised to draw on its bank accounts. You were a party to the removal of funds from this company and it remains to be seen whether or not a criminal offence has been committed'. 'Well, if he goes down on those cheques,' replies Buckley, 'I'll go down with him.'[25]

23

ENTER THE INSPECTORS

On 6 February, Stonehouse invites Ian Ward over for a chat and the pair discuss writing a book on Stonehouse's life. Stonehouse thinks he has found a friend and a journalist he can trust in the *Daily Telegraph*'s correspondent. Ward has written a helpful article and has offered to help Sheila Buckley. Although the Metropolitan Police have asked her not to leave the UK, she's planning her journey to Australia and will stop over in Singapore with a friend of Ward's.[1]

Stonehouse is excited about Buckley's imminent arrival and shows Ward a big metal trunk that he has just retrieved from Melbourne customs. Ward notices some women's clothing, and Stonehouse takes a black slip and holds it to his body. He takes a couple of steps as though he is dancing with the slip's owner and jokes how funny it would be if people thought it belonged to Buckley. Ward remarks that if so, Stonehouse should hide it as Barbara is due back in Australia the next day. He agrees to store some of the trunk's contents at his place.[2]

When Barbara does arrive, Stonehouse, dressed for an Aussie summer in light slacks and a floral beach shirt, is at Tullamarine Airport to meet her, along with the usual crowd of journalists. He protests mildly about the unwanted attention, but he needs all the friends he can get and shakes hands with every reporter before driving off with his wife.[3]

It has been a busy three weeks in England for Barbara. A

six-bedroom house in the country, bought for renovation in her name in 1972 – 'Stonehouse's Folly', the locals call it – is already on the market and she falls behind with the rent on Faulkners Down House. She is standing by her man, at least while he is in Australia and then, who knows?[4]

On Monday 10 February, the *Guardian* has new allegations. It runs a story about Stonehouse's business dealings with the two men who went missing at the same time as him, American financier J. David Shaver and Nigerian Sylvester Okereke, who drowned in the Thames two days before Stonehouse left London. His body was pulled from the Thames at Putney Pier on 28 December and family members have been getting threatening calls telling them to 'fold up' any enquiries into his cause of death. Both men were involved with Stonehouse in the Romania–Nigeria cement deal and the names of US Mafia enforcers are entering the picture.

The *Guardian* also reports that William Asturrizaga, the Fort Lauderdale go-between with the fictitious address, called his wife from Paris to wish her a happy new year but that's the last she's heard from him. Is it a case of there but for the grace of God for Stonehouse? Or is it one of the reasons he was so keen to disappear? Some British diplomats in the High Commission in Lagos are interested in getting to the bottom of it, but the Foreign Office isn't interested. Meanwhile the Fraud Squad know about it, but don't pursue it. While Stonehouse keeps quiet and the authorities don't enquire, he can't be implicated. But one thing is for sure: Barbara thought her husband was in a respectable industry and the international cement business is anything but that.[5]

She has been with her husband barely a week when he announces that he will be away for a few days. Her husband's lover thinks the promise not to come out in the immediate future has now expired. On 12 February, Buckley arrives in Perth in Western Australia and, having taken a four-hour flight across the country, Stonehouse is there to greet her. Another Australian airport, another woman. She is ecstatic at the prospect of seeing him again, but Ian Ward and his photographer have joined them. 'Stay away, don't get near,' Stonehouse shouts. 'I don't want to be in a picture with you.' He has promised Barbara there will be no photographs in the press. Eventually, the lovers lose Ward and fly another three hours to Adelaide, hire a car and go into hiding.[6]

But it is a short reunion. Stonehouse wants to keep Barbara happy – Buckley isn't the only recipient of a loving Valentine's Day card – and also check in with the Immigration Department. He drives Buckley to friends in Sydney and she comes to the bitter conclusion that the set-up is going to be the same as it was in London: Stonehouse back with Barbara and just seeing her when he can. Incredibly, she forgives him again. If that's the way he wants it, she tells herself, that's how he should have it – even though she knows it might appear she has no self-respect. No, she'll put up with it just to be able to see him.[7]

But Barbara is upset that Buckley is in the country and intends to fly straight back to the UK with Mathew – even though the 14-year-old has only just arrived. Stonehouse can't have those headlines – 'Wife flies out when mistress flies in' – and decides the three of them need to discuss the situation and should meet between Melbourne and Sydney. Under the cover of darkness, they drive together to a beauty spot on the out-skirts of Albury in the River Murray Reserve, with Mathew. Once there and satisfied that they have not been followed, Stonehouse and the two women leave Mathew in the car and walk to some benches. 'I want you both,' he blurts out. Barbara is appalled and says that Buckley joining them in Melbourne is unthinkable. 'I won't have that girl there,' she says and he gets progressively more agitated as his wife refuses to back down.[8]

Barbara reiterates that she and Mathew are packed and ready to fly back to England if he insists on Buckley coming to Melbourne. At that moment, she thinks she could quite happily jump on a plane and never see him again. 'If you leave me Barbara,' he says, 'I'll kill myself!' He runs into the night towards a nearby bridge as Barbara calls after him, 'You always say that, but you never actually do it.'

Buckley doesn't share her confidence. She chases him and finds him slumped against the bridge. She begs him to think of her sometimes. 'I've always thought of you,' he says. 'That's why I'm still alive.' *It's me he can't leave!* thinks Buckley and she persuades Stonehouse to return to the car where Barbara is in the driving seat. 'Get in the car,' she says. The family go back to Melbourne, while Buckley moves in with a friend in Sydney. Will there be no end to this heartache? she asks herself.[9]

For Stonehouse, his personal life soon becomes the least of his worries. At just before 9am on 25 February, two Englishmen in their forties leave the faded grandeur of the Windsor Hotel and join Melbourne's morning commuters. Many of the shop and office workers are wearing open-necked shirts and slacks or summer dresses; the two men stand out in their dark suits, crisp shirts and silk ties. They have been in town for five days and have already established a daily routine. Breakfast together in the hotel, a stroll in the park opposite, back to the hotel to collect their documents and then a short walk to the top of Collins Street, Melbourne's high-end shopping boulevard. They board one of the city's tram cars by the centre doors, remain standing and alight at the Elizabeth Street stop. It would have been possible to walk, but they are carrying heavy, double-sized briefcases and if anyone is going to be made to sweat that morning, it won't be them.[10]

Michael Sherrard – dark hair, side parting, serious black-framed spectacles, below average height – and Ian Hay Davison – six foot two, paler complexion, swept-back dark hair, lighter glasses – cross the street to Number 330, the Colonial Mutual Life Building, a 1960s tower block. Photographers are already gathering outside but don't recognise the two men who pass between the retail outlets either side of the entrance.

They take the lift, crowded with office workers. No one says anything. On the ninth floor, the pair get out. They have arrived at the Melbourne office of the accountants Arthur Andersen and they are here on behalf of the British Department of Trade to interview John Stonehouse. And they are a formidable pair.

Michael Sherrard QC is one of Britain's leading barristers. He is best known to the public for his defence of James Hanratty, the last man to be hanged in Britain in 1962, but these days the legal world know him as a brilliant prosecutor of business fraud. Ian Hay Davison FCA is managing partner of Arthur Andersen UK. A Conservative candidate in the 1964 general election, he is one of Britain's top accountants and has taken charge of the Department of Trade job personally. Appointed on New Year's Eve, they have been searching desks and files in Stonehouse's Dover Street offices ever since.

They are shown to Arthur Andersen's main conference room. There are four chairs on one side of the polished wood boardroom table and facing them are two chairs behind a smaller grey table. In the corner is a sound recording desk. Fluorescent strip lights add to the functional feel. The layout looks forbidding and that's precisely the intention.

The room slowly fills up. Bruce Pascoe, a recording engineer on loan from the Australian Court Reporting Service, sits behind the sound desk. At one end of the boardroom table, Bruce Picking of Arthur Andersen takes charge of the files; at the other end sits Arthur Andersen partner Brian Currie, secretary to the inquiry, taking notes and smoking Gauloises. Between them, Sherrard and Davison wait.

At nine o'clock, Stonehouse and Patterson arrive. Stonehouse wears a smart blue suit, silk handkerchief in the top pocket, dark coloured shirt and bright tie. He is still handsome, notes Davison, but looks haggard underneath the suntan. Jim Patterson, less well heeled and with a weather-beaten, ruddy face, looks older than his years. Introductions are made, hands are shaken and they get to work.

Stonehouse spends the whole day giving evidence. It is a story of breakdown, conspiracies and blackmail in which every man is against him. He says he is co-operating only as a director of a company under investigation, not as an individual, and claims the Companies Act does not apply to him because he is a privy counsellor. He trusts no one, especially not the Department of Trade who he thinks will show his evidence to the Commons select committee. Sherrard is gentle this first day and Davison says little. Both know that Stonehouse could simply walk out and they have no powers to make him stay.

The British High Commission has an office a few floors above and, after the day's proceedings, Sherrard goes upstairs. He dictates a cable for the attorney general in London, outlining their concerns and seeking permission to tell Stonehouse that this evidence will not be shown to the select committee. He needs a reply by 10.30pm and warns London that a walkout is a serious risk. He and Davison give a press conference, but it is the man who has left by the building's underground garage that the journalists really want to see. Whether he'll be back is anyone's guess.[11]

On 26 February, the inspectors are relieved to see Stonehouse reappear, but it's only a half-day hearing. In Canberra, the opposition have called a debate on the Labor government's handling of the Stonehouse affair and Cameron, already under fire for plans to track down and expel tens of thousands of illegal immigrants, is under pressure. He says more than London would like about the UK's problems in gathering evidence for extradition, before reading from a Commonwealth Department of Health psychiatric report. It says Stonehouse is in 'a depressed and paranoid state of mind' and the rules are clear: he should be refused permission to stay in Australia.[12]

Like Wilson in Britain, Prime Minister Gough Whitlam is juggling a tiny majority and in the face of such clear advice, the government needs to come off the fence. Cameron says that as Stonehouse is mentally unfit to be a permanent resident, he will have to leave Australia within seventy-two hours of ceasing to be an MP. It is, he says, the same decision he took in the middle of January. 'I was hoping that I would not have to tell him this until he ceased to be a member of parliament, but now he knows as a consequence of this debate.'[13]

News of Cameron's decision filters through to Melbourne and Stonehouse realises that he is sunk if the Commons select committee recommends his expulsion from the House. He takes the afternoon off and calls a press conference. He tells reporters he wants his passport returned and doesn't want to go back to Britain: 'I can expect neither justice nor understanding there.' With his arm round Barbara, he asks people to accept that he's suffered a breakdown and has been a sick man these past few months. Barbara adds that she has spoken to his psychiatrist and is now beginning to understand his condition. Going back to England, she says, would bring back all the pressures that made him ill in the first place.[14]

As the inspectors take the tram along Collins Street on the morning of Thursday 27th, Sherrard and Davison are still not counting on Stonehouse turning up. Following yesterday's publicity, photographers wait outside, writ servers hover in the Arthur Andersen lobby and there's no sign of the man they want. But up on the ninth floor, the goods lift arrives and out he pops, ready for more questions.[15]

Sherrard is the master of silent intimidation, menacing in tone and manner, ready to pounce on any mistake. For six days it goes on. The air conditioning cannot cope with the cigarette smoke, the air turns a faint blue and there is a slight hum from the strip lights, audible when Stonehouse falls silent to consider his answers. Brian Currie scribbles away, Bruce Picking passes files across to Sherrard, Bruce Pascoe fiddles with knobs. Patterson sits quietly, glasses on, making copious notes and occasionally objecting to certain questions. Stonehouse largely ignores him. Davison intervenes on technical points.

The inspectors believe that Stonehouse has been syphoning money from his public company to fund his new identity. He says the money was for business agents, mainly paid in cash, and there are no receipts. He can't remember who else was involved. 'You mean you know but you would rather not name them?' asks Sherrard. 'I cannot remember, I cannot recall who else was involved at this point of time'.[16]

It is relentless and it goes on day after day. Stonehouse takes another half day off to look at schools for his son who is still in Australia. The inspectors spend the evenings checking the day's transcripts, Davison playing the occasional game of squash at the nearby Athenaeum Club; in another life, that was Stonehouse's game too. The photographers lose interest, the writ servers wait in vain, the inspectors press on.

They want to know about his Liechtenstein and Swiss bank

transactions, particularly that of 20 September 1974 when Stonehouse's lawyer Oswald Bühler withdrew £14,000 in cash from one of the Liechtenstein accounts and handed it over to him. Sherrard asks: 'You said a few moments ago that there were transfers from the Liechtenstein accounts into the Swiss bank accounts for Markham. It is not very difficult for banks to make transfers.' 'They were not made by banks. They were made . . .' and Stonehouse hesitates. Sherrard finishes the sentence for him: '. . . by cash?' 'By cash.'[17]

Over in the corner of the room, Jim Patterson, who has been quietly weighing up the evidence against his client, has a serious change of heart. He is now under no illusions: extradition is inevitable for Stonehouse. There is no way he can remain in Australia. Patterson confides in Sherrard that he intends to advise his client to return to the UK voluntarily.[18]

After six days, the hearing closes. Sherrard and Davison take an afternoon off to watch some cricket in their shirtsleeves at the Melbourne Cricket Ground. The next day, they return to London to prepare an interim report, but they have already made up their minds. Stonehouse's memory lapses are too selective to be involuntary, especially when he's in danger of incriminating himself. There's no doubt about it: the MP for Walsall North has committed widespread fraud.[19]

24

STATE OF MIND

The state of Stonehouse's mind in March 1975 divides opinion between Britain and Australia. Whereas Clyde Cameron sees it as grounds to deny him citizenship, the Commons select committee see it as a reason to delay judgement. Or perhaps no one thinks it's a real problem and both countries are simply seeing whatever it is that they want to see.

Either way, the impasse gets tetchy on 17 March when the select committee reports. It recommends no immediate action on mental health grounds, but warns that expulsion from the House 'on grounds of non-representation' must remain a future option. That goes down well in Australia, but the committee's suggestion that in the meantime the Australian government should take the initiative touches old sensitivities.

An official in the Immigration Department responds on the record: 'What the select committee are trying to suggest is that we do the dirty work. It's the old "Heads the Poms win, tails the Aussies lose". Clyde Cameron is not a messenger to be winked and nodded at by a bunch of Pommy MPs who haven't got the guts to give a definite Yes or No on someone who concerns them more than us.'[1]

With the Department of Trade inspectors off his back, Stonehouse relaxes, thinking he has seen them off. But in London, wheels are turning and, on 19 March, the director of public prosecutions tells Etheridge and his Fraud Squad that there is sufficient evidence to apply for extradition.[2]

It is dark in Melbourne and everyone is still asleep when the phone in the Melbourne home of Commonwealth Police detective Bob Gillespie rings at 5am. Etheridge is on the line with news that, in London, Bow Street magistrates have issued a provisional warrant for Stonehouse's arrest. He asks for Commonwealth Police assistance. 'We are opposed to bail,' Etheridge says. It is going to be a busy day for Gillespie and there seems little point in him going back to bed.[3]

The Stonehouses – back together with their son and trying to lead a normal life – know nothing of this. Friday 21 March turns into a typically sunny autumnal day. The leaves are still on the trees and by lunchtime it is a pleasing twenty degrees outside. Barbara and Mathew leave their small, rented apartment on the Toorak Road in the Melbourne suburb of Hawthorn to go shopping. Stonehouse relaxes in the lounge, reading a copy of *Time* magazine. The Commons select committee delay has given him some respite and he is feeling optimistic. At 1.30pm, there is a knock at the door.[4]

Stonehouse opens up to be greeted by DI Gillespie. 'You know me,' says Gillespie, 'and this is Detective Inspector Craig. And you remember Detective Sergeant Coffey, don't you?' 'Oh, hello Bob,' says Stonehouse. 'Come on in.' Stonehouse is all too familiar with the policemen, especially John Coffey, who arrested him at St Kilda Station three months ago.

'I have here with me a warrant for the arrest of John Thomson Stonehouse. Are you the person, John Thomson Stonehouse, mentioned in this warrant?' 'Yes.' Gillespie reads out fifteen charges of uttering forged documents; obtaining pecuniary advantage by deception; theft; and obtaining property by deception. 'I am now arresting you by virtue of this warrant. I now warn you that you are not obliged to answer any questions or make any statement. As anything you say or any statement you may make may be used in evidence. Do you clearly understand that?' 'Yes. I don't wish to make a statement,' says Stonehouse. 'Can I ring my solicitor?' and he does so.

Barbara and Mathew return from their shopping trip and they can't fail to notice a police car parked outside the building. Their fears are realised when they go inside and find police turning their apartment upside down. Gillespie discovers a black briefcase containing items in the name of Markham. He tells Stonehouse he intends to seize the documents, credit cards and cheque books he's found inside and tells Coffey and Craig to make sure they take anything else like this that they can find. This includes an early draft of the book Stonehouse is writing.

'Is it necessary to take the papers relating to my book?' he asks. These are the precious chapters he has been crafting in every spare moment. Gillespie confirms that indeed it is necessary. 'Look darling!' he shouts into the other room. 'They're taking all the papers for my book!' The three policemen open every cupboard and drawer, collect all the papers they find, place them in a cardboard box and carry them to the boot of the police car downstairs. Craig looks behind pictures on the wall in case anything is concealed there.

Stonehouse says goodbye to Barbara and Mathew, and the detectives escort him first to the police station and then to Melbourne Magistrates' Court. Patterson makes much of the UK authorities' opposition to bail: 'The Bow Street Magistrates and Scotland Yard don't seem to be aware that Australia is now an independent country and cannot be instructed in the matter of bail.' The magistrate agrees, noting that Stonehouse has been in the country for three months and has been no threat to Australia. Stonehouse is bailed for the relatively low surety of A$1,000, but has to report daily to the police station.[5]

On Sunday 23 March, Stonehouse calls a press conference. With Barbara sitting silently at his side, he rages at the seizure of his memoirs. He accuses the Commonwealth Police of acting as the 'handmaidens' of the British government, which 'would be extremely embarrassed by the publication of my book'. Scotland Yard, he says, 'is engaged in a vendetta against me' and this is 'the beginning of police state intimidation'. When later asked for his reaction to this accusation, Etheridge responds: 'There's two sides to a vendetta, aren't there?' Patterson couldn't be less pleased with the press conference. It has been arranged without his consent and he feels that the coverage will do Stonehouse's cause no good at all.[6]

A couple of days later, on 25 March, Stonehouse is told by a journalist that Bow Street Magistrates' Court has now issued a provisional warrant for Sheila Buckley's arrest. She is staying with a friend, Denis Streeter, in Cronulla Bay, a beach resort twenty-six kilometres outside Sydney. Stonehouse gets his daughter Jane, now in Australia, to tip her off. Cronulla Bay is in New South Wales, so Buckley decides that she should do what Stonehouse has suggested: cross the state boundary to Victoria where Patterson could represent her too. Streeter agrees to drive her the 600 miles to Melbourne and they leave Cronulla Bay immediately.

Scotland Yard's Etheridge and DI David Townley, who have now made their way to Melbourne, decide they want to serve Buckley's warrant personally. Flights to Sydney are delayed by industrial action, but they are on a mission and book a private plane. It's an extravagant gesture that will need some explaining back at the Yard, especially as they arrive in Cronulla Bay just after Buckley has left. Crestfallen, they put out a search for Streeter's Volkswagen.

Buckley and Streeter are still on the road. After overnighting in New South Wales, by early evening on the 26th they are in Victoria, but still 130 miles short of Melbourne. Just outside the small town of Maffra, an inspector at a pest-control point recognises their vehicle and phones ahead to police. They spot the Volkswagen and pull it over. 'I don't know what this is all about,' Buckley tells Streeter, before being taken to Maffra police station. At 10.30pm, DI John Sullivan, a man who by now knows a lot about her, arrives and identifies himself to Buckley. 'Are you Mrs Sheila Elizabeth Buckley?' he asks. 'Yes,' says Buckley. Sullivan informs her he has a warrant on charges of theft and conspiracy to commit fraud, and arrests her. He drives her to the location where he interviewed Stonehouse three months ago – Commonwealth Police headquarters in downtown Melbourne.[7]

Arriving at 1.30am wearing a crocheted poncho and white flared jeans, Buckley manages a smile for waiting photographers before being escorted inside. She spends a night in a cell at the Melbourne watch house while Stonehouse rants about not being able to arrange bail for her. The following morning, wearing the same clothes and described as being 'of no fixed abode', Buckley is also bailed for surety of A$1,000. Stonehouse books her a room in one of Melbourne's largest hotels. 'I'm so sorry,' he tells her over and over. 'I swear I'll make it up to you one day. I promise.'[8]

To top off Stonehouse's disaster of a week, on 27 March he hears that Sir Charles Forte is resigning from the board of London Capital Group, the renamed BBT. He has been *in situ* less than a year and attended only two meetings. 'I never wanted to go on the board in the first place but was persuaded to do so,' says Forte. 'We all make mistakes and I have made mine. When you make a mistake, you try to rectify it. Now I have done so. I have resigned.'[9]

Good Friday, 28 March, is a public holiday in Australia, but at the offices of Patterson and Gabriel Solicitors, at 358 Lonsdale Street in Melbourne, a few people are hard at work, including Jim Patterson. He has a busy week ahead with four new cases as well as Stonehouse and Buckley to deal with. Before then, he needs to collect a copy of the select committee report and that afternoon stops off to do so with his teenage daughter at 31 Montalto Avenue in Toorak, the home of British consulate official Basil Harries.[10]

Harries invites them in and he and Patterson soon discover that they are fellow Liverpudlians. Patterson clearly wants to offload and he begins to talk openly about Stonehouse's suicidal tendencies, split personality and apparent belief in the existence of Joseph Markham. Patterson seems to believe that this is all genuine. Harries is surprised, for the police, with whom he is in frequent contact, have no truck with the idea that Stonehouse is suicidal. And although stories that Stonehouse suffers from schizophrenia have appeared in the British press – and have even been expounded by Stonehouse's mother Rosina – Harries's boss Ivor Vincent believes that it's all whipped up by Patterson to help his case.[11]

Harries is one of the many public servants, both British and Australian, who have been spending far too much time on Stonehouse. He hopes that, with Stonehouse and Buckley on bail until 5 May, there will be a let-up – but he is out of luck. After Easter, he receives a routine visit from Etheridge, Gillespie and Sullivan to update him. The policemen are in a talkative mood and Gillespie reports that Stonehouse is now being especially hostile towards him. Harries and Etheridge have also been on the receiving end of such antagonism and all three agree that it's probably best to stay away from the bail hearings.[12]

Stonehouse's anger at the authorities does not extend to the countries that might, just might, offer him citizenship. He is busy exploring his options and working his contacts, writing to eight countries whose leaders he knows personally in order to seek a passport. Sweden politely says that Stonehouse would require a resident's permit before he could be granted one. Botswana sends a curt rejection. A former London School of Economics acquaintance, Canadian premier Pierre Trudeau, discusses it with his fellow prime ministers Wilson and Whitlam before saying no. Stonehouse hopes that his Bangladesh citizenship comes with a Bangladesh passport, but little does he know that when James Callaghan hears speculation about the possibility, he tells British diplomats in Dacca to strongly express Her Majesty's government's displeasure. There is an ominous silence from Stonehouse's old East African stomping grounds of Zambia, Tanzania and Kenya.[13]

Mauritius, a country he has visited several times when he was in the Colonial Office, appears to be his best hope and, on 10 April, he sends his daughter Jane there. She visits the health minister, an old friend of her father, who publicly floats the idea of granting him asylum and a passport. Only seven years an independent country, the Mauritians check out the British government's attitude. Callaghan fears Stonehouse would use such a passport to go to Brazil, while Wilson bluntly expresses displeasure. The Mauritian cabinet duly decline the application. This, and his tell-all pieces in the *News of World*, have seen off any residual sympathy at cabinet.[14]

Now they have wind of what he's up to, the British authorities need to get Stonehouse home sooner rather than later. On

29 April, six new charges are brought against him, including a joint conspiracy charge with Buckley. New warrants are issued and seventy witnesses turn up at Bow Street Magistrates' Court to sign statements. They include Jim Charlton, Jean Markham, Elsie Mildoon and Bridget McBride, widow of the late Neil McBride, the former Labour MP whose forged signature had appeared on the Markham passport application.[15]

Once again Etheridge and Townley, by now the Fraud Squad's best-travelled coppers, take the warrants out to Australia in order finally to bring Stonehouse and Buckley back to face justice. A hearing on 5 May opens with the accused sharing the front benches of the tiny Melbourne Magistrates' Court with British and Australian journalists. Stonehouse offers to return to London voluntarily if extradition charges are withdrawn. Whispered negotiations in the corridors produce a surprising reply: the prosecution agrees, provided Buckley returns with him. Any relief Etheridge and Townley feel is premature, though. Buckley's counsel thinks it a ploy to strengthen the 'conspiracy' charge and declines. The court adjourns until 26 May.

Hot on the heels of this decision, the Commons select committee produces its second report and gives Stonehouse a month to either attend the House of Commons or resign. If he fails to do this, the committee says, the House will debate a motion to expel him. Wilson says that the government would take a neutral stance on such a motion and Chief Whip Bob Mellish seeks the prime minister's authority to prepare for a by-election.[16]

Time is running out for Stonehouse and he needs to reverse public opinion. The tireless Barbara, who has now returned to England, is his best asset and she agrees to go in front of the cameras again. She tells the BBC that, although it is hard to understand some of the things her husband has done, having spoken to his doctors, the family now accept that he has had a personality change and that he has been ill. She asks for compassion, understanding and an extension to the Commons timetable to give Stonehouse time to attend.[17]

Over on ITV, she describes a schizoid personality change in her husband over the past eighteen months and criticises the select committee for not going to Australia to assess his mental state for themselves. She is asked about reports she left Australia because of Stonehouse's continued daily meetings with Buckley. Barbara says that they have to meet because they report daily for bail and her husband accompanies Buckley to protect her from the press. Asked if she is happy about it, she pauses before explaining that 'it is something that is necessary at the moment but not something I'm prepared to discuss'. Meanwhile, Buckley is secretly delighted that, with Barbara gone, she can now see more of Stonehouse. He even takes her to the jazz club and introduces her to the old friends of Clive Mildoon.[18]

On 9 May, the man himself sits down for a twenty-five-minute television interview. He criticises the state of Britain, the press and Scotland Yard. He says that Barbara has delivered his book to publishers W. H. Allen and is negotiating terms on his behalf. She will rejoin him in Australia 'if' – he says after an almost imperceptible pause – 'I am here a very long time'.[19]

A Commons debate on expulsion is set for 12 June, but in Melbourne there are further court adjournments until the following day. Stonehouse writes to select committee chairman George Strauss claiming that, as a man of honour, he would have 'returned voluntarily to the UK if any indication had been given that criminal charges were to be brought. No such indication was given before my arrest.' He pleads for the debate to be moved so he can attend.[20]

But in Britain, power does not end with parliament which, as a privy counsellor, Stonehouse knows only too well. Desperate to put his case to the Commons in person, he composes a 4,600-word petition to the Queen. 'Your Majesty should now be made aware that your petitioner intends to exercise his rights and duties as a Member of Parliament [and] therefore now intends publicly and openly to leave Australia to travel to the UK to attend the House of Commons.'[21]

The Queen's representative in Victoria is the governor, Sir Henry Winneke, a former chief justice of Australia, and Stonehouse wants to deliver the voluminous handwritten petition personally. He telephones in advance and, at 4.05pm on 8 June, makes his way past the guard at the main gate of Government House. At the State Entrance, an aide reports Stonehouse's arrival. The governor sends word back: he does not 'regard it as being within my authority' either to 'receive the petition or transmit it as demanded'. Stonehouse thrusts the petition under the aide's arm and storms off.[22]

True to his royal word, Stonehouse books tickets for a flight back to London on 9 June for Mathew, Jane and himself. By the time they get to Melbourne's Tullamarine Airport, there's a crowd of press and cameramen waiting. Surrounded by popping flashguns and shouted questions, he berates one reporter: 'I've told you ad infinitum all I want to do is to perform my duties as an MP.' The Stonehouses collect their boarding passes for flight BA931 and pass through customs and immigration. It's all so smooth that Stonehouse wonders if a deal has been done between the British and Australian governments.[23]

But much as the Australians would like to see the back of him, the law must be respected and they are not going to let him jump bail. As he leaves the airport lounge, just a few steps from the plane, a familiar figure appears. It's Bob Gillespie, clutching a warrant for his arrest. The new charge is attempting to obstruct the course of justice under Section 43 of Australia's Crimes Act. 'You've gone as far as you can, Daddy,' says Jane as police bundle him away.[24]

Stonehouse is taken to the cells at the Melbourne watch house where, now that he is in custody, his tie and comb are removed. For once looking dishevelled, he appears before Melbourne magistrates in the afternoon and is remanded in custody until his scheduled court appearance four days later. He remains silent throughout the hearing, but hands the magistrate a pencil note protesting at the absence of the prosecuting counsel. The magistrate says this is irrelevant and sends him to Melbourne's notorious Pentridge Prison, site of Australia's last execution only eight years earlier. Stonehouse faces a much less severe fate than that, but he's desperate to get attention and still no one is listening. Once locked away, he goes on hunger strike and refuses to talk for three days.

Stonehouse is then transferred to a ward on the hospital wing where the prison psychiatrist Dr Allen Bartholomew sees him. Stonehouse shakes his proffered hand and then turns his back to the doctor. Bartholomew thinks his demeanour strange throughout the first half-hour examination. He considers him partly hysterical, with the possibility of an underlying schizophrenic illness, but partly malingering or manipulative. Bartholomew says that even if he is deliberately 'protesting', he is still mentally ill.[25]

At Heathrow, Jane and Mathew are met by Barbara in an emotional reunion. Tearful, Jane says it seems terribly unfair not to give a man a chance to put his side of the story when they could so easily just postpone the Commons debate for a month.

The select committee start to think the same. On the evening of 11 June, they decide that although responsibility for failing to return to the UK should be laid entirely at Stonehouse's door, it is for the government to decide whether the debate planned for the next day should be postponed given his mental state and the risk of prejudicing judicial proceedings.[26]

The prime minister has also been thinking about Stonehouse. Wilson is advised by the cabinet secretary not to comment on defector Josef Frolík's forthcoming book, which is believed to be an exaggerated account of his time as Labour attaché at the Czech embassy in London between 1964 and 1966. But it does refer to an unnamed Labour MP, Wilson is told, who was 'greedy for money' and 'involved in some sort of homosexual trap in Czechoslovakia. Both are believed to refer to Mr Stonehouse.' In his own neat hand, Wilson writes in the margin, 'Not, I think, homo.'[27]

At a cabinet sub-committee following the select committee's retreat, the prime minister tells Ted Short to announce that the debate has been postponed but will be held 'at the first opportunity'. The statement will need to make clear, he says, 'that there was no implication that the government condoned Mr Stonehouse's behaviour, in particular the deceptions he had employed; that they were however concerned not with alleged criminal actions but with his failure to perform parliamentary duties and in that connection greatly regretted the continuing non-representation of the Walsall North constituency'. The meeting notes that although Stonehouse's continuing absence will reduce the government's majority, it will not affect their position on select committees. But, a fortnight later on 26 June, the Conservatives win a by-election in Woolwich. It's a good start for their new leader Margaret Thatcher who replaced Heath in February, but it leaves Wilson with a majority of just one. The need for a resolution to the Stonehouse affair gets ever stronger.[28]

It's 30 June before the Melbourne magistrate finally announces his decision: the attorney general should extradite Stonehouse and Buckley after the statutory fifteen-day period. After hearing evidence of Stonehouse's depression and suicidal tendencies from the psychiatrist Dr Gibney, the magistrate rules that he has no power to extend bail. He commits Stonehouse to the Immigration Detention Centre rather than prison, but when Stonehouse learns that there are no facilities for Buckley there, he opts to spend the fifteen days with his 'new-found friends' back at Pentridge, where he entertains the reporter Bob Friend again, this time in his cell. 'Being away on this sabbatical, if one may call it that,' says Stonehouse, 'helps to clear the brain and understand things a little more clearly.'[29]

PART SIX

The Reckoning

25

THE HOMECOMING

It's the cool winter morning of Thursday 17 July. Buckley has been behind the old walls and gates of Fairlea Women's Prison for over two weeks, where she's shared a cell with prostitutes and a murder suspect. Soon after breakfast, she's told it's time to leave. She picks up her things, says goodbye to the women from her dormitory and is taken to the governor's office. There's something of a crowd waiting: the governor, DCS Etheridge and British WPCs Shields and Jackson, who have been specially brought to Melbourne to escort her home. Etheridge plays it strictly by the book. He has a warrant to take her to the UK, he says, and shows it to the governor. Shields and Jackson take Buckley into police custody.[1]

Now for the big one. Etheridge is driven five miles across the Melbourne suburbs to Pentridge Prison. He's seen that gatehouse before; it's modelled on the famous entrance to London's Wormwood Scrubs, a place where many of his previous customers have done time. Stonehouse is as ready to face Etheridge as he will ever be. Etheridge goes through the formal drill, shows the warrant to the prison superintendent and takes Stonehouse into police custody. Stonehouse neither likes nor trusts the man and is resolutely silent.[2]

The two heavily guarded police cars drive twenty minutes to the airport. At Tullamarine, they sneak in through the service entrance to avoid the cameras and reach a secure area of the airport at 10.30am. There's an hour to spare. But the hour turns into two, then six, as a cracked windscreen and then a faulty nosewheel delay the plane's departure. As a former minister of aviation, none of this is a surprise to Stonehouse. At nearly 5pm, they finally board.[3]

The cabin crew show Stonehouse and Etheridge to a row of three seats. Stonehouse takes the window seat, Etheridge leaves the middle seat empty and takes the aisle. A day and a half of silence in cramped economy seats is going to be a challenge. The row in front mirrors this set-up, with Buckley and her escort. The flight fills up with Brits returning from family visits and Aussies starting the trip of a lifetime. And it's one they won't forget: there's a media scrum of TV cameras, photographers and journalists fighting to get near the prisoners. 'I am in fine form and ready to face whatever is in store,' Stonehouse informs one. The cabin crew restore order and BA 979 finally departs, albeit five and a half hours late.

It is going to be a long night. They haven't even passed Alice Springs when dinner is served, but Stonehouse refuses to eat in his seat. 'I have no intention of breaking bread with Scotland Yard,' he says. Etheridge knows his prisoners can't do a runner while the plane is in the air and allows Stonehouse to move to another seat. There he has his first meal since leaving Pentridge, complete with wine. It's not Connoisseurs of Claret quality, and definitely not Connoisseurs of Claret quantity, but it's a decent drop of red. And at least he's away from Etheridge – if only momentarily.

Once they touch down to refuel in Tehran, Etheridge takes no chances. Stonehouse is still a flight risk and Tehran Airport has form when it comes to trouble: four months earlier, there was a shoot-out with hijackers on the runway. Etheridge and his team guard an exit each and Stonehouse decides it's a good time to investigate the facilities. He stays in the toilet an inordinate amount of time and when they knock, he refuses to answer. Just as they speculate on what stunt he might be pulling – and what to do about it – out he comes, newly shaven, tie perfectly knotted, ready for his reappearance in London.[4]

The plane touches down at Heathrow at 3.15pm on Friday 18 July, after thirty-five hours on board. It's the middle of the night Australian time and Stonehouse and Buckley haven't had much sleep. They were first on this plane and now they're going to be last off. The other passengers gather up their things and file out by the front exit while the two prisoners wait. Back on British soil, Etheridge repeats that he has warrants for their arrest, and he cautions both. Stonehouse can add an arrest on British soil to those in Africa and Australia, Buckley just the latter.

They disembark onto a barriered walkway lined with journalists, photographers and TV crews straining for a glimpse or a word. Etheridge leads the way, then Stonehouse and Townley follow a couple of paces behind. Etheridge shepherds Stonehouse into the first of two unmarked black cars and then Buckley follows into the second car as flashbulbs light up the cloudy sky. In among the crowd, there is no sign of Barbara. She claims to be spending the day with friends to avoid the chaos and her absence is well noted.[5]

The prisoners are driven to the British Airports Authority Constabulary – once Stonehouse's ministerial responsibility – where DS Bryan Martin waits for them. He frisks Stonehouse, a female colleague checks Buckley and they are asked to identify their luggage. The cases are unpacked and Martin itemises the contents with Buckley's help; Stonehouse refuses to assist and looks on in silence. There is one item in Buckley's brown suitcase on which Martin and Buckley can't agree. Martin describes it as a black full-length crepe slip. Buckley says it is an evening dress she wears with a jacket. Martin is not going to pick a fight and writes 'evening dress'. Their luggage goes off to New Scotland Yard to be stored with the rest of the evidence.[6]

Stonehouse is soon whizzing along the A4 in the opposite direction to the Friday-night hordes escaping the capital. His car goes past the turning for Hounslow, where he and Barbara had their first house, and continues down the familiar Art Deco Mile, reversing the route taken by the man who tried to make himself disappear seven months earlier.

As his and Buckley's cars reach the Cromwell Road, it starts to rain. The shops of Knightsbridge are visible through steamed-up windows and, at 5.30pm, they arrive at Bow Street police station to yet another press mob. 'Here they are, here they are,' yells one of the photographers popping away behind the crush barrier. 'Who's in that one?' asks another before the cars disappear into the station yard.[7]

Once inside, Stonehouse and Buckley are swiftly charged. Stonehouse knows that every word will be evidence in court and it's time to break his silence. 'Why has Scotland Yard made no attempt to interview me about these charges while they were in Australia?' he demands. 'Why did Scotland Yard not warn me that these charges were being considered against me so that I could return of my own volition, rather than have to be subjected to the unnecessary indignity of replying to an extradition charge?' Buckley is asked if she has anything to say. 'I do not,' she replies. Stonehouse and Buckley are confident of bail and just want to get on with things.[8]

Their solicitor Jim Patterson has flown over, together with Melbourne barrister George Hampel, and they have an application ready to go. In the streets outside, the bars and restaurants of Covent Garden are warming up for a busy Saturday night and, if the magistrates grant bail, Stonehouse and Buckley could be home before dark. But the five-hour delay in Melbourne has caught up with them. They find out the magistrates have left for the day and are ushered down for a night in the cells with assorted Friday-night drunks and miscreants.

The following morning, the presiding magistrate is Evelyn Russell. He is the most experienced of the Bow Street beaks – and he'll need it all with this case. The fugitives' return was all over the Friday-night news and the morning papers have revealed the time and place of today's hearing. The public gallery is packed and journalists cram into the tiny press box immediately behind the dock. Russell rattles through routine Saturday-morning cases of petty crime, prostitution and drunkenness, and then calls Stonehouse and Buckley.

There are no objections to bailing the demure Buckley. She is free to return to her parents' semi in Abbey Wood. Stonehouse, on the other hand, has serious form. It's too big a risk; the director of public prosecutions wants him in custody. The Australian barrister Hampel argues that Stonehouse could easily have skipped bail down under and didn't. And besides, he needs to be free to attend the House of Commons. It's a valiant attempt, but it doesn't play with Russell who declines bail and remands Stonehouse to Brixton Prison.

Stonehouse thinks the government is behind all this, a suspicion that hardens when he gets to Brixton to find that a cell has already been prepared for him. Over the weekend, he fumes at the political stitch-up and refuses to take food. Barbara visits him in jail on Saturday afternoon and, on her way out, tells journalists that he is not protesting against the prison authorities but at the refusal of bail which prevents him going to the House of Commons. As she walks off, she obligingly turns round for photographers.[9]

Buckley spends a more comfortable weekend at her parents' home where she has agreed to live. She calls Barbara for what she describes as 'a personal chat', but it is a frosty call. Barbara's support for her husband is increasingly guarded. She tells newspapers that she will stand by him and do everything to help: 'But I haven't a crystal ball and I can't say what the situation will be in the future. I cannot pre-judge the issue.' She also can't stop Buckley visiting her husband in prison. 'I don't care if Barbara's there or not,' Buckley tells everyone. 'I'm going.' But Stonehouse doesn't want to whisper sweet nothings. 'Write this down,' he demands, as he gets her to reply to constituents' letters instead.[10]

At 9am on 21 July, Remand Prisoner 334093 in Brixton's C-wing is told that there's a lawyer to see him and he's taken along to an area set aside for solicitors' visits. Stonehouse is expecting someone from his own legal team, but it is Kenneth Jones, solicitor for London Capital Group, carrying a writ for £198,426. Stonehouse turns away to go back to his cell, but a warder blocks his way, giving Jones the chance to tap Stonehouse on the shoulder, signifying that the writ has been served. Two prison officers try to get Stonehouse to sit down, but he slips and lashes out, sending an industrial metal ashtray flying across the room. He gets up, tries to charge past them and is restrained. A prison officer has a bruised elbow and Stonehouse is treated for a slight cut to a finger, which becomes his whole hand in the press's version of events.[11]

Across London, Mr Justice Gare, a High Court judge sitting in chambers, hears a fifty-minute submission from George Hampel. It is familiar ground – he's not a flight risk and needs to do his parliamentary duty – but Gare rules that the decision of the Bow Street magistrate stands and Stonehouse must remain in custody until the following Monday. Jim Patterson runs the political angle again on the BBC's *World at One* and, the following day, Stonehouse writes to the home secretary, his old boss Roy Jenkins, asking to be escorted from Brixton to the House to vote. But there's no love lost and Jenkins coldly replies that he has 'no authority to proceed in the way you suggest'.[12]

Hampel and Patterson can't do anything more and fly back to Australia, leaving Stonehouse to represent himself at the next bail hearing on 28 July. It is his fiftieth birthday but there are no good wishes and he is remanded in custody again. Sure that he's fighting a political case, he wants a lawyer who knows about persecution, and Australian-born Geoffrey Robertson has defended controversial psychologist R. D. Laing and the anti-apartheid activist Peter Hain as a junior barrister. Stonehouse invites him to Brixton and takes him on. At Bow Street, Robertson argues that Stonehouse can't run away – 'He has no money, no passport and a face that has launched a thousand Fleet Street headlines' – but the magistrates remain stony-faced.[13]

The Stonehouse show plays every Monday in Bow Street. The weekend's drunk and disorderly cases amuse the gallery, but there's nothing to lift Stonehouse's spirits. He complains to the Home Office that his mail is being censored, the Walsall North Labour Party votes not to readopt him, and there are growing calls for him to do the honourable thing and resign. There is further public outrage when he is granted legal aid.[14]

The summer grinds on. Stonehouse complains that he is getting worse treatment than other remand prisoners, being kept in a cell measuring eight feet by five feet for twenty-two hours a day with prison canteen food brought in. Like everyone else, he exercises briefly in the yard and slops out his bucket before the door is locked for the night at 4pm. But every day there is half a bottle of his own claret allowed, which he drinks from a plastic cup while, in the world outside, Connoisseurs of Claret bankruptcy administrators raise £3,500 for creditors at an auction of surplus stock.

On 18 August, Stonehouse makes his seventh and most impassioned application yet for bail. Clasping the Bible eighteen years after declining it when he was sworn into parliament, he asks: 'Why can't I as a human being have my freedom when we are locked in this jungle?' 'The answer is, at the moment Mr Stonehouse, you can't,' says the magistrate. Drawing his Bible closer, Stonehouse declaims, 'In God's name, how can a man make out his case for bail and for liberty?' The magistrate tells him 'we are not here to argue the case' and remands him for a further two weeks. It's a week longer than usual because of the upcoming August bank holiday and Stonehouse storms off to the cells below.[15]

Wednesday 27 August is shaping up to be another dull 24 hours in Brixton. Stonehouse's next bail hearing is not for five days and it will be a routine day of reading, slopping out, pacing the yard and staring at the walls. But then he is told that his solicitor Michael O'Dell needs to see him urgently. Without warning or explanation, the magistrates have suddenly granted bail of £40,000 and the hunt is on to find it.

All afternoon, O'Dell rings round Stonehouse's contacts looking for help. It is not easy. Some have been burned in the BBT fallout and who is to say that a man who has disappeared once won't do it again? It's early evening before they have the money. Stonehouse puts up £10,000 – it's £10,000 he doesn't really have – and two anonymous friends each put up £15,000. Stonehouse packs his few prison possessions into an empty Weetabix box and, at 8.40pm, is driven out of Brixton in O'Dell's sporty red saloon car back to Sancroft Street. It is the first time he has been in his own home since he left for

Heathrow on 19 November the previous year. The whole family are there and Stonehouse enjoys a glass of wine – it's too soon for champagne – and Barbara has put together some supper. His first meal at home for nine months is quiche Lorraine, French beans and new potatoes, followed by greengages – and it's lovely.[16]

26

BACK IN THE HOUSE

Stonehouse wakes up in his own bed the following morning, but a lie-in isn't an option as he has to report to Kennington police station before 10am. It's only a fifteen-minute walk down the Kennington Road, but the press will be hovering so Jane Stonehouse drops him off in her ageing Ford Anglia. He says good morning to the journalists outside and saunters up the steps of the station with five minutes to spare.

When he emerges, he takes questions from reporters who have been there for two hours. His priority, he says, is to make two speeches, one to the House of Commons, the other to his constituency. 'But your constituents say they don't want you,' comes the response. 'The constituency committee made that decision in most unusual circumstances,' says Stonehouse, 'and I'm not going to comment before discussing it with the chairman of the party.' He's rattled. 'Anyway I don't want to make off-the-cuff, on-the-pavement comments,' he says over his shoulder as a traffic warden writes a parking ticket for Jane. They drive off before he can complete it, leaving the bemused warden shaking his head at the departing Ford. Don't these people know what a yellow line means?[1]

Now that he's free, Stonehouse needs to turn public opinion his way. He takes time out to drop into Brixton with Barbara to see a friend he made on remand – 'a delightful chap,' he tells the *Daily Mirror* who are waiting with their photographer. 'Very nice and helpful while I was there.'[2]

Barbara sells her story to *Woman* magazine. It was a rags-to-riches love story, she says, and tells of her 'first real feelings of bitterness' at the thought of him having an affair with Buckley. She adds that 'being my husband's girlfriend could not have been all that marvellous for Sheila Buckley. He'd always come home to me no matter what time of night it was.' But she admits that, when he re-emerged in Australia, she realised how he had been ready to abandon the family and the time might come when she feels she has had enough.[3]

For now, she's the supportive wife and accompanies him to the Labour Party conference in Blackpool at the end of September. They are both going down with the flu, but it's part of his defence strategy to show he's a functioning MP so they struggle on. And when he gets a hostile reception at a conference fringe meeting, it's Barbara who snaps back to a heckler: 'Are you the judge in this case?' Most MPs, though, avoid being seen with him.[4]

On weightier matters, the party is far from united, but Harold Wilson's keynote speech – in which he rips into Labour's left wing – is a rousing performance and he leaves to a standing ovation. The hall quickly empties but Stonehouse remains: he really doesn't have anywhere to go. The ostracised MP cuts a lonely figure in a bank of empty seats, and it's left to an unelected, middle-aged woman to take pity on him. It's the always decent Mary Wilson who, ever since she told her husband to lend the Stonehouse family their Scilly Isles holiday home, has had a soft spot for them.[5]

The Stonehouses are not back from Blackpool long when shocking news arrives from Australia. Jim Patterson has died suddenly at his Melbourne home. Mrs Patterson says he had been suffering from heart trouble for ten years and had been under great strain while representing Stonehouse. The man who in public attributed Stonehouse's actions to mental illness has been a guiding light through the Australian justice system and someone Stonehouse listened to – a rarity from one who is always convinced he knows best. He will be missed in London as well as Melbourne.[6]

Stonehouse's London lawyers are now the tenacious solicitor O'Dell and the young barrister Robertson. Like Patterson, they find their new client demanding. He is obsessed with the idea of explaining himself to the House of Commons, a move that Robertson thinks will turn public opinion against him further, and he urges Stonehouse to resign. Perhaps, says Stonehouse, but only after he has made a statement to the House. He has been looking forward to this moment for months and has no intention of giving up now.[7]

But before he can face that particular audience of former colleagues, he is obliged to face another at a BBT/LCG shareholders' meeting and takes O'Dell with him for moral and legal support. The annual report reveals that large sums were transferred to Stonehouse and his nominees. The other directors are photographed together and Charlton speaks up: 'It was a terrible shock, what we thought was a terrible tragedy,' he says, businesslike in his pin-stripe suit and horn-rimmed spectacles. 'He is a man who has done great work and it was with great regret that we found his affairs to be in such a tangled skein.' When confronted by reporters, Stonehouse retorts, 'I think we want to get at the facts, and the facts are not in this report,' declaring that matters are being investigated and everything is sub-judice.[8]

Prime Minister's Questions are drawing to a close on Monday 20 October when Stonehouse enters the chamber and immediately creates a stir by sitting on the opposition benches. With his trial imminent, Stonehouse has spent three days negotiating with the speaker's learned clerks to get his statement cleared. Jane and Julia Stonehouse are in the public gallery, Buckley is sitting behind them and Robertson is close by. As she had done on touchdown at Heathrow, Barbara stays away.

After PMQs, Wilson makes a statement on setting up a royal commission on the NHS, but pointedly leaves the chamber before Stonehouse is called. The House is unusually crowded for a Monday and there have been rumours of a mass walkout by MPs but, for most of them, hearing from the returning MP first-hand is irresistible and they stay in their seats. Stonehouse has been warned that he must stick closely to the agreed script and Selwyn Lloyd, in his final stint as speaker, is not a man to be messed around. He soon has to interrupt. 'Let there be no misunderstanding about this,' he says. 'The right honourable member is entitled to say only what I have passed'. Stonehouse is on thin ice before he's properly begun.

He apologises for the trouble he's caused and sets the record, as he would wish it to be, straight: 'I deny the allegations that I was a spy for the Czechs. I can only regret that the original stories were printed.' In the third person, he takes his lead from Dr Gibney and his mental breakdown and 'reactive depression' becomes 'psychiatric suicide' which 'took the form of a repudiation of Stonehouse because that life had become absolutely unbearable to him'. He's getting his defence in early and Selwyn Lloyd interrupts Stonehouse six times in thirteen minutes, before he finally wraps up and sits down. The House empties; there is evidently less interest in Health Secretary Barbara Castle's speech on one-parent families than in the antics of the member for Walsall North.[9]

The next edition of *Private Eye* shows Stonehouse with a newspaper in hand under the caption 'Totally Innocent MP Wrongly Accused'. It's what he's come to expect from the satirical magazine he was planning to sue before he disappeared. It's the courts that will decide, he tells himself, and that will be very soon at his committal hearing.[10]

This is a preliminary public hearing where a magistrate decides if the prosecution have enough evidence to proceed, but the media are more interested in Buckley than in legal niceties. 'Sheila's Fashion Show ... The Buckley Collection,' teases the *Daily Mirror* above photos of her daily courtroom outfits. It's enough to send Barbara to Ireland for a short break and, while she is away, Jane Stonehouse moves into Sancroft Street to be with her father. Increasingly, as his other supporters lose patience, the pressure is on Stonehouse's eldest daughter to speak up for him.[11]

During the hearings, Stonehouse gets up every day at 5am and writes down – in green ink on House of Commons paper – the questions he wants Robertson to ask that day. At 9am, he takes them along to the defence counsel's room at Horseferry Road Magistrates' Court and listens as Robertson patiently explains why most of them are not relevant. After a morning in court, they both return to the defence room and unpack the picnic lunch that Barbara, now back from Ireland, sends in every day.[12]

Robertson comments that 'if somebody came from another planet, he might think it was a trial for adultery not theft and forgery' but, in court, legal arguments, not salacious gossip, are the order of the day. Alleged insurance fraud of £125,000 is the most serious allegation and Robertson argues that to complete the alleged crime, Stonehouse would have had to remain hidden for several years, beyond the period under which claims can be brought. The magistrate agrees and strikes out the insurance charges but it's a small victory.[13]

On 5 November, Stonehouse is sent for trial at the Old Bailey on sixteen remaining charges, and Buckley on five. He's not going to accept this quietly. In a twenty-minute outburst from the dock, he reads from a seventeen-page prepared statement. He declares it 'a political trial brought for political reasons' and protests his innocence: 'I am not a criminal. I am not a forger. I am not a thief. I am not a con man.' The next day's papers can't decide whether to focus on that or on the upcoming anniversary of one man who is still missing: Lord Lucan.[14]

Success in overturning the insurance charges goes to Stonehouse's head. He's now convinced he can win on all counts; maybe he won't resign his seat after all. But he needs a silk now that the case is going to trial at the Old Bailey and deputes Robertson to meet several leading counsel at the Inns of Court. When Richard Du Cann QC, one of London's top criminal barristers, takes the brief, it makes the BBC news. With someone of Du Cann's stature on Stonehouse's team, this case is far from over.

Du Cann's first priority is to find out if Barbara knew anything of her husband's plans; it would ruin his strategy if it were to later emerge that she was party to an insurance swindle. After an hour's tough questioning, Du Cann and Robertson are certain that her husband's disappearance was as big a shock to her as anyone else. Barbara is entirely innocent.

Robertson points out to Stonehouse that a guilty plea would spare Barbara and Buckley a fresh round of publicity – and Buckley the ordeal of a drawn-out trial. Stonehouse asks what kind of sentence he could expect. Robertson says that a guilty plea and a show of contrition might bring a maximum three-year jail sentence. He says a professional defence might result in five years or fewer if found guilty. But pleading guilty and showing contrition is not the Stonehouse way. He won't admit to or apologise for anything, nor, it turns out, will he keep a low profile.[15]

On 24 November, he holds a press conference to launch the book that was momentarily confiscated in Melbourne. Elegant and alert in a dark suit and patterned tie, he's at pains to point out that Death of an Idealist was not written for money. 'It was a form of therapy,' he says. 'It exposes public life today; the humbug and sham.' More of that comes his way on 2 January, when the director of public prosecutions orders the reinstatement of the five insurance charges. 'It's political,' says Stonehouse.[16]

Early in February, evidence given the previous year by Czech defector Josef Frolík to a US Senate sub-committee is released in Washington. Frolík had been asked if the Czech security services concentrated only on government departments dealing with intelligence or national security. No, he replied, they include holders of political posts, 'for example, Mr John Stonehouse, former minister of technology in Great Britain'. This is a specific accusation that sounds authoritative and comes at a sensitive time. Stonehouse knows he has to respond and there is only one place he wants to do it: the House of Commons. This time he isn't so bold as to issue an outright denial. He concedes that he did indeed associate with the Czechs in London in the 1960s – but he thought they were embassy staff, not intelligence officers, a mistake he says ministers of either party could have unwittingly made. If he still remembers the clandestine cash drops to his car, he does not mention them.[17]

Convinced that he will soon be a free man able to resume his political career and that he is being politically persecuted, he sends a stream of letters to Chief Whip Bob Mellish and the prime minister over Labour Party attempts to deselect him in Walsall North. Mellish is facing a weekly battle to get the government's legislation through the Commons and has no time for such nonsense. He forwards a file of the correspondence to attorney general Sam Silkin QC who responds, 'like yourself, I find his letters almost breathtaking'.[18]

The other silk with an eye on Stonehouse is his own, Du Cann, but Stonehouse can't work him out. Dark and brooding, the barrister always keeps his distance from clients, is never on first-name terms with them and never predicts the outcome of their case. He and Stonehouse have eight two-hour meetings, but it's not enough for Stonehouse who doesn't think he is being paid the attention he deserves and he does a bit of brooding himself.[19]

The rest of his legal team, Robertson and O'Dell, are trying to explain Stonehouse's attempt to fake his own death. If it is madness, it is too carefully thought-out to win over a jury and they need a better explanation. Robertson contacts a previous client, R. D. Laing, the controversial psychiatrist. The title of Laing's most famous book, *The Divided Self,* comes closest yet to describing the state of mind in which Stonehouse claimed that he really was Joe Markham. Laing tells Robertson that 'a man in public life begins to feel desperately trapped by the lie he is in and he acts by acting out a weird death-rebirth fantasy'. It is the most promising lead they have, but when Robertson reports it to Du Cann, he's deeply sceptical.[20]

Three weeks before the trial, there is a major political development that makes the future representation of Walsall North critical. On 16 March 1976, Harold Wilson suddenly announces his own resignation. It's the same day that Buckingham Palace announce the divorce of Princess Margaret and Lord Snowdon, a canny move by either Press Secretary Joe Haines or the Palace or both. Wilson is barely two years into his fourth stint as prime minister and is only sixty years old. Lobby correspondents float various conspiracies, including long-standing wild theories that he was a Russian agent, but Wilson maintains that this is a long-planned decision, as his inner circle confirm.

Wilson's departure puts even more pressure on Labour's fragile majority and the new prime minister, James Callaghan, is the man who has to hold it together. But on 5 April, the night before he takes over, he's bumped from the headlines. *Newsday*, BBC2's flagship early evening news programme, leads with the story that Stonehouse has resigned from the Labour Party and will now sit as an independent. Stonehouse's defection turns the government's overall majority of one in the House of Commons into a minority of one. The Conservatives demand that the composition of Commons committees be adjusted to reflect this and the cause of the problem is on standby in the studio to give his own view.[21]

Interviewed live by presenter Ludovic Kennedy, Stonehouse calls for a general election, saying that Callaghan has no legitimacy and that Labour has lost the right to govern. He cites the weak pound, roaring inflation, terrorism and British industry's deep malaise. Kennedy reminds him that his local Labour Party have just voted 47-1 to deselect him, but the MP insists his own postbag runs in his favour and he's staying put.[22]

A week later, the trouble-making continues and Stonehouse gets ordered out of the House of Commons after calling into question the activities of Sir Julian Hodge, the Cardiff banker who he believes let him down on BBT. Ignoring instructions to stop his speech on the grounds of irrelevance and tedious repetition, Stonehouse carries on and is sent from the chamber.

He tells journalists that he has been 'gagged', but really it is a cheap shot at revenge against a financier who wouldn't invest. He also announces that, following his resignation from the Labour Party, he's going to join the English National Party, a band of eccentric traditionalists who believe in a devolved parliament under the Cross of St George.[23]

The weekend of 24 and 25 April is the last before Stonehouse's trial begins. Sheila Buckley attends a wedding in Cornwall, where former prime minister Ted Heath is a fellow guest. Heath judiciously avoids being caught in the same press shot with the ex-Commons secretary who is soon to appear before an Old Bailey jury. Stonehouse, meanwhile, spends his time at home hatching a plan, one that Buckley hears of on her return to London. Stonehouse doesn't think Du Cann is giving him the attention he needs. He's better off ditching the middle-man and representing himself. No one can defend Stonehouse better than Stonehouse.[24]

On Monday morning, Du Cann, Robertson and Stonehouse make last-minute plans for the next day's trial. They are deep in conference when, shortly before lunch, Du Cann is called to the phone. It's Buckley's QC, who has heard reports on the midday news that Stonehouse has decided to defend himself. Can Du Cann confirm it?

The unflappable Du Cann flaps. Stonehouse is sitting in a room next door discussing with the rest of his legal team how to present evidence the very next morning. Du Cann returns to the meeting and confronts Stonehouse. He confirms it's true. Du Cann is astounded and Robertson remembers telling Stonehouse to forget it as an option: 'If you defend yourself and infuriate the judge, you could get seven years.' Stonehouse apologises to them both for his decision. It's the first time they have heard him apologise for anything. They call an immediate end to the meeting, tie pink tape around their briefs and wish Stonehouse the best of luck. He has just sacked his counsel on the eve of his trial and they are sure he is going to need it.[25]

2 7

THE CASE FOR THE CROWN

The Maguire Seven arrive at the Old Bailey in a windowless prison van with police outriders. Once inside the world's most famous criminal court, they have to be carried out of the cells up to the courtroom. The family from Willesden are then wrongly convicted of storing explosives for the IRA, but theirs is not the case that most fascinates the British public in the month of April 1976.[1]

The Central Criminal Court officials have reserved the Old Bailey's Court Number One for Stonehouse and Buckley. The old place oozes theatre. It's an ornate Edwardian masterpiece, all stained oak, green leather and Palladian columns under a high alabaster ceiling. The raised dock is the stage, sixteen feet by fourteen feet, waist-high dark wood walls and a glass screen to shoulder level. Defendants and judge face each other eye to eye across the well of the court.

Court business is already under way when Stonehouse and Buckley arrive separately on Tuesday 27 April. They are both smartly dressed as if for an important day at the office. Buckley is wearing a light-coloured trench coat, belt cross-tied at the waist and big-buckled black shoes. She is escorted by her father, Leslie. Stonehouse has a dark overcoat over a light shirt, suit and tie, and is accompanied by Barbara. She kisses him goodbye for the cameras but doesn't go into court. The supportive politician's spouse is yesterday's story and the burden of keeping him buoyant falls to daughter Jane and legal aid-funded solicitor Michael O'Dell.[2]

The accused meet inside and sneak into the back of the court for their first sight of Edward Eveleigh, the 58-year-old judge who will hear their case. Resplendent in a scarlet gown with a shoulder-length wig framing his bushy eyebrows and glasses, he rattles through the early morning bail applications. Stonehouse's first impressions of the man are good. He is courteous and considerate, and allows bail against police objections in a couple of cases. But his reputation as a firm sentencer precedes him and he has recently sent down bank robber Mickey 'The Fish' Salmon for twenty-two years.

After Eveleigh has wrapped up his outstanding business, Stonehouse and Buckley slip out of the courtroom and re-enter from stairs below. It's a gladiatorial entrance and the public spaces and press benches are packed. They take their places side by side in the dock, careful not to give reporters a cheap line by so much as glancing at each other.

The English National Party MP for Walsall North immediately seeks an adjournment to consider tapes of his Christmas Eve police interview in Melbourne, which the prosecution have just produced. Eveleigh says no and Stonehouse protests, but Ted Eveleigh is not one to be messed around in his own court: 'You will sit down or be taken down and there you will stay until you decide to obey the directions of this court,' says the judge. Stonehouse carries on, reiterating his line that 'this is a largely political case', and he keeps going until he receives a final warning: 'You will sit down or be taken down? Make up your mind here and now. You are not going to delay these proceedings.' It's only day one.[3]

Richard Du Cann advised Stonehouse to accept the birth certificate and passport charges as he'd already admitted the applications to the police, but now that the barrister has been dismissed, Stonehouse pleads not guilty to everything, as does Buckley. Eveleigh rules that the five charges of insurance fraud, dismissed at the committal, should be reinstated, taking the total against Stonehouse to twenty-one and six for Buckley. Fifty Londoners called for jury service are brought in to the back of the court. Stonehouse challenges four members of the jury and it's nearly the end of the day before seven men and five women are sworn in. The real action won't now start until the following morning. Overnight, it dawns on Stonehouse that annoying the judge might not have been the best opening move.[4]

On Wednesday morning, Michael Corkery QC opens the Crown's case. He has the upright bearing of a former Guardsman and the unassuming confidence of a barrister familiar with winning. Occasionally waving his reading glasses to make a point, he likes to keep things simple. Stonehouse, he says, faced bankruptcy, disgrace and ruin. He resorted to fraud, deception and the plundering of his companies during 1974 in order to finance a new life in Australia with Buckley.[5]

Corkery outlines the £125,000 insurance policies set up to benefit Barbara and the family, along with the stealing of the Markham and Mildoon identities. He tells the jury that the Stonehouse companies were riddled with debt and on the point of blowing up when he disappeared. He is careful to head off at the pass any idea that the MP is being persecuted. 'This is not a political case,' emphasises Corkery. 'It is a criminal trial for sheer, absolute, downright dishonesty.'[6]

After hearing Corkery's opening statement, Stonehouse decides he must make amends for yesterday's spat with Eveleigh and, when court resumes for the afternoon session, he immediately apologises. 'I want to apologise. Due to my misunderstanding about procedures yesterday, there appeared to be an altercation. I want to assure you I meant no disrespect,' he tells Eveleigh. 'Think no more of it,' says Eveleigh graciously. 'You will have to take it from me what the procedure is.'

Corkery goes on to outline the money-go-round between the Stonehouse companies, the activities at BBT, the recording of directors as present at Epacs board meetings when they weren't there and the appointment of directors without their knowledge. Even though many of these alleged crimes are excluded from the charges by extradition law, Corkery makes sure that the jury knows all about them.[7]

He then turns his attention to Stonehouse's co-defendant Buckley and the conspiracy charge. He explains a conspiracy is an agreement between two people to do something unlawful. One person cannot be guilty of conspiracy; it takes two to tango. In this case, they conspired to defraud Epacs' creditors and set up a new life together. She, says Corkery of Buckley, 'knew perfectly well that what she was doing was to help Stonehouse to remove these funds to hide them away until it was convenient to meet her in Australia'. At nearly four o'clock, it is time for the court to adjourn. Corkery has won the day hands down and he strolls down to his Thames-side chambers at 5 Paper Buildings to study tomorrow's brief.[8]

Stonehouse starts Thursday 29 April as he means to go on – with another appeal to Eveleigh. He cites a 1967 select committee report which recommends that an MP should be able to perform his parliamentary work while involved in criminal or civil proceedings. He wants dispensation to go to the House when he pleases, but Eveleigh is dismissive: 'If there is any course I can take I will no doubt give it proper consideration. But I very much doubt any report of the House has anything to do with these proceedings.'[9]

Now it's time for Corkery, still opening, to get stuck into

'Stonehouse, the big, big spender' as the headline writers have it. Corkery describes his spending spree in the weeks before his disappearance, a period when he had twenty-four separate accounts at seventeen different banks, along with an array of credit cards in the name of Markham, including a well-used Amex. 'He decided to have a good time at the expense of the credit card companies,' say the prosecution. 'Here was a man facing ruin and an enormous debt, hopelessly insolvent and spending money substantially in an utterly dishonest way.'[10]

Corkery concludes his opening address on Friday by reading to the jury the 'Dear Dums' letters from Buckley, using her third-person prose. 'She feels like a rat in a trap and loves him more than life,' Corkery recites. He uses the letters to allege that Buckley was 'more than just a loyal secretary following instructions blindly'. There is substantial evidence she was a willing participant, says Corkery, including moving into a hotel where Stonehouse could, if something went wrong, correspond with and ring her in a way he couldn't at the old flat in his name.[11]

By four o'clock on Friday afternoon, Corkery has held the jury's attention for fifteen hours over these three days. He times his finish to coincide with the weekend break and wants to give the jury something to think about as they head back to their London homes and to the weekend papers. 'In this case there is no sudden breakdown. This is a story of crime where a very able and talented man, over a period of at least four months, covers up his disappearance, and spins a web of deception in which almost every single strand is fashioned with ingenuity and great ability.'[12]

Stonehouse and Buckley are held back for ten minutes to allow the jury to clear the building, but as everyone heads for the tube, Stonehouse is in surprisingly good spirits. He isn't a football fan, but his hometown team, unfancied Southampton, are in their first-ever FA Cup final tomorrow. They're playing the famous Manchester United and, you never know, the underdog sometimes wins. He has spotted factual errors in Corkery's speech and fully expects to be acquitted once the jury understand the pressures he was under.

Next week, he will take the floor and it's the stage he has been waiting for. Excited at what lays ahead, that evening back at Sancroft Street he fries a supper of sausages and tomato, humming the melodies from Tchaikovsky's opera, *Eugene Onegin*. It's the story of a man who fell in love with an innocent younger woman and then, too slow to act, lost her to another man. It's not the kind of mistake a fellow like John Stonehouse would make.[13]

It's a dramatic Saturday afternoon at Wembley Stadium. The underdog has its day and Southampton win the cup with a goal from Bobby Stokes. But at the Old Bailey the following Tuesday, there is another Stokes in the spotlight; Albert 'Claud' Stokes is the first witness called by the prosecution. The Dixon Wilson partner and BBT auditor is more valued for his forensic skills than his client relationships and in court appears nervous. For an hour and a half, Corkery tries to put him at ease, unravelling Stonehouse's stock exchange dealings and the Black–Buckley identity switch and how he investigated it. The next morning, it's time for Stonehouse to cross-examine him.

The witness box in Court Number One is situated in a corner of the room between the judge and jury, and just a few feet from the dock. It's as close as Stonehouse ever wants to get to the rottweiler accountant. He couldn't bear the sight of him in Dover Street, but now he's got Stokes where he wants him.

It's chilly in court, but Stonehouse turns up the heat during seven and a half hours of cross-examination. It's a contest between the charismatic debater and the numbers man. Stonehouse accuses Stokes of playing 'amateur detective' in his evidence that Black was Buckley, but Stokes counters no; phoning up to find out if Black existed was the way he chose to investigate. Stokes admits that BBT was unusual among small property lenders in not needing a Bank of England bailout, but he says the lack of a provision for bad debts seemed impossible. Stonehouse has one ace up his sleeve: why is Stokes even here, when he audited BBT and it's the activities of Epacs that are in question? 'The prosecution asked me to come,' the accountant limply replies. It's enough to put a spring in Stonehouse's step and he allows his confidence to grow.[14]

On 10 May, he agrees that Mrs Markham and Mrs Mildoon do not have to undertake the ordeal of appearing in front of the man who stole their dead husbands' identities nearly two years ago. The same applies to Bridget McBride, whose terminally ill MP husband's signature was faked as a witness to the false passports. Their damning evidence is read to the jury, as details of the doorstep visits and the cunning questions two years ago in Walsall are relived and raked over.[15]

The following day, Stonehouse's nephew, family solicitor and co-director Michael Hayes steps into Court Number One and he's on the witness stand for nearly two days. Stonehouse reads out newspaper reports of the insurance policies he says Barbara took out claiming they are exhibits, but Eveleigh isn't having it. He tells him that if he wants the jury to understand what was in Barbara's mind, he should call her as a witness. But the prosecution cannot call a wife to testify against her husband and Stonehouse has no intention of exposing Barbara to cross-examination by calling her as a defence witness.

Stonehouse changes the subject and produces more news-paper reports. Eveleigh gets cross: 'I have allowed you a good deal of latitude and I am not going to let you prove facts other than in the proper way.' Eventually the judge tells Hayes and the jury to leave the court. He turns to Stonehouse, and wags his forefinger sternly: 'I hope you are not seeking to try me. Let me make that quite clear to you.'

When Hayes comes back in, Stonehouse – now routinely referring to himself in the third person – asks him why he didn't consult Mr Stonehouse before winding up Epacs. 'The major reason the company was insolvent was that Mr Stonehouse had withdrawn more money from the company than was available for anyone to take out,' replies Hayes. 'Did you ask Mr Stonehouse for an explanation?' asks Stonehouse. 'Mr Stonehouse wasn't there to be asked,' replies Hayes.[16]

The next day, the prosecution call Alan Le Fort, the chartered accountant who joined the Stonehouse companies in 1972 and who ended up with responsibility for Epacs, Global Imex and the wine business. He describes loans from Epacs to Stonehouse in contravention of the Companies Act 1948, complicated inter-company transactions, stock exchange transactions and liquidity problems, all of which made him 'extremely unhappy' and led him to resign in September 1974. He says he frequently got instructions from Stonehouse to draw up company cheques in his own favour which Stonehouse or Buckley would then sign and cash. Le Fort concedes that Stonehouse had worked hard, won business for Epacs and Global Imex, and used his own money to allow individuals to withdraw their deposits from BBT. But by the time Le Fort is finished in the witness box, Stonehouse looks down and out.[17]

Stonehouse hopes to use the appearance of all his old chums called by the prosecution to his advantage but, unlike in Dover Street, they are all under oath now and less obliging. On 18 May, Stonehouse loses it while questioning former company secretary Philip Bingham. He reaches down to the floor of the dock to produce plastic sacks containing post and tells Eveleigh that while he was in Australia, his confidential mail was thrown out without so much of a thought. 'This is what I'm up against,' he says, holding the sack. 'I have suffered at the hands of people who have not dealt with me fairly.' He tells Eveleigh he is too upset and emotional to go on, but Eveleigh has other ideas and tells him to stick to the point. He also stops Stonehouse's line of questioning about the *Sunday Times* and Anthony Mascarenhas: the BBT allegations are not relevant to this trial, the jury are reminded.[18]

Stonehouse's personal assistant Philip Gay is called on 20 May. He says he was told about company business 'on a need-to-know basis' and that it appeared Epacs and Stonehouse were 'very much the same thing'. He concludes that his old boss 'brought matters upon his own head'.[19]

James Charlton is quizzed about the disappearance. It's the details that the papers are happy to regurgitate gleefully: the pestering to join him on the trip to the Fontainebleau and Miami Beach when the business prospects were poor; the swimming out to sea that alarmed Charlton who thought it 'a great deal farther than suitable'; the talk of his future before his fake demise; the fear he had collapsed in his room.[20]

After the court adjourns at 4pm on 27 May, Stonehouse takes a short cab ride along the Embankment to the House of Commons. He feels that being seen there, speaking and voting, strengthens his case that this is a political trial. But there is no exchanging of pleasantries with old Labour colleagues following his defection to the English National Party. This evening he votes with the opposition against a bill to nationalise parts of the aircraft and shipbuilding industries. It ties the vote 303-303 and the government looks like losing until one Labour MP breaks an agreement he has with a Conservative counterpart to abstain. It's a breach of the Commons 'pairing' convention and enables the government to carry the day.

Nationalisation is an article of faith for Labour's left wing and they excitedly burst into a rendition of 'The Red Flag', prompting Tory shadow minister Michael Heseltine to grab the speaker's mace and brandish it menacingly. The House is suspended for twenty minutes, there's jostling between MPs and the next day's papers are full of 'Tarzan' Heseltine. Commons leader Michael Foot notices the role played by the member for Walsall North, elected as a Labour MP but who tied the vote by siding with the opposition. 'At times we did not know where our majority in the Commons was,' he said. 'Then it crossed the floor leaving us without one.'[21]

The Old Bailey seems tame by comparison. Friday 28 May is the last day before an extended Whitsun break and it has seemed a long five weeks. Stonehouse believes he's doing well, but he's floundering on technical issues and annoying the judge who reprimands him again this week for 'a gross waste of time'. Then, just before the break, Eveleigh announces that over the holiday, Stonehouse has to report twice a day on bail and remain in London. These are the most stringent bail conditions Stonehouse has faced and the judge is sending him a message.[22]

On 3 June, Stonehouse is back in court and faced with a line-up of eyewitnesses ready to expose the reality of his double life. It's a roll-call of travel agents and hoteliers from the summer and autumn of 1974. Mariella Zandstra from the Highfield House hotel is one, having witnessed the married couple booking a bedsit room for Buckley for when her husband was away and the subsequent Honolulu phone calls. She is witness to the alleged conspiracy. Then there's Jane Grubb from Pan American Piccadilly who sold the Markham flights, and Ole Andresen who booked Markham into the Grand Hotel in Copenhagen.

Next come the overseas police witnesses: Patricia Evans from Miami, followed by Coffey, Morris, Sullivan and Gillespie from Melbourne. The jury hears of Stonehouse's fatal error in using Markham and Mildoon at two nearby Melbourne banks, along with Coffey's Fontainebleau matchbook discovery. And then comes Ian Ward, an ally-turned-nemesis whose evidence under oath is crucial to the prosecution's charge of conspiracy.[23]

The *Telegraph* journalist recounts his visit to see Stonehouse in February 1975 when the latter was preparing for Barbara's return. Stonehouse was 'unpacking women's clothing which included a black slip,' says Ward. 'I asked him who they belonged to. He said they were Mrs Buckley's.' Stonehouse danced with the slip, says Ward, and he recalls telling him that he had better conceal her clothes from Barbara, due in the next day. Stonehouse agreed and asked Ward to take them back to his house and store them under the bed in a red Samsonite suitcase. Stonehouse retrieved the case, he said, before Buckley arrived in Perth.[24]

Stonehouse counters that Barbara was already in Australia on the day that Ward says the incident occurred. He maintains that the clothes were Barbara's and that he had been joking when he said they belonged to Buckley, but it's all going on a bit too long for Eveleigh. On 8 June, Ward's second day in the witness box, the judge interrupts Stonehouse. 'I have not clamped down on you doing this because it takes longer than to let you have your head. But if you think you are scoring over the court I shall remind the jury at the end of the day what I am saying and what you are doing. Don't forget it.' Stonehouse says he is just trying to establish the facts.

'The totality of the facts will come out by evidence which

is admissible, and you must be well aware of what is and what is not admissible,' says Eveleigh. 'Accede to your requests and we shall be here until Christmas.' 'It is not my wish to be here until Christmas,' Stonehouse shouts back. 'I did not request this witness to be brought here all the way from Singapore. It was the Crown's decision—' 'Take Mr Stonehouse down to the cells!' Eveleigh interrupts. 'Members of the jury, we will adjourn for half an hour.' It will allow everyone to cool off, including the judge.[25]

Before long, it's the entire country that needs cooling off. The summer of 1976 turns into the longest and hottest on record. The temperature hits thirty-two degrees and the heat-wave continues until the end of August. Tarmac on the M1 melts, forests burn and swarms of European ladybirds invade the country. Maxi dresses, flared trousers and cheesecloth shirts, high fashion in early summer, give way to short summer dresses, shorts and T-shirts. The beaches are packed and there is a new craze for grilling meat outdoors. Elton John and Kiki Dee's *Don't Go Breaking My Heart* is the sound of the summer.[26]

But Stonehouse and O'Dell have their minds on other things. They think they have found a way to counter Ward's testimony. Stonehouse has made an application to have Mr Hills, a Melbourne customs inspector, come and testify in person. When O'Dell finally tracks him down and asks if he could be in court within forty-eight hours, he is told that he has broken his legs and would need to be accompanied by his wife. It is agreed with Eveleigh that a statement from Hills can be read to the jury as part of Stonehouse's defence when the time comes.[27]

On 10 June, Michael Sherrard and Ian Hay Davison's days in Melbourne come back to haunt Stonehouse when Corkery plays tapes from their interview sessions. The jury hears Stonehouse say that 'money I took out and put into the resources of a new personality as Mr J. A. Markham was money I was fully entitled to from a legal and moral point of view'. It's the first time that the public gets an insight into what the Department of Trade has discovered. 'I want you to know that every single one of these transactions is legitimate,' Stonehouse is heard telling the inspectors.[28]

And there are more tapes from Australia just four days later, when Stonehouse reads out the transcription of the first call to Barbara from Australia. The details of what he went on to say to Mathew stick in his throat: 'It's going to be all right in the end. One day you'll appreciate what I've been going through in this life. I'm sorry I have caused you so much hell. Be brave now,' he reads and then starts to cry.[29]

In court, it's shirtsleeves and light frocks for the jury. And now there's another prosecution witness that Stonehouse has been waiting for: Kenneth Etheridge. The policeman is an experienced courtroom performer, but Stonehouse wants the jury to see how the police use the press. On 17 February 1975, Harry Longmuir, the *Daily Mail*'s ace crime reporter, had written a Stonehouse story so full of detail that Stonehouse believes Etheridge was the source. He knows that Etheridge had travelled out to Australia twice on the same plane as Longmuir, as well as visiting him at the Melbourne Hilton on the evening of 18 February. Stonehouse thinks Etheridge looks uncomfortable under his questioning.

Now it is half-time, the moment when the prosecution case ends and the defence begins. Stonehouse and his solicitor want all the counts dismissed. The insurance charges have been thrown out once already and they think it's worth another try. The theft charges amount only to stealing from himself, the credit cards were used when he was on company business and he's sure the conspiracy case is full of holes. There are lengthy legal arguments and Eveleigh abruptly tells Stonehouse that he is withdrawing bail. 'I think the point has been reached where you, as it were, have come to your turn to bat. For that reason your bail must cease,' and the judge walks out.[30]

'No bail after half-time' is not unusual in long cases, but Stonehouse and his solicitor Michael O'Dell are wrong-footed. Instead of going home to sausages and tomato, Stonehouse is handcuffed to another prisoner and taken to a holding block shared with thirty-five other men. There's music blaring out of a radio all night and he doesn't get much sleep, let alone time to polish his opening defence. What's more, O'Dell isn't allowed to visit.[31]

There's a small victory in the morning when Eveleigh agrees to dismiss the birth certificate charges as they're implicit in the passport charge, but that's the only concession Stonehouse achieves; all the other counts stand. Now it's his turn to spring a surprise. He declares that he's going to make his statement from the dock rather than the witness box, avoiding cross-examination as it cannot be considered sworn evidence. When this happens, defendants usually make a short statement of innocence and sit down, but that's not Stonehouse's plan at all.[32]

2 8

THE JURY'S OUT

Stonehouse wakes up on 1 July in his second home – HMP Brixton. As he comes to in his prison bed, he remembers that his bail has been withdrawn and that today is the first day of his defence. He is given breakfast, handcuffed and bundled into a prison bus. It trundles through central London into Newgate Street and turns into the yard of the Old Bailey. Still handcuffed, Stonehouse is escorted into the building, unshackled and meets O'Dell. He is then taken up the stairs leading to the dock.

Finally, his chance has come to tell the jury his story. His unsworn statement cannot be cross-examined and begins with the claim that the case is one of political persecution. He says that charges would not have been brought but for the fact that he was causing embarrassment to the Labour government and this persecution is the explanation for his mental illness and subsequent actions.

He has an excuse for everything. There was no financial reason to disappear; the business was about to come good; the loan account would have been paid off; the insurance policies were taken out by Barbara after the car bomb at Heathrow. 'I was under pressure and the pressure was tightening in a very physical sense,' says Stonehouse. 'My ideals were being destroyed by evil forces . . . [Markham] was a psychological device to get relief from John Stonehouse. I could have gone to a doctor and in retrospect I should have done.'[1]

It was all forced on him by circumstances. He had to pay 'inducements' to overseas agents 'to make it all happen'. Paying bribes – to people like Sylvester Okereke – was the norm, he says. 'I was taking out large sums of money as inducements for foreign agents and that is not the sort of thing you talk about, so we put it through my loan account. I was not doing anything in order to disappear.'

He goes on to talk of a sustained and vicious press campaign – including Soviet spy allegations, the Mafia cement accusations around Okereke and Shaver, and pressure to resign as a member of parliament. 'Those were persisted in,' he says, 'even though they had been proved to be without foundation.' He also declares that he will demonstrate the complete impossibility of a conspiracy between him and Buckley.[2]

The *Sunday Times* and Mascarenhas are excoriated, before Stonehouse goes on to settle further scores when he claims that Harold Wilson was a go-between to get his friend Joe Kagan's Gannex raincoats stocked in Co-op shops in the mid-1960s and that Ted Short pushed him to appoint a disgraced Labour councillor T. Dan Smith to handle PR at the Co-op. It's irrelevant to the case and is the kind of diversion that tries Eveleigh's patience.[3]

On the fourth day of his statement, Stonehouse finally elaborates on the long-standing blackmail claim. It's not the Czechs – or if it is, he's not telling. The alleged blackmailers were a pair of dissatisfied creditors threatening to expose BBT's money-go-round to the Bank of England and the Department of Trade unless he bought back £30,000 of BBT shares they had been landed with. 'You are an MP and you cannot afford any publicity,' Stonehouse says they told him. 'Think of what it is going to do to you.'[4]

Wednesday 7 July is his fifth and final day reading from the dock, and he saves this for Buckley. It's what the court reporters have been waiting for. Their intimate relationship, he tells the court, only started after her husband left her. Once she heard he was still alive, 'being the great woman she was, she coped and did what she was asked – she didn't tell this terrible thing to anyone'. 'Sheila the Great, by Stonehouse' runs the *Daily Mirror,* but the public have heard it all before by now and are more interested in the news that Princess Anne will be riding for Great Britain in the upcoming Montreal Olympics.[5]

Stonehouse is coming to the end now and tells the jury in a firm voice: 'I have been very active in the House of Commons, but I would like to make it perfectly clear that whatever the outcome of this case, whether guilty or innocent, I intend to resign my seat in the House of Commons just as soon as possible.' Politicians think it's an empty promise. If he's innocent, he has changed his mind before, and if he's guilty and jailed, he would be expelled. By the time he has finished a speech lasting thirty hours spread over five days, it is the longest dock statement in history. Even the super-optimistic Stonehouse now realises he has lost the judge's sympathy, but it's the jury that matters and he allows himself to believe most are still with him.[6]

Witnesses for the defence come next. First, it's time to counter Ian Ward's testimony on the black slip and the trunk. As agreed with Eveleigh, the statement of Melbourne customs officer Mr Hills is read out to the jury. They hear that, on 30 December 1974, Hills was examining trunks and cases. A trunk shipped to a J. A. Markham was opened 'in my presence or under my supervision', goes his testimony. 'I did not see . . . a blouse, a black slip or any ladies shoes or any article of ladies clothing. The item was passed for collection.'[7]

Stonehouse next moves on to his medical witnesses. Melbourne psychiatrist Dr Gibney is first and repeats his January 1975 diagnosis of adopting a parallel personality as a result of depression and 'paranoic attitudes to society around him', reiterating that 'it is sort of suicide in a psychiatric sense'. But when pushed by Corkery, Gibney agrees that the phrase 'paranoic' was not being used in the sense that it constituted a particular disease under the Mental Health Act. Rather that it's just a term to describe a symptom of depression.[8]

On 15 July, Dr Lionel Heywood joins the expert line-up. He analyses Stonehouse's abstract paintings for the jury and describes Stonehouse as having a 'hysteroid personality' with a strong need for social attention and a certain aggressiveness.[9]

R. D. Laing, a gift to Stonehouse from his former junior counsel Geoffrey Robertson, applies his divided self theory to the case, but Corkery ridicules his methods and Laing admits that if it was a parallel personality, he's never seen one like this before. The MP Maurice Miller confirms that he had prescribed Stonehouse sedatives in the months leading up to his disappearance when they were together in the House of Commons. 'I viewed him as suffering from depression,' says Miller and adds that he thought Stonehouse might have been suicidal.[10]

Corkery rips into the psychiatrists' evidence. Only the GP Miller has seen Stonehouse pre-disappearance and the other diagnoses are retrospective. Corkery concludes that Stonehouse had indeed suffered a breakdown before he disappeared – but it was a moral not a mental breakdown. Stonehouse hasn't handled the expert witnesses he has called at all well, failing to square the clever lawyer he is trying to be with the tortured soul he says he was. The canteen gossip is that the mental health defence hasn't stood up.[11]

Jane Stonehouse is his last witness. She and her father adore each other and she has been watching from the back of the court throughout, keeping Barbara updated by phone. She has been on standby for three days and the call could come at any time. She drinks endless cups of coffee in the austere Old Bailey canteen, feeling as if all eyes are on her. The tension is unbearable. She has even taken up smoking. Then it's time. She takes the stand, swears the oath and it's the cross-examination that really gives her the chance to open up.

She tells Corkery of her father's mental state when she joined him in Australia early in 1975. 'He started screaming and shouting and rushing about the flat. He seemed to have no control at all. I saw him lying on the floor beating his head against the floor, crying and screaming. I was terrified . . . I thought he had gone over the top, never to return.' It's as good as it gets for the Stonehouse psychiatric defence, but he's dejected by the treatment of his medical witnesses and he closes his defence after three weeks. For Judge Eveleigh, that's about three weeks too long and he rejects another request from the accused to go to the Commons to vote.[12]

The growing heat in the city triggers electric storms around London on Tuesday 20 July when Buckley makes her statement, like Stonehouse, from the dock. For an hour, she reads carefully from a 5,000-word written text. Her shock at his disappearance. The confused calls. The dash to Copenhagen. Misleading everyone because her loyalties were to him. She knew nothing of his plans to disappear and never answered the phone as Mr Markham's or Mr Mildoon's secretary. She did not know of those names or money being transferred into those accounts. 'I don't have a short or full-length black slip,' she says. She was a director and company secretary who knew nothing of book-keeping. She signed lots of cheques but relied on the professionals' advice. The affair started only after she broke up with her husband. The 'Dear Dums' letters were written out of loneliness and desperation. He is a gentleman and a true friend. 'If I had the same decisions to make all over again tomorrow,' she concludes, 'I feel certain that those decisions would remain the same. I have no regrets.'[13]

Now it's time for the summing-up. Corkery takes three days remorselessly restating the case: 'The object was to escape ruin, disgrace and bankruptcy, and start a new life in a new country with Mrs Buckley.' Stonehouse's summary takes another three and a half days, which include his fifty-first birthday on 28 July. 'The lying and cheating is as bad as anything I have seen in the House of Commons,' he says of the trial. 'But the humbug is even worse, because it is dressed up in this decorum and in that way you are not supposed to notice it.'[14]

Buckley's counsel, Liberal peer Basil Wigoder, a down-to-earth Mancunian highly regarded as a defence lawyer, sums up for her on the afternoon of Friday 30th and the following Monday morning. He reminds the jury that she is not charged with agreeing to disappear with Stonehouse – there is no such offence – and that in her eyes he was a 'big shot, and she would virtually do as she was told without question or without thinking'. She would not be aware of the distinctions between companies and the boards of directors, and someone in Mrs Buckley's position could not be expected to understand banking terms such as 'liquidity' and 'solvency problem'. As for conspiracy, he submitted to the jury that the business of the slip was a case of a reporter sticking to what he had originally thought to be a good story.[15]

The prosecution and defence have had their say and now it's Eveleigh's summing-up. It lasts a further three days; lawyers, defendants and court reporters listen anxiously for clues. Stonehouse does not like what he hears. The judge surprises lawyers by ruling that the very act of disappearing in Miami constitutes an attempt to obtain insurance money by deception. 'I am going to repeat,' says Eveleigh, 'that he falsely staged his death by drowning, dishonestly intending that a claim should be made and the money obtained in due course, sooner or later. If I am wrong about that, there is a higher court that will put me right.'[16]

Eveleigh undermines the medical evidence by reminding the jury that, although it's for them to decide, no psychiatrist had examined Stonehouse in 1974 and that their diagnosis of his state of mind when he disappeared can only be hypothetical. Every person is presumed sane and accountable unless proved otherwise: 'There has been no attempt in this case to prove the contrary.' Eveleigh then takes the jury through various financial transactions which Stonehouse thinks he has misunderstood. He leaps up to object. 'You've already addressed the jury,' snaps the judge and tells him to sit down.[17]

He's no kinder to Buckley. 'If she is to be believed in her statement from the dock when she says she thought he was distressed and she was worried about his condition, why did she not do something about it? Put yourselves, members of the jury, in the position of someone who has a very fast and dear friend whom you have no reason at all to suspect has done anything wrong, that friend is reported drowned and you can see no illegal reason for that friend wanting to disappear, that friend rings you up from 5,000 miles away in such distress that it distresses and worries you, do you not say, good heavens, we must get help there as soon as we possibly can? . . . Whether or not in those circumstances you would go to the police at once is one thing but would you not go to some mutual friend? . . . Mrs Buckley did not do that. She kept it to herself.'[18]

It all sounds bleak for the accused so far, but Eveleigh is careful to balance it. He reminds the jury that they are 'the judges of the facts, you decide whether the facts have been made out to substantiate the charges . . . If you cannot feel sure that charge has been made out, you must acquit.' Eveleigh tells them not to hold it against Stonehouse that he has been rebuked by the judge. 'Put it down to my old age,' he says. 'You see, it is not easy for a man to defend himself.'[19]

Eveleigh says that if the jury were to conclude that Stonehouse told Ward it was Buckley's slip, remember she was not there to challenge it and she is not to be held responsible for what Mr Stonehouse said. 'If this case depended on that slip and that slip alone to prove whether or not Mrs Buckley was going to join Mr Stonehouse, you would probably be of the opinion that it did not prove anything.'[20]

The Czech stories were introduced by Stonehouse and are to be ignored, says the judge. So too BBT: 'A great deal has been said about the Bank of Bangladesh,' says Eveleigh. 'There is no charge against Mr Stonehouse for irregularities in regard to the Bank of Bangladesh.' It's sounding better for Stonehouse and Buckley now and the speculation in the corridors is that they might get off.[21]

At 4pm on Wednesday 4 August, Eveleigh is not quite done and the court adjourns. It's another hot August night and a fitful one in both Brixton and Abbey Wood. At 3.45am on Thursday morning, Big Ben also gives in to the heat and grinds to a halt. It takes Eveleigh less than an hour to wind up, but Big Ben is more obdurate. Just before 11am, Eveleigh sends the jury out with the instruction to come back with unanimous verdicts. Still on remand, Stonehouse is taken down to the cell area below and served with an indifferent prison lunch, while Jane smokes and Buckley waits in her solicitor's room. Her parents and sister Olwen wait upstairs in the canteen. The verdict could be at any time.[22]

The afternoon wears on – there's a false alarm at 7pm but it's only the jury sending out for dinner – and then, just after 8pm, there's a scramble as word reaches the lawyers that the jury is coming back. The jury register is taken, all confirm that they are present and then Buckley and Stonehouse are called up to the dock. Side by side, they stand, eight feet apart, Buckley nearest the jury, Stonehouse to her right.[23]

The foreman – youngish, female, sleeves rolled up – gets to her feet. The birth certificate charges having been dropped, as Eveleigh considered them wrapped up in the passport forgeries, the first count to be heard is count three: the forged application for a Markham passport. 'Have you reached a unanimous verdict in respect of John Thomson Stonehouse on count three?' 'Yes. Guilty.' It's not a surprise; Stonehouse has virtually admitted it.

Count four: the theft of the Garrett Corporation $12,500 banker's draft. 'Yes. Guilty.' Stonehouse bites his lip and looks hard at the jury. Count thirteen: the forged American Express application. 'Yes. Guilty.' Count twenty one: deception to enable Barbara Stonehouse to claim £30,000 from Royal Insurance. 'Yes. Guilty.' There are no more unanimous verdicts for Stonehouse. The jury will have to consider the remaining fifteen charges tomorrow, but he knows he is already done for. Still, he waves to Jane at the back of the court as he is taken back down. She smiles back.[24]

They can't reach a unanimous decision on the remaining counts or on any of the charges Buckley is facing. It is not good news for her as a quick return would probably mean an acquittal. The judge tells the jury he will now accept majority verdicts and sends them under guard to a hotel for the night with instructions not to discuss the case with anyone else. Stonehouse is sent back to prison a guilty man and Buckley goes back to her parents' home.[25]

It's 'Stonehouse Guilty' in huge block headlines on Friday's front pages. The jury resumes at 10am. Stonehouse arrives unseen in the prison bus, while Buckley travels by black London taxi, looking anxious, her hair tied back in a ponytail and sunglasses on her head. The morning drags on. Outside it's another belting day, but downstairs it's cool and dark. Stonehouse knows he is likely to face prison and passes time playing backgammon with O'Dell. Buckley, with her legal team, still hopes to be acquitted. It is nearly four o'clock when word comes that the jury are coming back. The press dash down from the third floor cafeteria and the accused meet for the last time at the stairs below court.

The jury register is taken and, count by count, the verdicts are read out. Stonehouse shows no emotion as he is found guilty on a further fourteen counts. He knows he is going to jail and it's all about Buckley now. 'On count four of this indictment do you find Sheila Elizabeth Buckley guilty or not guilty of theft?' 'Guilty.' Five guilty verdicts are read out in all, but on the conspiracy charge, they are both acquitted.[26]

Before deciding on sentencing, there is something Eveleigh wants to know and Kenneth Etheridge is called back into court. The judge asks him whether there is any more information about the Swiss accounts in the name of Markham. There are assets in accounts set up by Stonehouse in that name in the region of £90,000, replies Etheridge. Stonehouse is given an opportunity to ask a question and unwisely asks, 'Can you confirm the monies available from Victa were withdrawn?'

'97,000 Swiss francs were withdrawn on 20 September 1974,' Etheridge replies. It's evidently a fraud of considerable scale and Eveleigh has all the information he needs before passing sentence.[27]

29

COMING CLEAN

It's Friday 6 August 1976. Jane Stonehouse is weeping at the back of Court Number One of the Old Bailey, Buckley is in the dock, looking terrified, and Barbara is nowhere to be seen. Stonehouse makes a final plea in mitigation: 'I have been the loser from so many points of view. My career is in tatters and cannot now be recommenced. My position in the public eye is destroyed. Indeed, I have now precious little private life left to me. I ask your lordship to bear in mind my lifetime's work for the community . . . I ask you to bear in mind also my service to the state, during which I gave of my best, in the years from 1964 to 1970.' Unbeknown to judge, jury, daughter and lover, it was this exact period when Agent Twister was in the iron grip of his Czech masters.[1]

Eveleigh doesn't interrupt Stonehouse, yet he's unimpressed. Delivering his defence from the safety of the dock has damaged Stonehouse's case and it's going to be a firm sentence. 'You did not simply decide to disappear because you were oppressed by business burdens,' says the judge. 'It is clear to me that self-interest has been well to the fore' – Mickey the Fish, for one, has heard this tone of voice before – 'and you aimed to get rich quickly. You falsely accuse other people of cant, hypocrisy and humbug when you must have known all the time that your defence was an embodiment of all three.' It's a judgement scripted to make headlines.

'You were not an unlucky businessman escaping from unde-served financial problems,' he continues. Stonehouse is in front of him, showing no emotion. 'It all arose from your initial devious behaviour, whatever its object may be . . . You know you are not an ill-fated idealist.' Eveleigh delivers a sentence of seven years: five for obtaining pecuniary advantage; six for theft charges; six for obtaining property by deception. All are to run concurrently. A further year is handed down for the passport application forgery. 'Take him down!' orders Eveleigh. Stonehouse steals one last look at Buckley, turns on his heel and disappears.[2]

Eveleigh's tone changes as soon as Stonehouse has gone. He's the courteous and considerate judge Buckley heard from the back of the courtroom that first day. 'I think you were extremely unfortunate that you met this persuasive, deceitful and ambitious man,' he tells the tearful Buckley. 'I do recognise that John Stonehouse's influence must have been tremendous. One had only to see the manner in which he sought to mesmer-ise the jury in this court to know that he could have told you anything, and while it is clear that you knew the situation, I have no doubt he persuaded you your duty was to go along with him.' Eveleigh gives her two years, suspended for the same. Buckley is free to go – but not before she collapses into a chair, only stopped from falling by two wardens.[3]

She eventually makes her getaway in a private car driven by the *Daily Express*, who has secured her story. The asking price is reported to be £20,000. Stonehouse leaves in a green, barred prison bus, the driver hooting at the photographers chasing it down Holborn. It is the distraught Jane Stonehouse who gets caught by reporters as she emerges from the Old Bailey. She has stood by her father when everyone else stood back. 'I'm very, very shocked and terribly sad,' is all she can manage. In the evening, there's an extended item on Stonehouse on the BBC news. While the reporter concedes that communist spy allegations contributed to his disappearance, the BBC man airily dismisses them with the words, 'not true, as it happens'.[4]

The trial over and freed from sub-judice, the papers can finally go to town. 'A conman, a liar and a thief,' declares the *Daily Mirror,* with Buckley reduced to 'shrewd and scheming', while the *Daily Express* splashes her story as 'Sheila: Love Was My Only Crime'. They were out to get John Stonehouse, she says, and she feels guilty only that she helped them. 'If I had my time over again,' says Buckley, 'I'd do the same.'[5] *The Times* says the police investigation alone cost £750,000, and the *Guardian* uses the colloquial to nail the accusation: 'John Stonehouse, Member of Parliament, Privy Counsellor, and twister'. If only they knew how right they were.[6]

Jean Markham, the joint victim of Stonehouse's most heinous crime, also lets rip on what she really thinks. It's slightly more than two years since she asked Stonehouse for his ID on her Brownhills' doorstep and told him to back off criticising their GP. She should have kicked him out there and then, she says. She is still livid that Joe's name has been abused and that she and her family has to live with this terrible insult to her late husband. 'He is a scoundrel and a blackguard,' she concludes. 'I shall never vote again.'[7]

It's left to Barbara to bring the curtain down. She hasn't been to court and has kept her feelings to herself – until now. She had slowly stepped back from her supportive role, but still she lived with Stonehouse as his wife. 'Now I am going to start proceedings,' she says, revealing that she actually made up her mind 'to divorce John when I first went to Australia', recalling that long plane journey over Christmas 1974. She attempts to explain her astonishing loyalty as not wanting to 'add to his personal problems', but in fact Barbara is still haunted by her father leaving so suddenly when she was just five years old. The one thing she always strove to avoid above all else was a broken home. Finally, she's let it go. And yes, she has a new man in her life.[8]

It is to this frenzied backdrop that Stonehouse arrives at the gatehouse and octagonal towers of Wormwood Scrubs, the infamous west London jail. It all looks oddly familiar, its design being the prototype for Pentridge Prison in Melbourne, and its twelve-foot walls have been keeping the most dangerous prisoners away from society since 1891. The convicted KGB double agent George Blake climbed a rope ladder flung over the walls en route to Moscow in 1966 but, for most, there is no escape from the Scrubs.

While he adjusts to residency in this high-security prison, Stonehouse's lover on the outside gets more than her *Daily Express* pay cheque. Buckley tees up her first-person account for serialisation across three issues of *Woman* magazine and it creates more acrimony than ever between the two women who have most shared Stonehouse's life. Buckley says the Stonehouses' relationship broke down years before he disappeared, that their 'miserable marriage' was just a pretence because Barbara liked the prestige of being a politician's wife. Barbara refused a divorce and never really loved him, claims Buckley.[9]

It's outrageous. Barbara knows there can only have been one source for all of this one-sided version of events. The realisation that her husband convinced Buckley his actions were justified with these lies hurts more than anything else, even the affair. She may be moving on, but she can't reconcile how easily Stonehouse betrayed her. Everything she had done to make her marriage a success, and standing by him for all those months, had counted for nothing. Her husband's absolute treachery against her is beyond doubt.[10]

Opinion is with Barbara and she receives hundreds of letters of sympathy from members of the public. 'Sheila Buckley saw it as a conspiracy between two lovers against the world,' writes a *Daily Mirror* columnist, 'when really it was him finding the biggest fool he knew to do the necessary dirty work.' Buckley's attempt to give her side of the story – 'I will wait twenty years for him' – brings a further blow: the Official Receiver demands her media fees to pay off her debts now that she is bankrupt.[11]

On Monday 8 November 1976, John Stonehouse is still one of the 1,000 prisoners doing time at the Scrubs. It's fewer than three months since he was frogmarched from the prison bus, given a quick medical and stripped of his personal effects, but it's not just his possessions that have gone. He resigned from the Commons on 27 August and, having tendered his resignation from the Privy Council, the Queen accepted it in less than a week during routine state business at Balmoral. Finally, nineteen years and six months after his maiden speech, and following nearly two years of clinging onto his seat against all odds, the Conservatives win Walsall North from the English National Party in a by-election. But it is in effect a loss for Labour, and two more quickly follow, reducing Callaghan's majority to one.[12]

Two miles across west London from Stonehouse, Michael Sherrard and Ian Hay Davison are getting ready for their day. Conspicuous in business suits and carrying briefcases, they weave their way past the casually dressed Japanese tourists thronging the lobby of the American-styled fancifully named Kensington Hilton. It's actually on the Shepherd's Bush–Holland Park boundary and, they note, lacks the style of Melbourne's Windsor. They are taking a black cab, not a

Melbourne tram, but the Department of Trade inspectors are on a familiar mission.

It's a fifteen-minute ride down the A3220, under the Westway, down Scrubs Lane, left along Du Cane Road and a right turn into the prison drop-off area. The pair are then led into a grim world of barred windows, clanking gates and jangling keys, but both know the score. The governor welcomes them. Lunch will be served by trusties in the officers' mess. 'You'll find it very good,' they are told, but the faint aroma of stale soup suggests otherwise.

A warder brings Stonehouse down from the South Wing where the long-term prisoners are kept. Now a convicted fraudster, his hair is shorter than they remember and his trademark two-piece suit has given way to the prison uniform of grey woolly sweater, grey trousers and black shoes. He says he likes it here; he's glad not to be commuting to the Old Bailey. And, just to remind them he was an important man, he says it's a relief to be free of all the phone calls.

At first, it's the old cocksure Stonehouse – I'm right, everyone else is wrong. Then gradually his attitude changes. He has already faced the judge and jury, and now he has nothing left to lose. Davison suggests that the criss-crossing of funds between his companies 'was presumably to comfort the bank manager with the thought that here was a busy company?' 'Certainly,' replies Stonehouse. Davison asks whether this was a sham. 'It was a sham, yes,' says Stonehouse. They ask if there was 'business substance in this flow of funds'. 'Absolutely not,' declares Stonehouse.[13]

His once-failing memory – never the product of mental illness, think the inspectors – has been restored and the admissions come thick and fast. He admits that Ronvale, a company he couldn't remember when quizzed by Sir Charles Hardie at

Dixon Wilson and the inspectors in Melbourne, was a cover-up for BBT's failed share issue. The plan was to sell the shares quickly, but when Sherrard suggests there was no purchaser in sight and that 'this was all being done hurriedly in the hope that something would turn up', Stonehouse concurs.

'Exactly,' he says. 'We genuinely thought . . . that those lovely printed accounts would help us to get the agreements with the bank in Beirut and with the Miami bank and other potential investors . . . and by the end of the year everything would be tied up,' Stonehouse explains. 'When you get one stroke of good luck, everything is cleaned up . . . And then everybody after the event would not be bothered with how it was done . . . You know that can happen.' But Sherrard and Davison really don't.

Friday 19 November is the inspectors' eighth and last day in the prison. Stonehouse won't be meeting them again but, before they go, there's another thing he wants to say. 'I didn't differentiate clearly between myself and the companies,' he confesses. 'I was prepared to throw my resources into the companies at will and similarly if one of my personal accounts was in trouble, the resources of the companies would be prayed in aid.' Finally, he admits this was not a way to conduct business. It's an explanation, of sorts. The inspectors pack up their things, say farewell to the governor and go off to write their report.[14]

In December, Stonehouse is moved from Wormwood Scrubs to HMP Blundeston, a low-security prison near Lowestoft in Suffolk. His appeal team of Louis Blom-Cooper QC and Geoffrey Robertson ask the prison for a medical report before they try to lodge grounds for appeal. On 21 December 1976, just shy of two years since Stonehouse's disappearance, Francis Eteng, senior medical officer at Blundeston, examines him.[15]

Eteng finds no signs of a psychotic illness and a normal memory, despite 'doubtful' insights into his own mental state and an 'attention-seeking personality'. 'I think he has a tendency to exaggerate the normal stresses and strains of life,' writes Eteng. 'He wishfully thinks he had a nervous breakdown which gave rise to his irresponsible conduct, and such, wants to be pitied.'

There will be little pity forthcoming from Sherrard and Davison. They've had thirty-two days of Stonehouse hearings since the trial and seventy days including their time in Melbourne. There are 4,000 typed pages of transcripts of interviews with witnesses. On 19 January, *Private Eye* leaks what it purports to be the findings, but it is 4pm on 12 February before it is finished. Sherrard's next brief is a mental health case and Davison gives him a copy of *One Flew Over the Cuckoo's Nest* as a parting gift.[16]

The next month, Stonehouse receives a day's release from prison – to appear at the London Bankruptcy Court. His debts are declared to be £816,000 and his assets are estimated to be £137,185, most of which are still in Switzerland and is subject to arrest proceedings there. As Buckley watches from the public gallery, Stonehouse launches into a familiar story of innocence, breakdown and wrongful conviction. For those who were at the Old Bailey, it's just like old times. 'I am listening to irrelevant answers,' the registrar responds. 'Meaningless answers, points you are trying to score off the Official Receiver.'[17]

The two men with the real inside track on Stonehouse's financial position also have his number. Sherrard and Davison's final report explains how it started with that *Sunday Times* article. In the beginning, BBT was going to be a rebirth of Stonehouse's old idealism; that's why the article needled so much. But he lost all sense of proportion, became increasingly bitter and 'repeatedly and with ingenuity broke the law'. On 30 November 1972, he crossed the line with illegal loans to fund the share issue.[18]

Thereafter 'the companies under Mr Stonehouse's control were saturated with offences . . . to conceal others even more objectionable'. Some associates were duped all too easily, while others, like chartered accountant John McGrath, should have known better. General manager Keith White, they conclude, knew what was going on at crucial times. Both of these men shared with Stonehouse 'a common and almost impenetrable psychological block of recognition'. McGrath, White's deputy John Broad, executives Philip Bingham and Alan Le Fort, and ledger clerk Vera Kemp all knew about Ronvale and its purpose. Kazi Ahmed, who first had the idea of a bank for British Bangladeshis, was young, easily influenced and failed to show the judgement expected of an independent director. Jim Charlton, a chartered company secretary and barrister, was naïve, casual and blinded by stardust.[19]

Dixon Wilson were 'thoroughly slipshod in dealing with material matters', while Eric Levine & Co's advice was littered with errors. Sir Charles Hardie and Eric Levine are criticised for their firms' failings and for their personal involvement: 'Sir Charles took a deliberate risk believing that no great harm would ensue. Mr Levine on the other hand seems to us to have lacked the objectivity appropriate to his position as the company's adviser.'[20]

As for Buckley, Sherrard and Davison did not interview her but say she participated in 'a serious and deliberate attempt to mislead the auditors' when she typed a letter to herself from company secretary Bingham's long-hand draft. They think that 'of the two, Mr Bingham probably realised more clearly the implications of the deceptions which was only one of several he practised at the time'. The inspectors pass no judgement on Buckley, but quote Judge Eveleigh: 'I have no doubt that you were fully aware of what was going on.'[21]

Stonehouse himself, of course, was the instigator of it all, the presiding conductor. He was a 'sophisticated and skilful confidence trickster' who used his reputation, charm and influence to deceive family, friends and business associates. 'Most held Mr Stonehouse in awe and great respect. He treated them well, took them for walks along the corridors of power and enabled them to rub shoulders with men and women of considerable eminence who were themselves impressed by his charm, confidence and seeming integrity.'

Extradition law and the director of public prosecutions' rush to get him out of Australia saved Stonehouse from being charged with the most egregious charges, those relating to BBT. The real extent of the 'serious wrongdoings' he was responsible for 'extends very considerably beyond the offences for which he was tried and convicted', say the inspectors. They conclude that he should count himself lucky he was in the dock before it all became apparent.[22]

Meanwhile Stonehouse's appeal team try to overturn the five insurance convictions on the basis that Eveleigh misdirected the jury, but the Law Lords are unconvinced. 'I am of the opinion that this is a clear case where no miscarriage of justice has resulted from misdirection,' rules Lord Diplock.[23]

In July 1977, Stonehouse's divorce from Barbara comes through. There has been no contact at all between them since he went to jail a year ago. She is now in a loving relationship with Dennis Flexney-Briscoe — her business partner at her burgeoning PR agency and soon-to-be husband. Buckley spends her weekends travelling to and from HMP Blundeston and weekdays working as an anonymous temp under her maiden name Black. It's clear who got the better deal. She had all the pleasure of the early years; Buckley is welcome to the misery they turned into.[24]

3 0

COVER-UP

By 1978, James Callaghan's minority government has been weakened by five by-election defeats, including that in Stonehouse's old constituency. He is clinging to power through the 'Lib-Lab' pact with the Liberals and, never having fought a general election as leader, is seen as a prime minister without a mandate. The Tories, led by Margaret Thatcher since 1975, smell blood. Backbench opposition MPs look for any excuse to discredit the government and former MI6 intelligence officer Cranley Onslow, member of parliament for the true blue constituency of Woking, thinks he has found one.

Onslow is one of the last Tory squires and has Stonehouse in his sights. He disapproves of idealistic causes such as the Campaign for Nuclear Disarmament and generous aid to the developing world and, as Ted Heath's aerospace minister between 1972 and 1974, deplored the cancellation of Britain's TSR2 spy plane when Stonehouse was aviation minister. With his security services background, he follows intelligence issues closely, none more so than the Stonehouse espionage story after Frolík's evidence emerged. It would be good to get one over on Labour, but for Onslow it's more than that. Traitors deserve to be outed.[1]

He bides his time for the right moment and, in June 1978, with Callaghan looking vulnerable after his latest by-election loss, Onslow writes to the prime minister. Based on the

Department of Trade report, he says there is no reason to believe Stonehouse 'in any area where there is good reason to suspect he may be lying' – espionage included. Drawing on both his security services and ministerial experience, Onslow says that Stonehouse's published account of his meeting with the Czechs at the ski hotel in the Low Tatras mountains – Robert Husak and Karel Pravec just ambushed him out of nowhere and then appeared in his hotel room – looks like a cover story.

Onslow doesn't know that this was where Husak handed over Stonehouse to Pravec back in 1968, but he knows enough about the intelligence world to doubt Stonehouse's version of events. In fact, he simply doesn't believe it. It's not, he says, how a visiting minister would be treated by foreign security services 'unless he had some sinister motive for collaborating with them'. Onslow concludes that 'espionage by a minister of the Crown can never be a light matter' and asks Callaghan to refer it to the Security Commission.[2]

Onslow and other Conservative MPs have already enlisted the help of their colleague Patrick Mayhew QC, the MP for Tunbridge Wells, and he has arranged to meet Frolík on a trip to Washington DC. He is travelling with his wife to attend a conference there, but has agreed to interview Frolík. Under cover of darkness, Mayhew drives out of Washington and arrives at the agreed rendezvous on the banks of the Potomac River. He is escorted to a car, in which sits Frolík. Mayhew spends more than six hours talking to the defector under this arrangement over two evenings, and with Frolík's agreement, he records the interviews. On his return to London on 19 June, Mayhew takes up the running from Onslow, and writes to the prime minister asking for an independent investigation and offering up the tapes for Callaghan to hear himself.[3]

Callaghan dutifully consults the cabinet secretary, Sir John

Hunt, who advises that 'we should first see what the tapes say'. On 27 June, Mayhew puts the six cassettes into a sealed package. He gives them to his secretary who takes the five-minute walk across Parliament Square to Downing Street and hands them over to Number 10. The tapes are then passed to Hunt, who orders for a transcript to be made. While Callaghan and MI5's new leader, Howard Smith – fresh from diplomatic stints at the British embassies in both Prague and Moscow – read the transcript, Mayhew ups the pressure, telling Callaghan he intends to share his correspondence with Thatcher. Callaghan is not one to be flustered and coolly notes to his officials that there is 'no need to treat this in any other way than normally'.[4]

After a fortnight, Mayhew gets impatient. On 11 July he writes to Callaghan again, threatening a motion in the Commons two days later, and this time the prime minister jumps to it. They meet at 8pm in Callaghan's room at the House of Commons the next day, when Callaghan jokingly enquires whether Mayhew is taping this meeting as well. He asks about Mayhew's impressions of Frolík. Mayhew says that despite the 'frightful crimes' that Frolík has committed – presumably espionage – he was more impressed by him than he expected. Callaghan says he has not yet made up his mind whether to refer the matter to the Security Commission, set up by Alec Douglas-Home after the Profumo scandal. Mayhew agrees to defer his Commons motion until 20 July to allow Callaghan time to think about this.[5]

The prime minister, a former navy man, is very cautious on intelligence matters and his time in charge of both the Home Office and the Foreign Office has given him more insight into the security environment than Harold Wilson ever enjoyed. He is seriously concerned that a prominent member of a former Labour government could have been disloyal to his country and is sympathetic to establishing the facts – even though he has a nagging dread that this could get political. He orders further investigations and decides to sound out both his predecessor and the leader of the opposition.

On 14 July 1978, shortly before lunch, Callaghan meets Wilson in the Cabinet Room on the ground floor of Number 10. The long green baize table can seat forty, but it's empty now save for the two men and a note-taker. It's just downstairs from the Number 10 sitting room where Wilson and MI5's Charles Elwell confronted Stonehouse. Wilson had carefully dismissed the rumours of Stonehouse's Soviet spying career in the Commons in December 1974 and had chosen not to say anything when he was told in June 1975 that the security services 'might now be just a shade more cautious in advising the prime minister on whether he could give Mr Stonehouse a clean bill of health from the security point of view'. He was briefed again on the matter in July 1977 after he had retired.[6]

Callaghan asks Wilson what he remembers of the allegations, but Wilson doesn't recall ever seeing Stonehouse about this matter. However, he does reveal that in 1970 he told Stonehouse that he did not intend to give him another front-bench appointment. This was because he disapproved of Stonehouse's handling of the Post Office pay claim in a way that had undermined the chancellor's economic policy and because he believed he had mishandled some charitable funds for a third-world country. It appeared then that if Stonehouse wasn't corrupt, he was certainly corruptible.[7]

Just four days later, at nine in the evening on 18 July, Callaghan briefs opposition leader Thatcher in his office in the Commons. The prime minister and the leader of the opposition traditionally work closely on matters of state security, and in this instance it will be helpful for Callaghan. Part-ownership of the problem reduces the risk of a hostile press briefing.

As summer rain drizzles outside the Houses of Parliament, Callaghan tells Thatcher the matter relates to the Stonehouse question that her MP Patrick Mayhew intends to raise in the House. Before he can finish, Thatcher interrupts and says she has asked Mayhew to withdraw the question as she understands the prime minister would not have time to respond. It's nearly an apology.

Callaghan then gets formal and establishes that the discussion is on 'privileged' Privy Council terms, a convention whereby the prime minister briefs the leader of the opposition on a confidential basis. He quotes Wilson's 'not in any sense a security risk' denial to the House on 17 December 1974 and Thatcher remarks that 'that was a very powerful statement'. Callaghan admits that there is now 'at least a possibility that John Stonehouse was an agent' and that 'he would not now accept that Stonehouse was not a security risk'. However, Callaghan says, there is no more in the Mayhew tapes with Frolík than that which MI5 already knows from its own conversations with the defector.

Thatcher asks if the security services had exercised what she describes as 'maximum due diligence'. Callaghan says there was 'no evidence which they could really sustain . . .' and Thatcher finishes the sentence for him, '. . . in a court of law'. Forced by expediency to keep many of Heath's supporters in the shadow cabinet, she is not yet secure as party leader. Thatcher says that her problem is to convince her people that she had not been taken in by all this and asks for time to think about it all.[8]

She does so for a few days. She certainly doesn't want to take lightly the suggestion that a former minister was a spy for the

Eastern bloc. But by the same token, she is not interested in scoring party political points by exploiting a security matter. The national interest must come first. She is also a relatively new leader with no real experience of security and intelligence matters. Who is she to argue with a political veteran like Callaghan who has lived through every single security scandal of the Cold War?

She agrees not to call for a referral to the Security Commission and Callaghan indicates that his officials will give her MPs enough of a briefing to keep them quiet. They do so and Mayhew then writes to Callaghan thanking him: 'I, too, concur in that view, on the basis of the advice given to you, and your own assurances which I naturally accept.' 'This, we hope,' says the prime minister's office, 'sees the end of the matter.'[9]

A couple of weeks later, it's nearly the end of everything for John Stonehouse. He has a heart attack in prison and is rushed to Lowestoft General Hospital. It's clear he needs more specialist care than Blundeston can provide and, in September, he's transferred to Wormwood Scrubs' hospital wing. The next month, he's moved up the road to Hammersmith Hospital where he is given a heart bypass. The operation is a success and soon he's back in Blundeston.[10]

Callaghan is also facing an existential crisis, albeit one of a professional rather than personal nature. The Lib-Lab pact ends in August and Callaghan decides not to call an autumn election in the hope that an economic recovery is just round the corner. But water, sewerage, ambulance and refuse workers go on strike. Piles of rubbish on the streets become a symbol of the government's problems and, on 1 March 1979, voters get the chance to make their feelings known about the 'Winter of Discontent'. It's not a general election, but two by-elections on the same day. Labour emphatically lose them both. Thatcher calls a 'no confidence' vote in the Commons, she wins by one vote and Callaghan is finally forced to call a general election. The electorate thinks the unions are running the country and, on 3 May, Thatcher wins a thumping majority.

By now, the man whose antics cost Labour the seat of Walsall North is nearly halfway through his seven-year stretch. He is eligible for parole and, at the second time of asking, the parole board decide he is of low risk to the public and release him on good behaviour.

He is moved to Norwich Prison prior to release and by dawn on Tuesday 14 August 1979, there's a gaggle of press waiting outside. At 6am, an hour before the parole prisoners' official release time, a prison warder brings out a suitcase and several boxes, and loads them into a waiting Volvo. Then Stonehouse appears. He runs to the car, jacket over his head, and lays down on the back seat out of view. The Volvo roars away, pursued by photographers on motorbikes. The car touches 100 miles per hour, screeches into U-turns and the chase goes on for an hour.[11]

Stonehouse goes to ground and, once again, it falls to Jane to speak up for her father. On BBC2's Sunday night programme *The Editors*, she is confronted with Fleet Street's finest and it's a tough gig. Veteran journalist George Scott is the presenter and she faces James Nicholson, the *Daily Star*'s crime reporter, the *News of the World*'s Stafford Somerfield and the most widely read diarist in Britain, the *Daily Mail*'s Nigel Dempster. She's outnumbered and out of her depth. Jane protests at the way the press are treating her father, but they all know her family have sold their stories over the years. Dempster insists Stonehouse has brought it on himself and predicts that this latest chapter will also be sold.[12]

Buckley and Stonehouse get a couple of weeks of peace

tucked away in a secluded East Anglian cottage but by the end of August, paparazzi track them down eating ice cream in the sun. Like Barbara in 1975, Buckley tells them that Stonehouse is still ill and needs peace. But also like Barbara, she knows that these people, while annoying, have large cheque books. Dempster has called it right: by October, Buckley's latest instalment fills the pages of *Woman* magazine. There were no popping corks or extravagant celebrations, says Buckley of their reunion, just a dance around their rented living room. She met other men while he was in prison, but lived alone and was never unfaithful. 'I still love John and I always will,' she says. He wants to marry her straight away.[13]

Excitement about the country's first female prime minister sustains Thatcher through a difficult first few months, which see unprecedented interest rates of 17 per cent and the IRA killing of twenty-one on a single day, including Prince Philip's uncle Lord Mountbatten. But in November, Thatcher has a different security problem to face. *Private Eye* names Sir Anthony Blunt, surveyor of the Queen's pictures, as a member of the notorious Cambridge spy ring. Other members – Guy Burgess, Donald Maclean and Kim Philby – had fled to the Soviet Union and the identity of the mysterious fourth man has always fascinated the public.

The security services have known since 1964 that it was Blunt, but with the agreement of then prime minister Sir Alec Douglas-Home, they did a deal, granting Blunt immunity from prosecution in return for a full confession. The Queen was told, successive governments stayed silent and Blunt retained his royal position until he retired in 1972.

Private Eye's revelation and the publication of *The Climate of Treason,* a well-researched book by Scottish journalist Andrew Boyle, are sensational. The security services advise Thatcher not to comment, but she is appalled that he was granted immunity. On 16 November, she tells the Commons that Blunt's behaviour had been 'contemptible and repugnant' and that when it comes to traitors 'our task is to guard against their counterparts today'. Blunt is stripped of his knighthood the same day and it's clear there will be no toleration of treachery under this prime minister.[14]

Or not. In July 1980, cabinet secretary Sir Robert Armstrong briefs Thatcher on information from a new Czech defector, Karel Pravec, who was Husak's successor in London in 1968. Pravec never recreated the success of Husak's relationship with Stonehouse, despite staking out Stonehouse's Potters Bar home and chasing him around the 1969 Labour Party conference.

But it's what he learned before then as Stonehouse's silent controller in Prague that interests the cabinet secretary. Armstrong tells Thatcher that this new defector, also residing in the US, claims he was the overseer of Stonehouse at HQ before he was posted to London, and that Stonehouse was a willing, paid agent from 1962. Pravec says that, on taking office in 1964, Stonehouse provided information on government plans and policies, and on technological subjects including aircraft. Thatcher asks to be kept informed while the matter is investigated.[15]

A few months later, on the morning of 6 October, Attorney General Sir Michael Havers reports to Thatcher and Home Secretary Willie Whitelaw at Number 10. He confirms that he is now sure Stonehouse was an agent for the Czech intelligence service, but there is still no convincing evidence he could put before a jury. They could challenge him again, but Stonehouse was interrogated at length by Charles Elwell in the late 1960s and had vehemently denied everything. Since then, he has served a prison sentence and undergone open heart surgery. If he was interviewed now, he is likely to make a public fuss and claim he is being persecuted by the government again. Havers believes that Stonehouse should not be confronted with the new evidence and, in a different stance to that he took on Blunt barely a year before, recommends that 'matters should be left where they were now'.

This is a tricky moment for Thatcher. While in opposition, she had assured her backbenchers that the Stonehouse story was not worth going after, even though she knew then that the allegations might have been true. As the new prime minister, she has since named Blunt, denounced traitors and told the House to be on its guard. She might look foolish if it emerged that she had been complicit in not pursuing an earlier matter involving a far more senior figure with much better access to confidential information than Blunt. Despite the fact that she is appalled that Stonehouse looks to have betrayed the interests of the UK by taking money from an adversary power, it is not a hard decision to accept Havers's advice.[16]

Stonehouse is blissfully ignorant of his narrow escape. He and Buckley tie the knot in a quiet registry office ceremony in January 1981, initially share the attic flat of a Victorian terraced house in Kilburn in north-west London, then buy a modern detached house near to Southampton, his hometown. He writes his first novel, convinced he will make a living as an author like Jeffrey Archer has done.[17]

The book is released in 1982; it later comes out in paperback as *Breach of Security* and concerns a bureaucrat who gets honey-trapped by a Soviet spy in East Germany. Once again, the chutzpah of this man is breathtaking. Within five years, he goes from denying being in the pay of the Czechs to writing about that very world – including settings, like St Ermin's Hotel, where he'd met with his own handlers. 'I must say,' he tells a magazine programme on the BBC, 'it's very, very amusing to be able to knit together some of the things that I know about from the inside and put them into a thriller.'[18] As such the book is read closely for clues as to his own spying career, but is slammed on the review pages.[19]

Stonehouse is undeterred; it took Archer a long time to be accepted as a writer.[20] Next up comes *The Baring Fault*, about a Soviet spy in the mould of the ideologically driven Cambridge Spies who goes on to become prime minister.

Stonehouse takes to the sofa circuit under the impression he'll be able to promote his books, but there are other things the talk-show hosts want to ask him about, and they're not fiction. Both Michael Parkinson and Russell Harty invite him onto their prime-time shows, where he dispatches the Czech spy allegations as usual; his relationship with Robert Husak was purely official.[21]

Then there's a major TV interview with the country's favourite psychiatrist, Professor Anthony Clare. But after an initial open discussion about his childhood, Stonehouse becomes as irritated and hard done by as ever and trots out the same old lines: the gulf between the idealism learned from his parents and the reality of political life led him to live a lie, and the only way out was to develop parallel personalities and commit psychiatric suicide. He is still completely without remorse.[22]

In between these appearances, his daughter Jane is interviewed by the *Sunday Mirror*. She speaks of the strain of supporting her father in Australia, during his trial and while he was in prison. It made her, she says, become a chainsmoker, and her hair started falling out. And she felt that when he was cast out, she became an outcast too.[23]

On 8 August 1987, Stonehouse uses the launch of his new novel *Oil on the Rift* as an opportunity for a press conference, the first, he claims, in eleven years. Far from talking about his new novel, which details the takeover of an African country using 'manipulation by corrupt practice', he demands an inquiry into MI5's 'dirty tricks', of which he believes himself to be a victim. The allegation that he was a Czech spy? 'That is an absolute lie,' he declares again. 'I think it is important that the air is cleared and that the allegations are mopped up.'

In March 1988, Stonehouse is booked to appear on Central Television's *Weekend Live* programme. He's still trying to promote his books, rather than discuss his past, and is still being asked the same questions. 'What about the people you left behind and the distress you caused?' the host says. Stonehouse begins to answer, repeating his defence of 'psychiatric suicide', then loses his thread and slowly loses consciousness, lolling in his chair. The live show goes dark as a doctor in the studio audience rushes to help. Three weeks later, Stonehouse dies in Southampton General Hospital at the age of 62.

Buckley, now 41, is interviewed exclusively by the *Daily Mail* at her Romsey home the next day. When asked, she says she can't explain why she remained in such a sacrificial relationship for so long, and instead points to 'a deep-seated maternal instinct' as the reason she could never desert Stonehouse. 'Many people have called me a fool,' she says, 'but he needed me so much.' For twenty-seven years, Barbara had stayed too. These two women's protective tendencies, combined with the emotional blackmail of a charming yet narcissistic man, kept Stonehouse loved even when he behaved appallingly. 'There will never be another John,' Buckley adds. 'You have to understand.' But no one really can.

The other papers dub his death 'the final chapter in the unreal life and death of John Stonehouse', but they don't know everything. On 15 January 2006, the *Mail on Sunday* reveals that Stonehouse had worked for the Czechs as a spy throughout the 1960s. Other publications pick up the story, but by this time the public is more concerned about Islamic terrorists than reds under the bed. It is treated as an embarrassing episode from another age but without much historical significance. At the beginning of 2008, the Czech government opens its security services archive and begins releasing its StB files. Rumours about Stonehouse are finally substantiated with documentation.[24]

But then, in December 2010, papers released under the thirty-year rule reveal the 1980 meeting between Thatcher, Havers and Whitelaw. The left-leaning *Guardian* seizes on Thatcher's involvement saying that she 'agreed to a cover-up' of allegations that Stonehouse was a spy. Quick to defend a Tory icon, the *Daily Mail* responds that 'far from being a cover-up, the truth is that Mrs Thatcher was advised that neither [Czech] source had provided information that could be used as evidence. And on that basis, she agreed that he could not be prosecuted for espionage.' The *Mail*'s version pleases the embarrassed security services and custodians of the Thatcher legacy, but misses the significance of the meeting with Callaghan in the summer of 1978 and her agreement to call off her Tory backbenchers.[25]

This casts a very different light on her meeting with Havers and Whitelaw two years later. If it had been decided in 1980 to challenge Stonehouse, let alone charge him, as Havers had said, Stonehouse would have made a public fuss and her earlier acquiescence would very probably have emerged. That would have been an embarrassment after her very public stance in the similar case against Blunt. The question would have been asked: 'Why call out Blunt and go easy on Stonehouse?' That, and the way she played her backbenchers to Callaghan's tune, would have dented the Iron Lady's reputation before she had fully exerted her authority over the country or her party.[26]

Stonehouse was never appointed to the cabinet, but he is the only British politician known to have acted as a foreign agent while holding senior ministerial office. By failing to press the security services for answers, three prime ministers buried his treachery, each for their own different reasons. Thatcher would have suffered reputational damage, but for the two Labour leaders it could have been much more serious. Wilson never shook off the stories that MI5 suspected him to be a communist sympathiser at best, or in the pay of the KGB at worst. Confirmation that one of his ministers and one of the Queen's privy counsellors was an enemy spy in the 1960s, that Wilson's 1974 Commons statement was wrong and that he did nothing with subsequent warnings would have caused acute embarrassment. For Callaghan, who under Wilson held all three great offices of state – foreign secretary, home secretary and chancellor – guilt by association and acquiescence would have been even more damaging to his precarious premiership. Had Stonehouse's espionage become public during either of their times in Number 10, it could have done for Wilson and Callaghan what Profumo did for Macmillan.

AUTHORS' NOTE

Keely: March 2020, first lockdown. Philip and I were corresponding about a completely different idea when I mentioned the Stonehouse story. I sent across my documentary treatment and straight away he came back: 'This should be a book'. Within weeks we had a chapter overview and within months we had signed with Simon & Schuster.

Philip: What makes a documentary-maker and a historian who don't know each other work together on a book? The answer is a shared interest in story-telling and the discovery of a fascinating tale that yielded more and more secrets the further we looked into it. From then on, the richness of the archive material, the twists and turns of the story and the realisation that this was a remarkable window into sixties and seventies Britain, swept us along.

Keely: Two years after we first spoke on the phone, we have produced a non-fiction narrative on perhaps the most outrageous saga of the 20th century. Every time you think it can't get any more outlandish, it does. In that sense, it's a writer's dream. We believe this is the first non-partisan, comprehensive account of the John Stonehouse story.

Philip: At the time of writing, we have met in person on only three occasions and have spent a total of less than three hours in each other's company. But the need to observe lockdown and social distancing have made us expert in electronic communication and may even have helped our productivity.

Keely: Thanks to Rubina and Satema, two-thirds of No BDIs, the most supportive group chat in existence; my parents, for their love and understanding; and my incredible girls, Afiya and Eleni, experts in cheering up the woman who spends too much time at her desk.

Philip: Once more at book-writing time, Denise has supported me with love, patience and tolerance. I plan for this to be the last but as she reminds me, I have said that before.

We are grateful to Ian Marshall and Kaiya Shang at Simon & Schuster for their guidance and support, to Toby Mundy at Aevitas UK for introducing us to them and to Nige Tassell for copy-editing. We'd also like to thank Milan Rydvan, the guardian angel of Czech translation, Tanya Dendis, Thomas Santarius and Jani Santarius for meticulously interpreting the Czech Security Services (StB) files for us. Also, the staff and archivists at the Czech Security Services Archive, for sending countless DVDs, and those at the National Archives at Kew, the British Library, Cambridge University Library, Churchill College, Cambridge and Lizzie Richmond and her colleagues at the University of Bath.

We spoke to a number of John Stonehouse's contemporaries, some of whom wish to remain anonymous. Our respect for their wishes in no way diminishes our thanks for the time they spent with us. Robin Butler, Ian Hay Davison, Bernard

Donoughue and Joe Haines were generous with their time and insightful in their comments and we thank them for that.

Methodology

The immense public interest in the Stonehouse affair is reflected in voluminous contemporaneous records. It was a story that wholly gripped the public's imagination. The smooth operator with a political profile, a secret lover, a wronged wife, espionage, fraud, Mafia cement deals and the daring escape plan filled the broadsheets and the tabloids – and that was before he was back on British soil. John, Barbara and Jane Stonehouse and Sheila Buckley gave regular interviews to newspapers, contributed lengthy first-person pieces for magazines and conducted numerous radio and television interviews. John Stonehouse wrote three autobiographical books, four novels (one under the pen name James Lund) that he claimed drew on his own experiences and there was a steady stream of additional revelations as official records were released in the UK and Czechoslovakia.

Labour's perilous position in the House of Commons – compounded by Stonehouse's absence and then defection to the English National Party – combined with the real risk of a diplomatic stand-off with the Australians, saw diplomats, civil servants and politicians preoccupied with Stonehouse for nine months from December 1974 to August 1975. The National Archives contains hundreds of relevant files and thousands of relevant cables, minutes and inter-government correspondence between Number 10, the Foreign Office and the Home Office and their representatives and opposite numbers in Australia. Dozens of witnesses then gave evidence for the trial of John Stonehouse and Sheila Buckley and these and other trial records remain, as does the Department of Trade's 392-page report on John Stonehouse's business dealings.

We have tried to ensure that our observations are accurate by using these multiple sources, together with newspaper reports (the dedication of the West Midlands press in following the every move of one of their more high-profile MPs was invaluable), first-hand contemporaneous testimony (especially witness statements), interviews with individuals who were present at the time and television and radio clips. Where we attribute emotions – love, relief, anger, joy, frustration, grief – we do so on the basis of how that person described their feelings in articles or interviews or on how other people present in the room or on the call observed them at or soon after the time. Barbara Stonehouse and Sheila Buckley declined to be interviewed for this book.

Where the participants disagree about what happened, we have used our judgement as to the most likely chain of events. We have applied two overarching principles: firstly, is it beyond all reasonable doubt that the event in question happened? If not, is it likely, on the balance of probabilities, that it did? These are the two tests applied in the courts of law, the former for a criminal conviction and the latter for a civil charge.

For example, did the Stonehouses drive to the airport from Sancroft Street on the morning of 19 November 1974, or from their home in Hampshire? On the balance of probabilities, we believe the former as it was a Tuesday and Stonehouse was already in London buying airline tickets the previous day. Was Barbara Stonehouse immaculately turned out when they left? We think so as we have never seen her looking less than this in the many photographs of her we have studied.

Some questions we faced were easier to answer. What happened, for example, when John Stonehouse was detained on a waiting train at St Kilda Station by three officers on the morning of Christmas Eve 1974? Despite reports of trousers being pulled down to compare scars with those of Lord Lucan, we have the unanimous contemporaneous testimony of four separate individuals, including John Stonehouse. There can be no reasonable doubt that it happened as we write it here.

We make reasoned assumptions about the context for certain events. For example, did Harold Wilson travel to Cornwall by train on Christmas Eve 1974 and, when he arrived at Penzance, did he step off the train? Given that he went to Cornwall on that date, usually took the train, and was never reported to have been carried off or fallen from a train, we think it highly likely that he did so. This is not the dramatisation of events, but reaching a logical conclusion with the intention of bringing the story to life and giving it immediacy. For the same reason, on a handful of occasions we have truncated events to make our story more readable.

Sources and references

Our base document for this book eventually contained more than 3,000 references as we strove to stand up every single fact and assumption, holding ourselves to the highest combined standards of both journalism and academia. However, as this is intended to be read as a non-fiction narrative, rather than an academic book, we have omitted most of the individual citations from this published edition. The remaining citations, some 650 in total, are detailed in the Notes section, where we also provide a note of the main sources for the individual chapters.

Political context and the National Archives

In addition to speaking to surviving politicians, special advisers and civil servants who worked at Number 10 and the Home Office, some of whom requested anonymity, we have drawn on academic accounts of the Wilson years and participants' memoirs. We have also studied numerous TV and radio interviews with the participants.

The Department of Trade inspectors' report

The drama of Stonehouse's espionage, escape and love affair has deflected attention from his fraudulent business dealings, of which there is an impeccable account in the form of the Department of Trade inspectors' report, compiled at the time by Michael Sherrard QC and Ian Hay Davison FCA. They had no axe to grind, no political masters to please and no external deadlines to meet. What emerges is a balanced, objective report that has been a valuable source to us in reconstructing the timeline of the events we describe. The inspectors' work runs throughout the relevant chapters of our book and numbered references are given only for important and specific passages.

Czech Security Services Archive

The Security Services Archive (Archiv Bezpečnostních Složek) in Prague gives a full account of Czech intelligence officers' dealings with Stonehouse and other politicians and public figures at this time. Stonehouse's file – more than 500 written pages dedicated to him and his various aliases – is an authentic record of the relationship between intelligence officers working under diplomatic cover at the Czech embassy in London and John Stonehouse. It also includes letters and documents from the head of the overall ministry in charge of security activities at home and abroad – the Ministry for the Interior – as well as the divisional leaders. These files are regularly referenced by Czech and UK scholars, including leading Czech security expert Dr Daniela Richterova, associate professor of intelligence studies at Kings College, London. You can find out more about the files here: www.abscr.cz/en/

We assessed the value of the verbal information Stonehouse gave to the Czechs by checking across many sources whether or not it was in the public domain at the time they recorded receiving it. This reveals that while in general the Czechs were disappointed with what he gave them, on occasion his intelligence was strong and based on confidential information. An example of this is when Stonehouse revealed that the Americans were building a military base on Diego Garcia, then a British territory, as outlined in Chapter 9, confirming what had previously been only an unsubstantiated rumour. This betrayal of defence intelligence – fewer than five years after the US–Russian Cuban missile crisis – was not the only time he gave certainty to an enemy for whom any information edge was valuable. That, of course, is why they kept him on the payroll.

We have studied the files of contemporaries including his friend Donald Chesworth, Will Owen MP and Ernest Fernyhough MP, who were also in the pay of the Czechs. In 2019, an Independent Press Standards Organisation (IPSO) investigation – Sutcliffe vs *The Mail on Sunday* – of a complaint on grounds of accuracy ruled that the StB file on Ernest Fernyhough contained a genuine and correct record of exchanges between Fernyhough and the Czech security service officers who handled him. The IPSO investigation concluded that the *Mail on Sunday* was accurate in describing Fernyhough as a 'spy'. This ruling sets a precedent that we follow in our assessment of the evidence.

All reports were seen and signed off in Prague at the highest levels. We find no proof that the Czech officers habitually falsified the files of individual Britons in order to personally pocket the money they claimed was paid to informants and agents. If they claimed cash for an invented lunch with an informant, it was the exception rather than the norm. The officers in question were on two- to three-year rotations and then were made to return to Prague. There they found an increasingly autocratic, authoritarian regime that thought little of 'disappearing' undesirables. Officers – including two of Stonehouse's handlers, Vlado Koudelka and Robert Husak – were sent home and into career purgatory for much lesser crimes than falsifying meetings with high-profile agents. They simply did not and dare not invent agents.

We have corroborated and triangulated the movements of John Stonehouse as detailed in his StB file with contemporaneous newspaper reports both local and national, Hansard records of parliamentary activity, files detailing Stonehouse's ministerial business in the National Archives in Kew and his own description of his movements in his book *Death of an Idealist*. We believe there is no more reason to question the validity of the Czech Security Services Archive than the archives of the UK Security Services.

The John Stonehouse books

We have used John Stonehouse's autobiographical books to illuminate practical detail, such as what he was reading, the interior of a particular house and his various journeys to and around Europe, the US and Australia. But because his version of events was contested in the UK's Central Criminal Court and led to his conviction, we have not used his books as a basis for factual assertions unless they can be corroborated by other sources or seem so highly probable as to be trustworthy. Two books published by family members in 2021 have not been used for any source material.

In the final analysis

The Stonehouse story is one of the best-documented of all scandals in public life and we have used this good fortune to write as though from behind the camera, showing the reader what John Stonehouse did and how he did it. Our intention is for the reader to decide whether Stonehouse was a wicked trickster or a well-intentioned man who just got sucked in too deep. Or something in between.

We observe a pattern of aberrant behaviour long before the 1970s. Evidence of mishandling money starts at the International Union of Socialist Youth and the farming co-ops of Uganda in the early 1950s, as did his extra-marital affairs. Stonehouse refused to take responsibility for any of these actions.

Yet in the early days his affinity with the underdog saw him establish a connection with the needy that other politicians struggled to pull off. He was also undoubtedly dedicated to his constituents until his disappearance in 1974 and after his release from prison he campaigned for prisoners' rights and reform of the judiciary. He may not have been the idealist he claimed to have been, but there was a streak of decency there no matter how much it later became tarnished.

His was clearly a complex personality. He exhibited signs of a possible psychological disorder, but it is impossible to label John Stonehouse retrospectively so we have resisted trying. Instead, we provide the diagnoses of those who treated him at the time.

Was Stonehouse a spy? It is hard to think of any other term to describe a senior politician who secretly accepted money from an adversarial foreign power in return for information. In the context of the Cold War, and regardless of the information he handed over, there is no escaping the fact that he betrayed his country as soon as he agreed to be on the Czech's payroll.

We believe that, like Will Owen before him, Stonehouse could have been put up before the courts on charges of breaching the Official Secrets Act. Whether those charges would have stuck is a matter of debate. We know he was careful not to hand over written classified information and that securing a conviction on hearsay evidence is difficult. But all of this is moot: Stonehouse was extremely lucky his case was never tested and that he died before the Czech Security Service files were released, at which point evidence that might previously have been disallowed as 'hearsay' would have come right into play.

As we see in our concluding chapter, three British prime ministers, on the advice of the security service and the attorney general, decided that there was not enough evidence to charge Stonehouse. Politically this was very convenient and they all had good cover stories for looking the other way. They could claim to be reluctant to re-question Stonehouse given his ailing health and, less understandably, because he was already disgraced and had served a prison sentence on an unrelated matter. They could tell themselves that the evidence against Stonehouse was not dissimilar to that used in the unsuccessful 1970 prosecution of Will Owen and that another failure would have been embarrassing politically and internationally; all parties could agree on that.

But what message did this inaction send to Britain's enemies or to others contemplating betraying their country, when it came to light? Here we had an ex-minister, blatantly writing and publishing spy novels which he said he enjoyed writing because he could draw on real-life experience. As evidence from Eastern bloc defectors mounted, the authorities did not even re-question him, let alone charge him. That certainly suited the Establishment; whether that was in the public interest is quite another matter.

Was Stonehouse a white-collar criminal? Undoubtedly – and again, it could have and should have been a lot worse for him, as is evidenced in the Department of Trade inspectors' report. In the director of public prosecution's rush to find charges that would definitely stick and get him out of Australia before he fled again, the authorities charged Stonehouse with lesser offences than those he committed. We agree with the view of the inspectors that 'the serious wrongdoing extends very considerably beyond the offences for which Mr Stonehouse was later tried and convicted . . . [and that] the companies under Mr Stonehouse's control were saturated with offences, irregularities and improprieties'. Twister by name . . .

REFERENCES

Note on abbreviations: The National Archives of England and Wales is referred to as TNA. Within these National Archives references, CAB is Cabinet Office, DEFE is Ministry of Defence, FCO is Foreign and Commonwealth Office, FO is Foreign Office, HO is Home Office, J is Supreme Court of Judicature and related courts, KV is the Security Service, PREM is records of the Prime Minister's Office. DOT refers to London Capital Group, Department of Trade Report by Michael Sherrard and Ian Hay Davison. HC Deb refers to a House of Commons debate as recorded in Hansard.

Note on style: We have, where possible, put our references at the end of the relevant paragraph, rather than within paragraphs. If a source is listed at the top of the chapter, it can be assumed that it is used throughout and not specifically referenced each time.

Note on monetary values: Monetary figures are shown in actual prices throughout. As an approximate guide, readers should multiply the given values by 25 in the 1950s, 20 in the 1960s and 10 in the 1970s to calculate the modern day equivalent.

NOTES

1. MIAMI BEACH

This chapter draws on the witness statements of:
- James Charlton, director and chairman of London Capital Group Limited
- Patricia Evans, police officer, Miami Beach Police
- David Bretton, detective chief inspector, UK police
- Anthony Sait, ticket agent, British Airways
- Helen Fleming, secretary, Fontainebleau Hotel (all J 267/707, TNA)

We also used the following sources multiple times in this chapter:
- Stonehouse, first person account, *News of the World*, Sunday 16 March 1975; his book *Death of an Idealist,* W H Allen, 1975
- Hansard, the official report of parliamentary debates
- Barbara Stonehouse interview with Robin Day, *Newsday*, BBC, 19 December 1974
- Barbara Stonehouse, first person account, *Woman* magazine, September 1975
- Miami Dade College's Wolfson Archives (on Miami and Fontainebleau)
- *Horizon* documentary, BBC, 3 May 1973 (on Heathrow Airport)

1   *Miami Herald*, 18 December 1974; Barbara Stonehouse, *Woman*, September 1975
2   *Daily Mirror*, 29 November 1974
3   BBC News, 6 August 1976
4   *Nationwide*, BBC, 19 May 1982
5   *Miami Herald*, 18 December 1974

2. DEAD OR ALIVE?

Witness statements:
- James Charlton, director and chairman of London Capital Group Limited
- Patricia Evans, police officer, Miami Beach Police
- Philip Gay, Stonehouse's personal assistant and director of Export Promotion and Consultancy Services Limited (all J 267/707, TNA)
- Prime Minister's Office records, PREM 16/587, TNA
- ITN News, 4 December 1975
- *Daily Express*, 22 and 25 November 1974
- *Daily Mirror*, 27 November 1974
- Barbara Stonehouse, interview with Robin Day, *Newsday*, BBC, 19 December 1974
- Barbara Stonehouse, first person account, *Woman* magazine, September 1975
- Sheila Buckley, first person account, *Woman*, 30 October and 6 November 1976

Author interviews:
- Bernard Donoughue, head of the Policy Unit at No. 10, 1974–1979
- Joe Haines, prime minister's press secretary, 1969–1976

1   Barbara Stonehouse, *Woman* op cit
2   Sheila Buckley, *Woman* op cit
3   Philip Ziegler, *Wilson: The Authorised Life*, Weidenfeld & Nicolson, 1993, pp 472–473; Lord George Bridges, 'A Tribute to the Consummate Diplomat: Thomas Bridges', *Civil Service World*, 11 July 2017
4   Author interview with Bernard Donoughue
5   *Miami Herald*, 22 November 1974
6   *The Times*, 23 November 1974; *Guardian*, 23 November 1974
7   Francisco Gordillo, lifeguard, Fontainebleau Hotel, *Daily Mirror*, 27 November 1974 and ITN, 4 December 1974
8   *Miami Herald*, 25 November 1974; *Daily Mirror*, 27 November 1974; *Daily Mail*, 27 and 28 November 1974
9   *Daily Mirror*, 27 November 1974
10 *Private Eye*, 15 November 1974. See above, 'Note on monetary values.'
11 *Daily Mirror*, 13 December 1974
12 PREM 16/587, 27 November 1974; *Daily Mail*, 28 November 1974
13 PREM 16/587, 27 November 1974
14 *Daily Mail*, 27 November 1974
15 *Daily Mirror*, 28 November 1974

3. THE PROBLEM THAT WON'T GO AWAY

- Prime Minister's Office records, PREM 16/587, TNA
- Barbara Stonehouse, interview with Robin Day, *Newsday*, BBC, 19 December 1974
- Barbara Stonehouse interview, BBC News, 29 November 1974
- ITN News, 4 December 1974

Author interviews:
- Bernard Donoughue, head of the Policy Unit at No 10, 1974–1979
- Joe Haines, prime minister's press secretary, 1969–1976
- Robin Butler, private secretary to Harold Wilson, 1974–75.

1   *Daily Mirror,* 29 November 1974
2   *Newsday* op cit; Barbara Stonehouse interview, BBC News, 29 November 1974
3   Tony Benn, *The Benn Diaries, 1973–76*, Hutchinson, 1989, p 273; *Daily Mail*, 28 November 1974; author interview
4   PREM 16/587, 27 November, 2 and 21 December, 1974
5   *Daily Express*, 2 December 1974; *Newsday* op cit
6   PREM 16/587, 9 December 1974
7   Betty Boothroyd, *The Autobiography*, Century, 2001, p 98
8   PREM 16/587, 4 December 1974
9   *Daily Express* and *Daily Mirror*, 11 December 1974
10 *Daily Mirror*, 11 December 1974; *Guardian*, 17 February 1974
11 *Guardian*, 13 and 19 December 1974
12 *New York Times*, 15 March 1975; *Guardian*, 19 December 1974 and 10 January 1975; *Los Angeles Times*, 24 March 1975; correspondence from Sylvester Okereke/Unafrique Industrial Consultants to John Stonehouse, 15 November 1974, 'Inquiry into Death of Sylvester Okereke', JWN 14/1, TNA
13 *Daily Express*, 22 June 1975
14 *Newsday* op cit
15 PREM 16/587, 27 November 1974
16 *Daily Mirror*, 16 December 1974; *Guardian*, 18 December 1974
17 PREM 16/587, 27 November 1974
18 *Daily Mirror*, 17 December 1974, *Daily Express* 17 and 18 December 1974, *Newsday* op cit
19 *Daily Express* and *Guardian*, 18 December 1974
20 PREM 16/587, 17 December 1974; *Guardian* and *Daily Mirror*, 18 December 1974
21 PREM 16/587, ibid; *Daily Mirror* and *Guardian*, 18 December 1974; BBC News, 17 December 1974

4. TWENTY-SEVEN YEARS EARLIER

- *Jive Dance At the Hammersmith Palais*, 1943; *Hammersmith Palais History*; both British Pathé
- John Stonehouse interview, *Motives* with Anthony Clare, BBC, 1 August 1983
- Barbara Stonehouse interview, *Newcastle Evening Chronicle*, 17 September 1971
- *Light of Experience: Barbara Stonehouse*, BBC, 24 October 1977
- *Prohibited Immigrant*, John Stonehouse, Bodley Head, 1960
- Fenner Brockway's security service files, KV 2/1920, October 1942, and 17 November 1950, KV 2/1920

1   Barbara Stonehouse, first person account, *Woman*, September 1975
2   John Stonehouse interview, *Motives* with Anthony Clare, BBC, 1 August 1983
3   Clare op cit; *Birmingham Daily Post*, 13 March 1959; Barbara Stonehouse, *Woman* op cit
4   Barbara Stonehouse, *Woman* op cit
5   Barbara Stonehouse interview, *Newcastle Evening Chronicle*, 17 September 1971; *Light of Experience: Barbara Stonehouse*, BBC, 24 October 1977
6   *Luton News and Bedfordshire Chronicle*, 20 April 1950
7   *Ibid*
8   Clare op cit
9   *The People*, 14 October 1951; *Newcastle Evening Chronicle* op cit
10 *Evening Herald*, 19 March 1951
11 *Burton Observer and Chronicle*, 12 April and 17 May 1951
12 *The People* op cit; *Burton Observer and Chronicle*, 18 October 1951
13 *Burton Observer and Chronicle*, 25 October 1951
14 *Burton Observer and Chronicle*, 22 November 1951
15 *The People* op cit; *Guardian*, 14 August 2012; *Daily Mirror*, 7 August 1976
16 Fenner Brockway file, KV 2/1920, TNA
17 Barbara Stonehouse, *Woman*, op cit; John Stonehouse, *Prohibited Immigrant*, p 17
18 John Stonehouse, *Prohibited Immigrant*, p 26; *Burton Observer and Chronicle*, 6 March 1952

5. THE NEW RECRUIT

This chapter is based on the StB (Czech Security Service) files, particularly John Stonehouse's StB file, Fonds Foreign Intelligence Main Directorate,

Operative Files, personal file reg. no. 43075 I. S, Codenames Kolón, including MTH 21968 I. S.

We organised this file chronologically ahead of translation. The reverse date references are ours, not those of the StB (Czech Security Service), whose digital files are arbitrarily named and many of the 1,000-odd pages are blank reverse pages. Some dates are after the events described as intelligence officers backfilled case information.

The contents of the document is clear from the referenced passages in the book.

- Barbara Stonehouse interview, *Newcastle Evening Chronicle*, 17 September 1971
- John Stonehouse, *Prohibited Immigrant*, Bodley Head, 1960
- John Stonehouse, *Death of an Idealist*, W H Allen, 1975
- Donald Chesworth StB file, Fonds Foreign Intelligence Main Directorate, Operative Files, personal file reg. no. 42480 I. S, Codename Knight, including 11465 I. S
- Hansard, the official report of Parliamentary debates

1 *Newcastle Evening Chronicle* op cit; John Stonehouse, *Prohibited Immigrant*, p 85; *Daily Mirror*, 7 August 1976

2 *Newcastle Evening Chronicle* op cit

3 *Reading Evening Post*, 13 June 1968

4 John Stonehouse's StB (Czech Security Service) file 630228

5 StB (Czech Security Service) file 591125

6 *Birmingham Daily Post*, 25 January 1957

7 *Birmingham Post and Gazette*, 28 January 1957; *Birmingham Daily Post*, 19 and 25 February 1957

8 *Birmingham Daily Post*, 2 March 1957

9 Hansard HC Deb, 14 March 1957; 16 April 1957; 3 May 1957; StB (Czech Security Service) file 630228

10 *Birmingham Daily Post*, 7 October 1957

11 John Stonehouse, *Death of an Idealist*, p 86

12 StB (Czech Security Service) file 580114

13 StB (Czech Security Service) file 580114

14 *Birmingham Daily Post*, 22 January 1958; *Birmingham Daily Post*, 1 February 1958; *Coventry Evening Telegraph*, 31 January 1958; Hansard HC Deb, 20 February 1958

15 *The Times*, 8 January 1959; John Stonehouse, *Prohibited Immigrant*, op cit p 124

16 John Stonehouse interview, BBC News, 13 March 1959

17 John Stonehouse, *Prohibited Immigrant*, pp 142–189; *Daily Herald*, 6 March 1959; Hansard HC Deb, 13 March 1959

18 StB (Czech Security Service) file 591125; author interview with Bernard Donoughue; StB (Czech Security Service) file 630228

19 StB (Czech Security Service) file 630228
20 StB (Czech Security Service) file 621012, a retrospective report on how he
knew when he was recruited in 1960 he was working with them and his
main motivation is money.

6. SUCKED IN

- John Stonehouse StB (Czech Security Service) file
- Security case of Will Owen, DEFE 23/203, TNA
- Pavel Žáček, *The Little Sister*, Pamięć i Sprawiedliwość, Instytut Pamięci
  Narodowej 2017
- Hansard, the official report of Parliamentary debates
1 *Leicester Evening Mail*, 18 February 1960
2 *Birmingham Daily Post*, 10 May 1960
3 *Guardian*, 20 June 2016; Le Matelot review, Fanny and Johnnie Craddock,
   Bon Viveur's London & the British Isles, Dakers, 1955
4 StB (Czech Security Service) file 600222
5 Will Owen op cit
6 StB (Czech Security Service) file 600222
7 StB (Czech Security Service) files 600222, 600301, 600331 and 600413
8 StB (Czech Security Service) 600413
9 *Liverpool Echo*, 8 April 1960; *Birmingham Daily Post*, 9 April 1960
10 *Birmingham Daily Post*, 25 March 1960
11 *The Times*, 18 September 1961
12 StB (Czech Security Service) file 600530
13 StB (Czech Security Service) file 600620
14 *Birmingham Daily Post*, 10 May 1960
15 Hansard HC Deb, 29 June 1960; *Birmingham Daily Post*, 30 June 1960; StB
    (Czech Security Service) file 600701
16 Žáček op cit
17 *Birmingham Daily Post*, 1, 12 and 15 September 1960; *Coventry Evening
    Telegraph*, 14 September 1960; *Halifax Evening Courier*, 28 September 1960
18 StB (Czech Security Service) file 601123
19 StB (Czech Security Service) file 601123
20 StB (Czech Security Service) file 610324; *The Independent*, 14 August 1998
21 The Lonsdale Case, KV-2-4466, March 1961; Christopher Andrew, *Defence
    of the Realm: the Authorised History of MI5*, Penguin, 2010, p 488
22 StB (Czech Security Service) file 610204, 610324 and 610522; *Birmingham
    Daily Post*, 9 March 1961
23 StB (Czech Security Service) file 610204 and 610620
24 *Birmingham Daily Post*, 21 June 1961

25 StB (Czech Security Service) file 610620

26 StB (Czech Security Service) file 610620 and 610711; *Birmingham Daily Post*,
   10 July 1961

27 StB (Czech Security Service) file 611023, 611127, 611025, 611115 and 611211

7. ON AND OFF THE HOOK

- John Stonehouse StB (Czech Security Service) file op cit
- Pavel Žáček, *Czechoslovak and Soviet State Security Against the West Before 1968*,
  Pamięć i Sprawiedliwość, Instytut Pamięci Narodowej 2016
- Bridget Kendall, *The Cold War: A New Oral History*, BBC Books, 2017
- DEFE 23/203 op cit
- Various papers, London Co-operative Society (LCS) Archives,
  Bishopsgate Institute

1 *Birmingham Daily Post*, 15 January 1962; John Stonehouse, *Death of an
   Idealist*, W H Allen, 1975, p 36; StB (Czech Security Service) file 630228;
   LCS archives

2 StB (Czech Security Service) file 620213

3 StB (Czech Security Service) file 620115

4 StB (Czech Security Service) file 620115 and 620319; John Stonehouse,
   Death of an Idealist, pp 87–88

5 *Birmingham Daily Post*, 5 March 1962

6 StB (Czech Security Service) file 620319; John Stonehouse, *Death of an
   Idealist*, p 87

7 StB (Czech Security Service) file 620319 and 620402

8 StB (Czech Security Service) file 620402; *Birmingham Daily Post*, 7 May
   1962; John Stonehouse, *Death of an Idealist*, p 37

9 *Daily Mirror*, 14 June and 3 September 1962

10 StB (Czech Security Service) file 620507; *Birmingham Daily Post*, 31 July 1962

11 StB (Czech Security Service) file 620720 and 621012

12 *Birmingham Daily Post*, 10 September 1962; *Daily Herald*, 24 September 1962

13 *The Independent*, 25 September 2013 and 23 October 2011; *The Times*, 16
   January 1963

14 StB (Czech Security Service) file 620801

15 StB (Czech Security Service) file 630306; John Stonehouse, *Death of an
   Idealist*, p 48

16 StB (Czech Security Service) file 630228

17 StB (Czech Security Service) file 630515

18 Security case of Will Owen, DEFE 23-203; StB (Czech Security Service)
   file 630228

19 StB (Czech Security Service) file 630515

20 LCS archives

21 LCS archives; John Stonehouse, *Death of an Idealist*, pp 38–39; *Birmingham Daily Post*, 19 February 1963

22 *Birmingham Daily Post*, 18 February 1963; *Coventry Evening Telegraph*, 6 May 1963; *Daily Herald*, 6 May 1963

23 *Daily Herald*, 30 July 1963; *Daily Mirror*, 30 July 1963; Tony Benn, *The Benn Diaries, 1963–67*, Hutchinson, 1987, p 21; Richard Crossman, *The Crossman Diaries*, vol 3, Hamilton Cape, 1977, p 339

24 *Birmingham Daily Post*, 13 September 1963

25 *Birmingham Daily Post*, 14 November 1963; *Liverpool Echo*, 20 November 1963

8. AGENT TWISTER

- John Stonehouse StB (Czech Security Service) file op cit
- Election coverage, BBC, 16 October 1964
- PREM 13/444, TNA
- FO 371/182564, TNA
- *Czechoslovak and Soviet State Security Against the West Before 1968* op cit
- John Stonehouse, *Death of an Idealist* W H Allen, 1975
- *Yesterday's Men*, BBC, 17 June 1971

1 *Daily Herald*, 10 January 1964; *Daily Mirror*, 5 May 1964

2 *Birmingham Daily Post*, 8 October 1964

3 *Birmingham Daily Post*, 12 October 1964

4 *Sunday Mirror*, 11 October 1964

5 David Butler, BBC, 16 October 1964

6 Ben Pimlott, *Harold Wilson*, William Collins, pp 327–328; Harold Wilson, *The Labour Government 1964–70*, Weidenfeld and Michael Joseph, 1971, pp 4, 11–13, 27

7 Roy Jenkins, *A Life at the Centre*, Macmillan, 1991, p 156

8 John Stonehouse, *Death of an Idealist*, p 46

9 Jenkins op cit, p 158; John Stonehouse, *Death of an Idealist*, p 47; *The People*, 15 November 1964

10 Josef Frolík, *The Frolík Defection*, Leo Cooper, 1975, p 102

11 Communist Bloc Intelligence Activities in the United States: Frolík Testimony, Committee on the Judiciary, United States Senate, 12 April 1976, p 51; John Stonehouse, *Death of an Idealist*, pp 88–89; Chapman Pincher, *Dangerous To Know*, Biteback, 2014, p 328

12 StB (Czech Security Service) file 641203; John Stonehouse, *Death of an Idealist*, p 89; Tony Benn, *The Benn Diaries, 1968–72*, Hutchinson, 1988, p 251

13 FO 371/182564 and FO 371/182565; *Birmingham Daily Post*, 20 March 1965 and 29 April 1966; *Daily Mirror*, 22 December 1965

14 PREM 13/444, 1 April 1965

15 FO 371/182564, 24 June 1965

16 Ian Mikardo, *Back-bencher*, Weidenfeld & Nicolson, 1988, p 178; FCO
    371/182565, 23 and 25 June 1965; Andrew, *Defence of the Realm*, op cit p.758

17 FO 371/182564 and /182565

18 FCO 371/182565, various dates

19 Žáček op cit; *The Czech Connection*, Thames TV, 1977

20 *Birmingham Daily Post*, 25 September 1965

21 FCO 371/182565, 12 October 1965

22 StB (Czech Security Service) file 651010 and 660108

23 *Birmingham Daily Post*, 11 March 1966; *Coventry Evening Telegraph*, 7
    March 1966

24 Wilson op cit, p 218

25 StB (Czech Security Service) file 660625

26 StB (Czech Security Service) file 660625, 660720 and 660802

27 *Coventry Evening Telegraph*, 22 July 1966; *The People*, 24 July 1966

28 StB (Czech Security Service) file 661129 and 670105

29 *Coventry Evening Telegraph*, 16 January, 26 January and 21 February 1967

9. FALLING STAR

We establish the value of the verbal information Stonehouse gave to the
Czechs by checking multiple sources to see if it was in the public domain
at the time. For example, our research reveals that Stonehouse's specific
information on Diego Garcia, Polaris and West Germany's nuclear plans
was not in the public domain at the time. At best it was mooted – but never
confirmed.

* John Stonehouse StB file op cit
* John Stonehouse, *Death of an Idealist*, W H Allen, 1975
* Barbara Stonehouse interview, *The Observer*, 8 June 1975
* FCO 7/867, 20 October 1967, TNA
* Bridget Kendall, *The Cold War: A New Oral History*, BBC Books, 2017
* Tony Benn, *The Benn Diaries, 1968–72*, Hutchinson, 1988
* Sheila Buckley, first person account, *Woman*, 30 October and 6
  November 1976
* Author interview

1 StB (Czech Security Service) file 670224, 670306 and 670309

2 StB (Czech Security Service) file 670427, 670615, 670507, 670504
   and 670629

3 *The Observer*, 8 June 1975; Barbara Stonehouse, first person account, *Woman*,
   September 1975

4   StB (Czech Security Service) file 670713, 670725 and 670805

5   *Liverpool Echo*, 14 October 1967; FCO 7/867, 21 October 1967

6   Daniel Harari, '"Pound in your pocket" devaluation: 50 years on', House of Commons Library, 2017

7   StB (Czech Security Service) file 671219

8   StB (Czech Security Service) file 680108

9   Sheila Buckley's first-person account, *Woman*, 30 October and 6 November 1976

10   *Birmingham Daily Post*, 15 and 19 February 1968

11   StB (Czech Security Service) file 680306 and 680326; *The Observer*, 24 March 1968

12   'Carbon Fibres for the Reinforcement of Structural Plastics' report, Mintech (Ministry of Technology) / RAE (Royal Aircraft Establishment), StB (Czech Security Service) file 680220; *Birmingham Daily Post*, 29 March 1968

13   StB (Czech Security Service) file 671219 and 680430; John Stonehouse, *Death of an Idealist,* p 90

14   John Stonehouse, *Death of an Idealist*, p 78; Tony Benn op cit p 91

15   StB (Czech Security Service) file 680716

16   *Daily Mirror*, 1 July and 9 September 1968; *Sunday Mirror*, 27 October 1968; *Birmingham Daily Post*, 1 and 20 July, 5 September; *Coventry Evening Telegraph*, 19 July 1968; *Walsall Observer*, 16 August 1968

17   Bridget Kendall, *The Cold War: A New Oral History*, op cit, pp 279-280

18   StB (Czech Security Service) file 681004

19   *Daily Mirror*, 5 October 1968; *Birmingham Daily Post*, 8 October 1968

20   StB (Czech Security Service) file 681205 and 681005; *Daily Mirror*, 7 August 1976

21   *Daily Mirror,* 21 November 1968; *Coventry Evening Telegraph,* 19 November 1968; *Daily Mirror*, 16 and 27 January 1969; *Coventry Evening Telegraph*, 15 January 1969; *Newcastle Evening Chronicle*, 27 January 1969

22   Richard Crossman, *The Crossman Diaries*, vol 3, Hamilton Cape, 1977, pp 341–342; *Daily Mail*, 27 January 1969

23   Crossman op cit, p 348

24   Author interview

25   Crossman, op cit; *Newcastle Journal*, 28 January 1969; Barbara Castle, *The Castle Diaries Vol 1*, Weidenfeld and Nicolson, 1984, p 599

26   *Daily Mirror*, 13 March 1969; *The People*, 2 February 1969

27   *Birmingham Daily Post*, 27 and 28 March 1969

28   StB (Czech Security Service) file 690521

29   *Daily Mirror*, 5 May 1969; John Stonehouse, *Death of an Idealist*, pp 80–81, Tony Benn op cit, p 152

30   David Leigh, *The Wilson Plot,* Heinemann, 1988; John Stonehouse, *Death of an Idealist*, pp 80–95

31   Paul Routledge, *Wilson*, Haus Publishing 2006, p 140; Christopher Andrew, *Defence of the Realm: the Authorised History of MI5*, Penguin, 2010, pp 540

32   Author interview with Bernard Donoughue, head of the Policy Unit at No 10, 1974–1979; *Daily Mirror*, 25 September 1969; Chapman Pincher, *Dangerous To Know*, Biteback, 2014, p 330

10. THE IDEALIST RIDES AGAIN

Witness statements:
* Philip Gay, Stonehouse's personal assistant and director of Export Promotion and Consultancy Services Limited

Other sources:
* John Stonehouse StB file op cit
* *London Capital Group, Department of Trade Report*, Michael Sherrard and Ian Hay Davison, 1976
* London Co-operative Society (LCS) Archives, Bishopsgate Institute
* DEFE 23/203 op cit
* Hansard, the official report of Parliamentary debates
* Judge Eveleigh's summing-up, J 82/3714, TNA
* Sheila Buckley, *Woman* op cit
* Barbara Stonehouse, first person account, *Woman*, September 1975

1   The Official Secrets Act and Official Secrecy, House of Commons Library, CBP 07422, May 2017, p 33

2   Christopher Andrew, *Defence of the Realm: the Authorised History of MI5*, Penguin, 2010, p 542

3   Agency reports, *Newcastle Journal* and others, 17 January 1970

4   Tony Benn, *The Benn Diaries*, 1968–72, Hutchinson, 1988, p 252

5   Sheila Buckley, *Woman* op cit; *Daily Mail*, 16 April 1988

6   LCS Archives; DOT p 31

7   *The Observer*, 8 August 1976

8   DOT, pp 31–33

9   *Daily Mirror*, 7 May 1970

10   *Newcastle Journal*, 7 May 1970; Ministry of Defence file on Will Owen, DEFE 23/203, TNA

11   Pimlott op cit, p 557

12   Pimlott op cit, pp 528–529

13   *The Times*, 16 and 17 June 1970

14   Marcia Williams, *Inside Number 10*, Weidenfeld & Nicolson, 1972, p 1; Harold Wilson, *The Labour Government 1964–70*, Weidenfeld and Michael Joseph, 1971, pp 789–790

15 Chapman Pincher, *Dangerous to Know*, Biteback, 2014, p 330; PREM 16/1848; Andrew op cit, p 707

16 *Evening Standard*, 27 June 1970

17 *Evening Standard*, 25 February 1971; Hansard, HC Deb, 30 November 1970

18 StB (Czech Security Service) file 700120

19 DOT, pp 30–33

20 Suhail Aziz, *Breakthrough: Memoir of a British-trained Bangladeshi*, Book Guild, 2020, pp 216–217; Lorraine Boissoneault, 'The genocide the US can't remember but Bangladesh can't forget', *Smithsonian Magazine*, 16 December 2016

21 John Stonehouse, *Death of an Idealist*, W H Allen, 1975, p 102

22 *The Times*, 8 June 1971; Mark Dummett, 'Bangladesh war: the article that changed history', BBC News, 16 December 2011

23 Hansard HC Deb, 18 January 1972; John Stonehouse, *Death of an Idealist*, pp 108 and 113

24 The inside of Concert for Bangladesh, S.I.X T; Birth of the rock benefit concert, *Financial Times*, 20 March 1971

25 *Guardian*, 25 September 1971

26 *The Times*, 24 June 1971; *The Times*, 25 January 1974

27 Sheila Buckley, *Woman* op cit; Barbara Stonehouse first person account, *News of the World*, 8 August 1976

28 John Stonehouse, *Death of an Idealist*, p 111

29 HC Deb, 18 January 1972; *The Times*, 17 January 1972

11. DIRTY WORK

Principal source:
- *London Capital Group, Department of Trade Report*, Michael Sherrard and Ian Hay Davison, 1976

Other sources:
- Hansard HC Deb
- John Stonehouse, *Death of an Idealist*, W H Allen, 1975
- Judge Eveleigh's summing-up, J 82/3714, TNA
- Sheila Buckley, first person account, *Woman*, 30 October and 6 November 1976

1 DOT, p 10; John Stonehouse, *Death of an Idealist*, pp 117–118

2 DOT, p 53

3 Judge Eveleigh op cit; DOT, pp 348–349

4 Sheila Buckley, *Woman* op cit

5 *The Times*, 5 April 1972

6 *New York Times*, 13 July 1970

7 DOT, pp 59–61

8 *The Times*, 9 June 1972

9 DOT, p 58; John Stonehouse, *Death of an Idealist*, p 129

10 DOT, pp 68–9

11 DOT, p 12

12 DOT, pp 61–65

13 DOT, p 68

14 HC Deb on Finance Bill, 20 April 1972; on Rhodesia, 15 June 1972; and on thalidomide, 16 and 29 November 1972

15 *Sunday Times*, 19 November 1972; DOT, pp 68–69

16 DOT, p 71

17 DOT, pp 69–70; John Stonehouse, *Death of an Idealist*, p 128

18 *The Times*, 20 November 1972

19 DOT, p 75

20 DOT, pp 95–97 and 100

21 DOT, pp 106–114

22 DOT, p 71

23 DOT, pp 83–89 and 94–98

12. NO ONE ARGUES WITH MR STONEHOUSE

Principal sources:
- *London Capital Group, Department of Trade Report*, Michael Sherrard and Ian Hay Davison, 1976
- John Broad, assistant general manager, BBT/LCG, witness statement, J 267/707, TNA.

1 *Daily Mirror*, 7 August 1976; Judge Eveleigh summing-up, J 82/3714, vol 2 p 35

2 John Stonehouse interview, BBC News, 21 January 1975

3 DOT, p 128

4 DOT, pp 115–120

5 Broad op cit; John Stonehouse, *Death of an Idealist*, W H Allen, 1975, pp 132 and 138

6 DOT, pp 122–126

7 DOT, pp 128 and 134–135

8 DOT, p 137

9 DOT, pp 137–140

10 DOT, pp 143–144

11 DOT, pp 144–146

12 DOT, pp 143–153

13 DOT, p 165
14 DOT, passim

13. THE UNACCEPTABLE FACE OF CAPITALISM

Principal sources:
- *London Capital Group, Department of Trade Report*, Michael Sherrard and Ian Hay Davison, 1976
- Judge Eveleigh's summing-up, J 82/3714, TNA
- John Stonehouse, *Death of an Idealist*, W H Allen, 1975

1   DOT, p 204
2   James Charlton, witness statement, J 267/707, TNA; DOT, p 228
3   DOT passim, especially pp 211–215 and 33–38
4   Sheila Buckley first person account, *Woman*, 30 October and 6 November 1976
5   DOT passim, especially pp 203–215 and 220–221
6   DOT passim, especially pp 222–224
7   DOT passim, especially pp 222–233
8   DOT passim, especially pp 236–239
9   DOT, pp 211–215
10 DOT, pp 236–237
11 *The Times*, 25 January 1974
12 For example, the existence of Stonehouse's StB (Czech Security Service) file and the corporate fraud
13 DOT, pp 238-239
14 *Birmingham Daily Post*, 1 March 1974
15 DOT, pp 246–248 and p 224
16 Eveleigh summing-up, op cit, vol 2, p 11
17 *Daily Mirror*, 12 December 1974
18 DOT, pp 242 and 248–249

14. BECOMING JOE MARKHAM

Witness statements:
- Keith Dalton, assistant manager, Lloyds Bank
- Alfred Gundry, manager, Lloyds Bank
- Derek Perks, patient services officer, Manor Hospital, Walsall
- Jean Markham, wife of Joseph Markham
- Elsie Mildoon, wife of Clive Mildoon

- Christine Ash, supervisor, General Register Office
- James Robson, manager, Midland Bank
- William White, director, Stanley Gibbons
- Michael Dixon, chief passport officer
- Martin Christie, clerical officer, Passport Office
- Howard Smith, clerical officer, Passport Office
- James Mitchell, executive officer, Passport Office
- Margaret Reilly, manager, Astoria Hotel
- David Ellen, principal scientific officer, UK police
- Raymond Lock, director, National Giro Bank

(all J 267/707, TNA)

1 John Stonehouse, *Death of an Idealist*, W H Allen, 1975, p 151; Dalton and Gundry op cit; *Birmingham Daily Post*, 25 June 1974
2 Francis Eteng medical report to the Court of Appeal, 1977, J 82/3714; John Stonehouse, *Death of an Idealist*, p 149
3 Perks op cit
4 Markham op cit
5 Mildoon op cit
6 Markham op cit; Ash op cit
7 DOT, pp 257–264, 236 and 241–243
8 Ash op cit
9 DOT, p 260
10 Markham op cit; Ellen op cit; *The Times*, 11 May 1976
11 HO 306/149/3
12 Reilly op cit
13 Robson op cit
14 Lock op cit
15 HC Deb, 22 July 1974
16 DOT, pp 259–262
17 White op cit, 12 February 1975
18 DOT, pp 262–263
19 Christie and Smith op cit
20 Mitchell op cit
21 DOT, pp 273–281
22 *Daily Mirror*, 6 January 1975

15. CASHING OUT

Witness statements:
- Keith Dalton, assistant manager, Lloyds Bank
- Margaret Reilly op cit

- Alfred Gundry, manager, Lloyds Bank
- Peggy Bierke, supervisor, Bank of America, Los Angeles
- David Miles, life assurance consultant, Royal Insurance, London
- Arthur Jones, accountant, Bank of New South Wales, London
- Kenneth Betts, inspector, American Express
- Geoffrey Honess, bank clerk, Lloyds Bank
- Robert Lewis, detective inspector, UK police

(all J 267/707, TNA)

Principal sources:

- Judge Eveleigh's summing-up, J82/3714, TNA
- *London Capital Group, Department of Trade Report*, Michael Sherrard and Ian Hay Davison, 1976

1   Eveleigh op cit, vol 2, p 18
2   Harry Wetzel obituary, *San Francisco Chronicle,* 19 August 2008; letter to Ronald Reagan's deputy chief of staff, Reagan Library, 10 July 1984
3   Bierke and Bemiller op cit
4   Eveleigh op cit, vol 2, p 51; DOT, p 346
5   Witness statements, TNA J 267-707-3, especially Miles
6   DOT, pp 345–346
7   Reilly op cit
8   DOT, p 374
9   DOT, pp 243–244
10 DOT, pp 277–279
11 Betts op cit
12 DOT, pp 278–279
13 DOT, p 283
14 DOT, pp 286–297
15 Jones op cit
16 DOT, 236–245
17 James Robson, manager, Midland Bank, witness statement, J 267/707, TNA
18 Robson ibid; Betts op cit
19 Gundry op cit
20 Philip Ziegler, *Wilson: The Authorised Life*, Weidenfeld & Nicolson, 1993, p 419
21 DOT, p 352; Lewis op cit
22 *Private Eye*, 20 September 1974
23 Gundry op cit; Honess op cit
24 Jones op cit; Robson op cit
25 *Birmingham Daily Post*, 11 October 1974

16. WHAT THEY DIDN'T KNOW

Witness statements:

- Jane Grubb, ticket agent, Pan Am
- Garry Wakefield, director of shipping agents, Clowhurst Limited
- Ian Ward, journalist, *Daily Telegraph*
- Peter Street, bank officer, Bank of New South Wales
- Mariella Zandstra, receptionist, Highfield House
- Sally Richard, ticket agent, National Airlines
- Robert Lewis, detective inspector, UK police

(all J 267/707, TNA)

Other sources:

- *London Capital Group, Department of Trade Report*, Michael Sherrard and Ian Hay Davison, 1976
- John Stonehouse, *Death of an Idealist*, W H Allen, 1975

1   DOT, pp 245 and 320–321
2   James Robson, manager, Midland Bank, witness statement, J 267/707, TNA
3   Grubb op cit
4   Wakefield op cit
5   Arthur Jones, accountant, Bank of New South Wales, London, witness statement, J 267/707, TNA
6   William White, director, Stanley Gibbons, witness statement, J 267/707, TNA
7   Zandstra op cit; ITN News, 3 January 1975
8   Lewis op cit; *Daily Mirror*, 7 August 1976
9   Jones op cit
10   Street op cit
11   Richard op cit
12   Lewis, op cit
13   John Stonehouse, *Death of an Idealist*, p 152
14   HC Deb, 4 November 1974
15   *Daily Mirror*, 6 January 1975
16   John Stonehouse, *Death of an Idealist*, p 167

17. CAN I GET A WITNESS?

Witness statements:

- James Charlton, director and chairman of London Capital Group Limited
- Helen Fleming, secretary, Fontainebleau Hotel

- Anthony Sait, ticket agent, British Airways
- (all J 267/707, TNA)
- Other sources:
- 'Inquiry into Death of Sylvester Okereke', JWN 14/1, TNA
- Barbara Stonehouse interview with Robin Day, *Newsday*, BBC, 19 December 1974
- Judge Eveleigh's summing-up, J 82/3714, TNA
- John Stonehouse, *Death of an Idealist*, W H Allen, 1975

1   *Death of an Idealist*, pp 171–173
2   *Miami Herald*, 18 December 1974
3   Patricia Evans, police officer, Miami Beach Police, witness statement, J 267/707, TNA. We assume that the dummy run was identical to the actual disappearance
4   John Stonehouse, *Death of an Idealist*, pp 174–176; Eveleigh, op cit, vol 2 pp 21–22
5   Letter from Sylvester Okereke to John Stonehouse, 15 November 1974, 'Inquiry into Death of Sylvester Okereke', JWN 14/1, TNA; *Miami Herald*, 20 February 1975; *The Observer*, 23 March 1975; Philip Gay, Stonehouse's personal assistant and director of Promotion and Consultancy Services Limited, witness statement, J 267/707, TNA
6   Fleming op cit
7   *Newsday* op cit
8   Charlton op cit
9   HC Deb, 14 November 1974
10 Eveleigh, op cit, vol 1 p 72; Okereke letter op cit; *Guardian*, 10 February 1975
11 *Private Eye*, 15 November 1974
12 Sait op cit
13 *Newbreed* magazine, Nigeria, June 1975; *Guardian*, 17 February 1975; *Daily Express*, 18 February 1975; Nigel Newman witness statement, JWN 14/1, TNA
14 Letter from Sylvester Okereke to Nigel Newman, 6 November 1974, 'Inquiry into Death of Sylvester Okereke', JWN 14/1, TNA
15 Fleming op cit; *Daily Mirror*, 27 November 1974

18. ON THE RUN

Witness statements:
- James Charlton, director and chairman of London Capital Group Limited
- Helen Fleming op cit
- Robert Lewis, detective inspector, UK police

- Kenneth Etheridge, Detective Chief Superintendent, UK police
- Caroline Gay, Philip Gay's wife
- Lauren Ramiscal, front office cashier, Sheraton Honolulu
- Patricia Makeau, chief telephone operator, Sheraton Honolulu
- Kathleen Elia, bank teller, Bank of Hawaii
- Richard Wolfish, travel agent, Hampstead Travel Agency
- Janne Olsen, ticket agent, SAS

(all J 267/707, TNA)

Primary sources:

- Barbara Stonehouse, *Newsday* op cit
- Judge Eveleigh's summing-up op cit
- *Death of an Idealist* op cit
- *London Capital Group, Department of Trade Report*, Michael Sherrard and Ian Hay Davison, 1976
- Sheila Buckley first-person account, *Woman*, 30 October and 6 November 1976

1 *The Times*, 1 May 1976; *Death of an Idealist*, pp 184-185
2 John Stonehouse, *My Trial*, Wyndham, 1976, p 190; Lewis op cit
3 Ramiscal op cit
4 Buckley, *Woman,* op cit
5 Makeau and Etheridge op cit; Buckley op cit
6 Elia op cit
7 Gay op cit
8 Buckley op cit
9 John Stonehouse, *Death of an Idealist*, pp 189–196
10 *Daily Mirror*, 29 November and 2 December 1974; *Daily Mail*, 28 November 1974; *Guardian*, 5 December 1974
11 Wolfish op cit
12 Olsen op cit
13 Buckley op cit; Barbara Stonehouse first person account, *News of the World*, 8 August 1976
14 Barbara Stonehouse first person account, *Woman*, 13 September 1975
15 *Daily Mirror,* 2 November 1976; *Guardian*, 7 August 1976; Etheridge op cit
16 Sebastian Whale, 'Betty Boothroyd: I am a bit timid. But I'm dealing with the giants', politicshome.com, 26 April 2018

19. A NEW LIFE IN THE SUN

Witness statements:
- Kenneth Etheridge, detective chief superintendent, UK police
- Robert Lewis, detective inspector, UK police

- John Coffey, detective sergeant, Victoria Police
- Hugh Morris, detective sergeant, Victoria Police
- Barbara Tilley, police officer, Metropolitan Police

(all J 267/707, TNA)

Sources:
- 'Inquiry into Death of Sylvester Okereke', JWN 14/1, TNA
- Judge Eveleigh's summing-up, J 82/3714, TNA
- John Stonehouse, *Death of an Idealist*, W H Allen, 1975

1   Letter to Nigerian high commissioner from FCO, JWN 14/1; *Newsbreed* magazine, Nigeria, June 1975; *Sunday Punch* newspaper, Nigeria; *West African Pilot* newspaper, Nigeria, 3 January 1975
2   *The Age*, 26 December 1974; John Stonehouse, *Death of an Idealist*, p 203
3   Etheridge, op cit; *Daily Mirror*, 7 August 1976
4   Lewis op cit; Etheridge op cit; *Daily Mirror*, 7 August 1976
5   Etheridge op cit; Eveleigh op cit vol 2, p 45; *Daily Mirror*, 7 August 1976; John Stonehouse, *My Trial*,Wyndham, 1976 p 83
6   Lewis op cit; *The Age* op cit
7   Eveleigh op cit vol 2, pp 45 and 47; Etheridge op cit
8   Coffey op cit, 23 October 1975; *The Age* op cit
9   John Stonehouse, *Death of an Idealist*, pp 209–210; *Guardian*, 14 June 1975
10 Coffey op cit
11 Etheridge op cit; *Daily Mirror*, 1 May 1976 and 7 August 1976
12 Coffey op cit
13 *The Age*, 18 December 1974
14 Morris and Coffey op cit
15 Tilley op cit
16 Coffey op cit
17 Morris witness statement op cit; Coffey witness statement op cit
18 Ibid

20. THE GAME'S UP

Witness statements:
- John Coffey, detective sergeant, Victoria Police
- Hugh Morris, detective sergeant, Victoria Police
- John Sullivan, detective inspector, Victoria Police
- Alan Plant, constable, Victoria Police

(all J 267/707, TNA)

Primary sources:
- Barbara Stonehouse interview with Robin Day, *Newsday*, BBC, 19 December 1974

- Barbara Stonehouse interview, *Daily Express*, 27 December 1974
- BBC News, 6 August 1976 (tape of phonecall)
- FCO 53/402
- FCO 53/434
- PREM 16/587

1   The opening pages of this chapter use Coffey op cit and Morris op cit; BBC News, 6 August 1976 (verbatim from the tape of the call); *Daily Express* exclusive with Barbara Stonehouse, 27 December 1974
2   *Newsday* op cit; *Daily Express* op cit; *The Times*, 15 June 1976
3   Coffey op cit
4   *The Age*, 26 December 1974
5   FCO 53/402, 24 December 1974
6   PREM 16/587, 24 December 1974
7   Sullivan op cit; *The Age* op cit
8   Sullivan op cit; www.abc.net.au, 13 December 2014
9   FCO 53/434, 9 April 1975
10 *Daily Mirror*, 2 November 1976
11 FCO 53/434, 9 April 1975; FCO 53/402, 24 December 1974
12 FCO 53/402, 24 December 1974; PREM 16/587, 29 January 1975
13 Plant op cit; *The Age* op cit
14 Bernard Donoughue, *Downing Street Diary*, Pimlico, 2006, pp 267–268
15 *Daily Mirror*, 24 December 1974
16 PREM 16/587, 24 December 1974; FCO 53/402, 24 December 1974
17 FCO 53/402, 24 December 1974

21. MERRY CHRISTMAS

Witness statement:
- John Sullivan, detective inspector, Victoria Police
(J 267/707, TNA)
Other sources:
- FCO 53/402
- PREM 16/587
- HO 306/148
- Judge Eveleigh's summing-up, J 82/3714, TNA
- *Light of Experience: Barbara Stonehouse*, BBC, 24 October 1977
- Barbara Stonehouse interview, *Hard Knocks*, BBC Radio, 22 December 1986
- Barbara Stonehouse interview, *Daily Express*, 27 December 1974
- Jane Stonehouse interview, ITN News, 28 December 1974
- Sheila Buckley interview, ITN News, 28 December 1974

1   PREM 16/587, 2 January 1975; *Daily Express*, 27 December 1974
2   *Light of Experience: Barbara Stonehouse* op cit; BBC News, 18 July 1975; *Hard Knocks* op cit
3   FCO 53/402, 24 and 25 December 1974
4   HO 306/148, 26 December 1974; FCO 53/402, 26 December 1974; ABC News, 29 January 1975
5   ABC News, 26 December 1974; *The Observer*, 29 December 1974
6   *Daily News*, 26 December 1974; *Guardian*, 27 December 1974
7   ABC News op cit; *The Observer* op cit
8   *The Times*, 27 December 1974; *Sydney Morning Herald*, 27 December 1974
9   British Pathé, 26 December 1974; *Sydney Morning Herald*, 26 December 1974
10 John Stonehouse, *Death of an Idealist*, W H Allen, 1975, p 228
11 FCO 53/433 and HO 306/148, 2 and 22 January 1975; British Pathé, op cit; *The Age*, 28 December 1974; *Hard Knocks* op cit
12 Barbara Stonehouse, *Woman* magazine, September 1975; *Daily Express* 27 and 28 December 1974; PREM 16/587, 7 and 10 January 1975; *Light of Experience: Barbara Stonehouse*, op cit
13 *Daily Express* op cit; interview with Jane Stonehouse op cit
14 *Daily Express*, 27 December 1974
15 ITN News, 27 December 1974
16 *Daily Express*, 27 December 1974; *Sydney Morning Herald*, 28 December 1974
17 Interview with Jane Stonehouse op cit
18 PREM 16/587, 25 and 29 December 1975; *Sydney Morning Herald*, 30 December 1974
19 Sullivan op cit; PA News, 29 December 1974; ABC News, 29 December 1974
20 ABC News, 29 December 1974
21 Eveleigh op cit vol 2, pp 34–35
22 *The Age*, 30 December 1974
23 *The Times*, 27 December 1974; PREM 16/587, 31 December 1974
24 Prem 16/587, 27 December 1974
25 Prem 16/587, 31 December 1974; DOT press release, 17 January 1975
26 Prem 16/587, 31 December 1974

22. FLIGHT RISK

Witness statement:
• John Sullivan, detective inspector, Victoria Police
(J 267/707, TNA)
Primary sources:

- Judge Eveleigh's summing-up, J 82/3714, TNA
- HO 306/148, TNA
- CAB 128/58/3, TNA
- John Stonehouse, *My Trial*, Wyndham, 1976

1 *The Age*, 4 January 1975
2 Eveleigh op cit, vol 2, pp 34–35; *The Age* op cit
3 FCO 53/433, 3, 4 and 6 January 1975
4 Eveleigh op cit, vol 2, pp 27–28
5 Kenneth Etheridge obituary in *Guardian*, 2 June 2011
6 PREM 16/587, 10 January 1975
7 PREM 16/587, 10 January 1975
8 HO 306/148/1 and -2, 9 January 1975
9 FCO 53/433, 9 and 13 January 1975
10 FCO 53/433, 13 January 1975; British diplomat oral histories, interview with H H Tucker, chu.cam.ac.uk
11 PREM 16/587, 13 January 1975
12 PREM 16/587, 14 January 1975
13 Sullivan op cit
14 PREM 16/587, 15 January 1975
15 PREM 16/587, 15 January 1975
16 PREM 16/587, 16 January 1975
17 CAB 128/58/3, 16 January 1975; Barbara Castle, *The Castle Diaries Vol 2*, Macmillan 1993, p 279; Tony Benn, *Diaries 1973–76*, Hutchinson, 1989, p 301–302
18 Eveleigh op cit, vol 2, p 23; BBC News, 21 January 1975
19 PREM 16/587, 17 January 1975; *The Age*, 17 January 1975
20 PREM 16/587, 19 January 1975
21 FCO 53/433, 28 January 1975
22 *Daily Express*, 29 January 1975
23 Sheila Buckley, *Woman*, 30 October and 6 November 1976
24 Kenneth Etheridge witness statement op cit; Eveleigh op cit, vol 2, p 35; Buckley op cit
25 Etheridge witness statement op cit

23. ENTER THE INSPECTORS

Witness statements
- Ian Ward, journalist, *Daily Telegraph*
(J 267/707, TNA)
Primary sources:
- PREM 16/588

- FCO 73/201
- FCO 53/434
- JWN 14/1, TNA 'Inquiry into Death of Sylvester Okereke'
- *London Capital Group, Department of Trade Report*, Michael Sherrard and Ian Hay Davison, 1976
- Diary of Ian Hay Davison

1   Ward op cit; *The Age*, 7 February 1975
2   Ward op cit; Judge Eveleigh's summing-up, J 82/3714, TNA, vol 1, pp 40–41
3   *The Age*, 7 February 1975
4   Author correspondence
5   *Guardian*, 10, 17 and 18 February 1975; letter from FCO to Nigerian high commissioner, JWN 14/1, 23 January 1975; Letter from Crompton to West African Dept, FCO, JWN 14/1, 26 July 1975
6   Sheila Buckley, *Woman*, 30 October and 6 November 1976; *Daily Mirror*, 2 November 1976; *Daily Express*, 12 February 1975; *Sydney Morning Herald*, 14 February 1975
7   Sheila Buckley op cit
8   Ibid
9   *Daily Mirror*, 2 November 1976
10 Author interviews and Ian Hay Davison diary
11 FCO 73/201, High Commission to FCO, 25 February 1975
12 Author interviews and Ian Hay Davison diary
13 FCO 53/434, 26 February 1975; *The Age*, 27 February 1975; *Sydney Morning Herald*, 27 February 1975
14 *The Age*, 28 February 1975; BBC News, 28 February 1975
15 Author interviews
16 DOT, pp 341–344
17 DOT, pp 349–352
18 FCO 53/434, 19 March 1975
19 DOT, pp 14–15; author interviews

24. STATE OF MIND

Witness statements:
- John Coffey, detective sergeant, Victoria Police
- Robert Gillespie, detective inspector, Victoria Police
- John Sullivan, detective inspector, Victoria Police

(all J 267/707, TNA)

Primary sources:
- PM 16/588

- FCO 73/201
- FCO 53/434
- FCO 53/435
- HO 306/150
- CAB 130/815
- PM 18/648
- J 82/3714
- DOT op cit
- John Stonehouse, *My Trial*, Wyndham, 1976
1   FCO 53/434, 21 and 28 March 1975; *Daily Express*, 21 March 1975
2   FCO 53/434, 20 March 1975
3   FCO 53/434, 20 March 1975
4   Coffey op cit; John Stonehouse, *My Trial*, pp 3–5
5   Coffey and Gillespie op cit; FCO 53/434, 21 March 1975
6   *The Age*, 24 March 1975; FCO 53/434, 9 April 1975
7   Sullivan op cit; *Daily Mirror*, 27 March 1975
8   *Daily Express*, 27 March 1975; *The Age*, 29 March 1975; *Woman* op cit
9   *Guardian*, 27 March 1975
10 FCO 53/434, 9 April 1975
11 *Daily Mirror*, 21 March 1975; HO 306/150, 14 April 1975
12 FCO 53/434, 9 April 1975
13 FCO 54/435, 12 May 1970; PREM 16/588, 12 May 1975
14 FCO 53/434, various, 19 March, 10, 12 and 17 April 1975; *Daily Telegraph*, 19 April 1975; Tony Benn, *Diaries 1973–76*, Hutchinson, 1989, p 359
15 *The Times*, 30 April 1975
16 FCO 53/435, 6 May 1975; PREM 16/588, 6 and 7 May 1975
17 BBC interview, 6 May 1975
18 ITN interview, 6 May 1975; Buckley, *Woman* op cit
19 FCO 53-435, 15 May 1975
20 FCO 73-201, 19 May 1975
21 FCO 53-435, 9 June 1975
22 FCO 53-435, 9 June 1975
23 ABC News, 9 June 1975; PREM 16-588, 9 June 1975
24 ABC News, 9 June 1975
25 Bartholomew to the Court of Appeal, J 82/3714
26 *Daily Express*, 11 June 1975; ; TNA PM 16-588, 10 June 1975; CO 130-816, 12 June 1975
27 PREM 18/648, 3 June 1975
28 CAB 130/815, 12 June 1975
29 HO 306/150, 30 June 1975; ABC TV, 12 July 1975

25. THE HOMECOMING

Witness statement:
- Kenneth Etheridge op cit
- Bryan Martin, detective sergeant, Company Fraud Squad, UK police (both J 267/707, TNA)

Primary source:
- PREM 16/589

1　Sheila Buckley, *Woman*, 30 October and 6 November 1976
2　Etheridge op cit
3　*Birmingham Daily Post*, 18 July 1975; ABC News, 17 July 1975
4　BBC News, 19 July 1975; BBC News, 18 July 1975
5　*Birmingham Post*, 18 July 1975
6　Martin op cit
7　BBC News, 19 July 1975
8　Etheridge op cit
9　Barbara Stonehouse interview, BBC, 21 July 1975
10　*Birmingham Post*, 18 July 1975; *Daily Mirror*, 21 July 1975; Buckley, op cit
11　*Daily Mirror*, 22 July 1975; HO 391/431, 21 July 1975
12　PREM 16/589, 24 July 1975
13　Geoffrey Robertson, *The Justice Game,* Vintage, 1999, p 64
14　*Daily Mirror*, 25 and 29 July, 6, 9 and 15 August 1975
15　*Daily Express*, 9 and 19 August 1975; *Daily Mirror*, 25 July 1975
16　*Daily Express*, 28 August 1975

26. BACK IN THE HOUSE

1　ITN, 28 August 1975
2　*Daily Mirror*, 6 September 1975
3　*Daily Mirror*, 9 September 1975
4　*Daily Mirror*, 2 October 1975
5　*Daily Mirror*, 1 October 1975
6　*Daily Mirror*, 6 October 1975
7　Geoffrey Robertson, *The Justice Game*, Vintage, 1999,pp 65 and 68
8　ITN News, 26 September 1976
9　HC Deb, 20 October 1975, *The Times*, 21 October 1975; *Daily Mirror*, 21 October 1975
10　Robertson op cit, p 66
11　*Daily Mirror*, 17 October 1975
12　Robertson op cit, p 65

13 Robertson op cit, p 66
14 *Daily Mirror*, 6 November 1975
15 Robertson op cit, pp 67–68
16 *Daily Mirror*, 3 January 1976
17 *The Times*, 10 February 1976; *Daily Mirror*, 9 and 10 February 1976; HC Deb 9 February 1976
18 PREM 16/589, Stonehouse to Mellish, 16 February 1976, and Silkin to Mellish, 24 February 1976
19 Robertson op cit, p 67; Stonehouse, *My Trial*, Wyndham, 1976, p 89
20 Robertson op cit, pp 69–70
21 *Daily Mirror*, 29 April 1976
22 BBC, 7 April 1976; *Newsday*, 4 April 1976
23 *Daily Mirror*, 14 April 1976
24 *Daily Express*, 26 April 1976
25 Robertson op cit, p 70

27. THE CASE FOR THE CROWN

1 BBC, 28 April 1976
2 *Daily Express*, 28 April 1976
3 *The Times*, *Daily Express* and *Daily Mirror*, all 28 April 1976
4 *The Times*, 28 and 29 April 1976
5 Judge Eveleigh's summing-up, J 82/3714, TNA, vol 1, pp 28–29; *The Times*, 29 April 1976
6 *The Times*, 29 April 1976
7 Ibid
8 Eveleigh op cit, vol 1, p 15; *The Times*, 29 April 1976
9 *The Times*, 30 April 1976
10 *The Times*, 30 April 1976; *Daily Mirror*, 30 April 1976
11 Eveleigh op cit, vol 2, pp 35–36; *The Times*, 1 May 1976; *Daily Mirror*, 1 May 1976
12 *The Times*, 1 May 1976
13 John Stonehouse, *My Trial*, Wyndham, 1976, p 99
14 *The Times*, 6 May 1976; Stonehouse, *My Trial*, pp 102–105
15 *The Times*, 11 May 1976; *Daily Mirror*, 11 May 1976
16 *The Times*, 11, 12 and 13 May 1976; *Guardian*, 13 May 1976; *Daily Mirror*, 13 May 1976
17 TNA J267-707-2, Alan Le Fort witness statement; *The Times*, 14 and 15 May 1976
18 *The Times*, 19 and 20 May 1976; *Daily Mirror*, 19 May 1976
19 TNA J267-707-2, Philip Gay witness statement; *The Times*, 22 May 1976

20   *The Times*, 25 May 1976
21   *Daily Mirror*, 6 May 1976; *Guardian*, 27 May 1976
22   *Daily Mirror*, 26 May 1976
23   *Daily Mirror*, 12 June 1976
24   Ian Ward, journalist, *Daily Telegraph*, witness statement, J 267/707, TNA;
     The Times, 8 June 1976
25   *The Times*, 9 June 1976; *Daily Mirror*, 9 June 1976
26   *Guardian*, 30 July 2016
27   Eveleigh op cit, vol 1, pp 21–22
28   *The Times*, 11 June 1976
29   *Daily Mirror*, 15 June 1976
30   *The Times*, 1 July 1976
31   *The Times*, 2 July 1976
32   Eveleigh op cit, vol 2, p 25

28. THE JURY'S OUT

1   Judge Eveleigh's summing-up, J 82/3714, TNA, vol 2, p 20
2   *The Times*, 2 and 3 July 1976
3   *Daily Mirror*, 6 July 1976
4   *The Times*, 7 July 1976
5   *Daily Mirror*, 8 July 1976
6   *Daily Telegraph*, 9 July 1976; John Stonehouse, *My Trial*, Wyndham, 1976,
     pp 175–176
7   Eveleigh op cit, vol 2, p 34
8   *The Times*, 13 July 1976
9   *The Times*, 16 July 1976
10   *Guardian*, 7 August 1976
11   Ibid
12   *The Times*, 16 and 20 July 1976; *Daily Mirror*, 21 July 1976; *Guardian*, 6
     August 1976; *Sunday Mirror*, 20 March and 20 July 1983
13   Eveleigh op cit, vol 2, pp 50 and 53; *The Times*, 21 July 1976
14   *The Times*, 21, 22 and 28 July 1975
15   Eveleigh op cit, vol 2, pp 54–55
16   Eveleigh op cit, vol 1, p 13
17   Eveleigh op cit, vol 1, p 22 and vol 2, p 25
18   Eveleigh op cit, vol 2, p 36
19   Eveleigh op cit, vol 1, p 9
20   Eveleigh op cit, vol 1, p 46
21   Eveleigh op cit, vol 2, p 56
22   *The Times*, 3 August 1976

23   *Guardian*, 7 August 1976

24   *The Times*, 6 August 1976; Eveleigh vol 2 pp 60-63

25   *Daily Mirror*, 6 August 1976; *Guardian*, 7 August 1976

26   *Guardian*, 7 August 1976; Eveleigh vol 2 pp 63-70

27   Eveleigh op cit, vol 2, pp 71–72; *The Times*, 7 August 1976

29. COMING CLEAN

1   Judge Eveleigh's summing-up, J 82/3714, TNA, vol 2, pp 72–73; *Daily Mirror*, 7 August 1976; *Sydney Morning Herald*, 8 August 1976

2   Eveleigh op cit, vol 2, pp 75–76; *Guardian*, *The Times*, *Daily Mirror*, all 7 August 1976

3   Eveleigh op cit, vol 2, pp 58 and 77

4   *Guardian*, *Daily Mirror*, *Daily Express*, all 7 August 1976; BBC News, 6 August 1976

5   Sheila Buckley, *Woman*, 30 October and 6 November 1976

6   *Guardian*, *Daily Mirror*, *Daily Express*, *The Times*, all 7 August 1976

7   *Guardian*, 7 August 1976

8   Barbara Stonehouse, *Woman*, September 1975; *Guardian*, 7 August 1976; *Sydney Morning Herald*, 8 August 1976

9   Buckley op cit

10 *Light of Experience: Barbara Stonehouse*, BBC, 24 October 1977; *Daily Mirror*, 26 October 1976

11 *Birmingham Daily Post*, 26 October 1976; *Daily Mirror*, 27 and 28 October 1976

12 *Birmingham Daily Post*, 18 August 1976; *The Times*, 28 August 1976; *Daily Mirror*, 6 November 1976,

13 DOT, pp 218–219; author interview

14 DOT, pp 15, 281, 336; Ian Hay Davison diary and author interviews

15 J 82/3714, letter to Criminal Appeal Office from Francis Eteng, 21 December 1976

16 DOT, p 5; Ian Hay Davison author interviews; *Daily Mail*, 16 April 1988

17 *The Age*, 1 April 1977

18 DOT, p 71

19 DOT, passim, especially pp 2, 109–110 and 252

20 DOT, pp 177 and 185

21 DOT, pp 14 and 243

22 DOT, pp 1, 3 and 7

23 J 82/3714, appeal ruling

24 *Daily Mirror*, 19 October 1977 and 27 February 1979; *Daily Express*, 9 October 1979

30. COVER-UP

1   Communist Bloc Intelligence Activities in the United States: Frolík
    Testimony, Committee on the Judiciary, United States Senate, 18
    November 1975

2   PREM 16/1848, 7 June 1978

3   PREM 16/1848, 19 June 1978; author interview with Jerome Mayhew,
    Patrick Mayhew's son, re. his mother's recollections

4   PREM 16/1848, 21, 27 and 30 June 1978

5   PREM 18/1848, Mayhew to Callaghan, 11 July 1978

6   PREM 16/1848, Hunt to Wilson 3 June 1975; 14 July 1978; 4 July 1977

7   PREM 16-1848, 14 July 1978

8   PREM 16/1848, 18 July 1978

9   PREM 16/1848, 18 and July 1978

10 *Daily Express*, 11 September 1978 and 10 October 1978; *Daily Mirror*, 27
    February 1979

11 *Daily Express*, 17 August 1979

12 *The Editors*, BBC, 19 August 1979

13 *Daily Mirror*, 1 September 1979; *Daily Express*, 9 October 1979

14 Charles Moore, *Margaret Thatcher, The Authorized Biography*, vol 1, Penguin,
    2014, pp 483–485

15 PREM 19-360, 7 July 1980

16 PREM 19-360, 6 October 1980

17 *Daily Mail*, 16 April 1988

18 *Nationwide*, BBC, 19 May 1982

19 *Sydney Morning Herald*, 15 January 1983

20 *Daily Mail*, 15–16 April 1988

21 Russell Harty, BBC, 26 January 1982

22 John Stonehouse interview, *Motives* with Anthony Clare, BBC, 1
    August 1983

23 *Sunday Mirror*, 20 March 1983

24 ITN obituary, 14 April 1988; *Daily Express*, 26 March 1988; *New York
    Times*, *Sydney Morning Herald* and *The Age*, all 15 April 1988; *Guardian*,
    14 January 2006; *Daily Telegraph*, 17 January 2006; www.abscr.cz/en/
    work-of-the-archive/; *Mail on Sunday*, 15 January 2006

25 MailOnline, 8 January 2011

26 PREM 19/360, 6 October 1980; Geoffrey Levy, 'Was Labour minister John
    Stonehouse – the real Reggie Perrin – a spy?', MailOnline, 8 January 2010;
    Daily Telegraph, 17 January 2006,

27 Tony Benn, *The Benn Diaries, 1963–67*, Hutchinson 1987, p 160

INDEX

JS indicates John Stonehouse.